Pat   Xmass   2019

G000245606

SOPHIA

MOTHER OF KINGS

THE FINEST QUEEN BRITAIN NEVER HAD

To Debra, for being even more fabulous than Sophia.

SOPHIA

MOTHER OF KINGS

THE FINEST QUEEN BRITAIN NEVER HAD

CATHERINE CURZON

PEN & SWORD
HISTORY

AN IMPRINT OF PEN & SWORD BOOKS LTD.
YORKSHIRE - PHILADELPHIA

First published in Great Britain in 2019 by
PEN AND SWORD HISTORY
An imprint of
Pen & Sword Books Ltd
Yorkshire – Philadelphia

ISBN 978 1 52675 534 6 hb
ISBN 978 1 52676 298 6 pb

A CIP catalogue record for this book is available from the British Library.

Printed and bound in the UK by TJ International
Typeset in Times New Roman 11.5/14 by
Aura Technology and Software Services, India

Pen & Sword Books Limited incorporates the imprints of Atlas, Archaeology,
Aviation, Discovery, Family History, Fiction, History, Maritime, Military, Military
Classics, Politics, Select, Transport, True Crime, Air World, Frontline Publishing,
Leo Cooper, Remember When, Seaforth Publishing, The Praetorian Press,
Wharncliffe Local History, Wharncliffe Transport, Wharncliffe True Crime and
White Owl.

For a complete list of Pen & Sword titles please contact
PEN & SWORD BOOKS LIMITED
47 Church Street, Barnsley, South Yorkshire, S70 2AS, England
E-mail: enquiries@pen-and-sword.co.uk
Website: www.pen-and-sword.co.uk

Or
PEN AND SWORD BOOKS
1950 Lawrence Rd, Havertown, PA 19083, USA
E-mail: Uspen-and-sword@casematepublishers.com
Website: www.penandswordbooks.com

Contents

Illustrations

Acknowledgements

Once again, it's a rather massive merci to the team at Pen & Sword, with a sound and serious nod of recognition aimed right at Jon. Yet more thanks are going out to the ever fierce and fabulous Lucy, editor extraordinaire!

To those friends, readers and marvellous correspondents all over the world, you continue to rock. There are a few extra special thanks to liberally distribute too, of course, and Adrian, you are never less than epic. Come through Rob, you glorious fellow, and Kathryn, get that clapper clapping!

To Pippa, Nelly and the Rakish Colonial - never, ever change.

Introduction

'The princess SOPHIA, who was a daughter and mother of a king, was herself mistress of every qualification requisite to adorn a crown. [Sophia was] the most accomplished lady in Europe.'[1]

Sometimes, history just *happens*. With as little planning and forethought as the turn of a card or the throw of a die something shifts; a butterfly flutters its wings and the course of the world changes forever.

In the case of Sophia of the Palatinate, it was all down to a marriage. Or rather, a marriage that wasn't.

When Sophia sat down to write her memoirs in 1680 she was in her fiftieth year. The idea of ruling Great Britain wasn't even a distant dream and she little knew what the future might hold for her. She finished her memoirs a year later, with more than three decades left to live. What exciting decades they would turn out to be.

From exile to electress to taking the throne of England, this is the tale of perhaps the finest queen that Great Britain never had, Sophia, Electress of Hanover.

Act One

Princess

'I was born, they tell me, October 14, 1630, and being the twelfth child of the King my father, and of the Queen my mother, I can well believe that my birth caused them little satisfaction.'

Meet the Parents

Once upon a time there lived a ruler who knew all about dynasty. He was Frederick V, Elector Palatine of the Rhine, a minor cog in the mighty wheel that was the powerful Holy Roman Empire. So far, so grand. Grander still, he later added to his portfolio of power by becoming King of Bohemia in 1619, but we'll come to *that* unfortunate episode later. Despite his fine titles, Frederick wasn't destined for a long and peaceful life and from almost the first moment of his reign, he struggled to keep his lands protected and united under his rule. It was a difficult balancing act and a thankless task.

Ultimately, Frederick failed.

Frederick's father, helpfully named Frederick IV (get ready for a lot of not at all unique names like this, but we'll hack our way through the forest together), was not a man who liked a quiet and uneventful life. He enjoyed the trappings of wealth and *indulgence* might have been his middle name. Known as *Frederick the Righteous*, he might more accurately have been called *Frederick the Extravagant* or perhaps even *Frederick the Alcoholic*. With an addiction to the hard stuff that eventually ravaged his health, Frederick IV's life was short and when he died aged 36 in 1610, his 14-year-old son was just that little bit too young to assume the mantle of sovereign. This meant that the electorate would need a regent to keep things ticking over.

Perhaps Frederick IV had been aware that his high living lifestyle would mean that he wouldn't see old bones, or perhaps he was just a born planner. Either way, he had already made plans for a regent to serve until his son reached the age of majority. The immediate family of the elector was part of the House of Palatine Simmern, a cadet branch[1] of the ancient House of Wittelsbach, and it was from this illustrious family that the regent was expected to come. The Golden Bull of 1356[2] decreed that Frederick's closest male relative would automatically be appointed regent and guardian of the young prince, but things had changed in the two and a half centuries since the Golden Bull was created and the boozy Frederick IV had other plans.

It was all a matter of religion.

The closest male relative, Wolfgang Wilhelm, Count Palatine of Neuburg, was a Catholic, and for the Protestant Frederick IV, that would never do[3]. Instead, Frederick IV chose John II, Count Palatine of Zweibrücken, to fulfil the important role instead. No doubt all of this looked fine on paper but when Frederick IV died, theory became practice and suddenly things were pretty damned far from fine as far as Wolfgang Wilhelm was concerned.

Regardless of what the late and rather well-prepared elector had wanted, Wolfgang Wilhelm came to Heidelberg, the electoral capital, with every intention of ruling as regent and assuming the guardianship of young Frederick V. Instead he found himself turned away from the city and John II, Frederick IV's preferred choice, already firmly installed. Understandably, Wolfgang Wilhelm took deep and very personal offence and a feud erupted that echoed across the Holy Roman Empire.

Matthias, who just happened to be the Holy Roman Emperor at the time the Houses of Palatine Simmern and Wittelsbach started feuding, had no choice but to intervene. When it came to emperors, Matthias wasn't the strongest leader and rather than choose between Wolfgang Wilhelm and John II, he decided to let Frederick V begin his reign one year early in 1613.

After all, he was already a husband…

The year before, Frederick's marital fate had already been decided for him. You're going to see a lot of that sort of thing as we travel through Sophia's life and times. Due to young Frederick's position, it was vital that he marry the right sort of candidate to ensure the strength of the

Palatinate and for *right*, read *Protestant*[4]. With this in mind, a team of hand-picked negotiators had left for London with the intention of winning the hand of Elizabeth Stuart for the young Frederick. At just one week Frederick's senior, Elizabeth was a ripe age for marriage, but a union with her promised far more than simple heirs and spares.

The matter of Elizabeth's marriage could have huge implications for England and the decision had to be right. As a highly-titled Protestant in possession of plenty of continental territory, not to mention being an ancestor of Henry II of England, just as Elizabeth was, Frederick looked like the perfect candidate. Elizabeth's father, King James I of England, was keen to extend his country's alliances in Europe and fancied that, through judicious marriage agreements, he might actually be able to gain influence in both Catholic *and* Protestant kingdoms. The delicate negotiations eventually resulted in an agreement and Frederick left his homeland and travelled to England to meet his bride.

He made an impact as soon as he arrived, delighting courtiers with his friendly manner and conversation. Marriages for the sake of dynasty were not always happy, as we shall see later, but Elizabeth swiftly became very keen indeed on her young suitor and he returned the sentiment with enthusiasm. In fact, though it wasn't quite love at first sight, it didn't take too long for mutual adoration to blossom.

Just as the king and court took to Frederick straight away, the young couple became swiftly smitten by one another. The verdict wasn't unanimous though for Elizabeth's mother, Queen Anne, had more aspirational plans in mind. In fact, she was sure that her daughter could capture the heart of a king rather than a mere elector. Indeed, Gustavus Adolphus of Sweden was an early and serious contender for the hand of the young princess. Ultimately, however, he was passed over due to the small matter of Sweden's very shaky relations with Denmark, Queen Anne's native land.

Even as Frederick was delighting English courtiers with his looks and charm, Sir John Chamberlain wrote an account of the visit to his friend, the ambassador and statesman, Sir Ralph Winwood. He informed Winwood that not everybody was thrilled with Frederick's dazzling approaches and darkly warned that, 'The Queen is noted to have given no great Grace nor Favour to this match'[5]. Yet what the queen wanted was immaterial in this case because her husband, King James I, thought the young man quite the perfect candidate and nobody dared to disagree *too* loudly.

Chamberlain, whose letters have left us with an invaluable record of the era, clearly took great delight in appraising Winwood of events at court. Breezy, playful and bristling with undisguised Protestant pride, his letter promised a very happy ending indeed.

> 'You have heard long since of the *Count Palatine's* prosperous Passage [and he] doth carry himself so well and gracefully, *that he hath the Love and Likeness of all, saving some Papists of popishly affected*, whereof divers have been called *coram* for disgracefull [sic] speeches of him, and among the rest, as I hear, Sir *Robert Drury*[6]; who (because he was not entertained perhaps by him or his, as in his Vanity he expected) began to talk maliciously. But the King is much pleased in him, and so is all the Court; and he doth so address himself and apply to the Lady *Elizabeth*, that he seems to take delight in nothing but her Company and Conversation.'[7]

Frederick's caring presence certainly seems to have brought his English betrothed some comfort when she lost her beloved brother, also the heir to the throne, Henry, late in 1612 just a few months before his nineteenth birthday. Henry had warmed to Frederick upon their very first meeting and Elizabeth adored nobody more than she did Henry. His death shattered her. Frederick's attentiveness and support not only to Elizabeth, but to her parents, did much to enhance his standing in the eyes of the queen who had thought him a rung below her daughter. A love match was surely blossoming.

In fact, it was fortunate indeed that James I thought highly of his future son-in-law, for the death of Henry cast a new light on Elizabeth's possible future. With Henry's passing, only two of James and Anne's seven children remained[8]. The next in line to the throne was now young Charles, later to reign as the ill-fated King Charles I, but his succession was by no means guaranteed thanks to his frail health. Should Charles die, then Elizabeth would come to the throne as Queen Elizabeth II, so the matter of choosing her husband suddenly became a very delicate one indeed. Catholic opponents of the marriage had already been summoned before the Privy Council to account for the volume with which they had voiced their reservations and now those reservations grew louder.

Yet James silenced any doubters by treating young Frederick as though he was already his son. The decision had been made.

Elizabeth and Frederick were married at Whitehall Palace on 14 February 1613. It seems apt that the ceremony took place on Valentine's Day for this was a royal couple who were truly in love, which, as we shall see, wasn't always the case in dynastic marriages. The nuptials were celebrated with enormous public festivities including, 'a naval fight, to be made upon the river of Thames, together with masks, fireworks, buildings and divers other preparations, necessary for such princely triumphs.' With the wedding lauded by poets and balladeers, perhaps the most famous work of art it inspired was John Donne's adoring and very lengthy poem, *An Epithalamion, or Marriage Song, on the Lady Elizabeth and Count Palatine Being Married on St Valentine's Day*, which commemorates and celebrates the wedding in epic style.[9]

The newlyweds remained in England until April, when they made the journey home to Heidelberg. No longer ruled by regents and ready to take the reins, Frederick was now the elector. Thanks to this and the bona fide royal princess at his side he took on a new importance amongst his fellow German princes and Elizabeth, always fond of the limelight, was delighted by this turn of events. As daughter of the king of England she insisted on taking precedence over her new courtiers, including her husband's own family, for she was second in line to one of the most important thrones in the world. A focus on precedence and adherence to protocol was something that her daughter inherited too, and it comes through vividly in Sophia's own memoirs. These women were *always* assured of their place in the world, regardless of what life threw at them.

Yet though Frederick's rank *did* elevate him amongst his peers, he let that elevation go to his head. As history would tell, it cost the Elector Palatine dearly.

Into Exile

Over the next five years, the political world in which Frederick moved became ever more unstable. A period of ill health left him suffering from depression and even the birth of his first son did little to lift his spirits[10]. He was set on making his electorate one to be reckoned with and that began at home. Frederick spent a fortune improving his castle and its estates, eventually creating the *Hortus Palatinus,* a breathtaking garden that became the talk of Europe thanks to the pioneering techniques employed in its creation[11]. Yet as Frederick and Elizabeth admired the beauty of their awe-inspiring landscaped estates, the world around them was in flux.

The Palatinate was situated in central Germany and with its rich mining industry it was economically very strong indeed. From across borders powerful members of the House of Habsburg looked on hungrily, whilst behind the scenes, those who fancied getting their hands on some of the lucrative mining territory were waiting for a moment of weakness in which they might strike. The seeds of disaster were sowed in 1617 when Archduke Ferdinand of Styria was crowned king of Bohemia. This Catholic, Habsburg king faced opposition from the Protestant majority in the realm over which he ruled and eventually, this opposition broke out into deafening dissent.

The Habsburg dynasty wielded immense power on the continent, as did the Church of Rome. Though Bohemia was an elective monarchy and Ferdinand *had* been elected by the Bohemian diet, his Protestant subjects watched in increasing anxiety as their new king hoovered up title after title. As well as taking the Bohemian crown, he also became king of Hungary and, ultimately, the Holy Roman Emperor in 1619. Even before he became emperor though, alarm bells were ringing for those who feared the march of absolutism and Catholicism across the continent. They believed nothing demonstrated it as well as Bohemia, where Ferdinand had casually cast off promises of freedom of worship[12] for his subjects and had set about imposing his devout religious beliefs on the populace.

In May 1618, Protestant nobles under the command of Count Jindřich Matyáš Thurn stormed Prague Castle where a meeting of senior Catholic Lords Regent was taking place. The Protestants charged the Catholics with violating the promise of religious freedom made by Holy Roman Emperor Rudolf II in 1609, and demanded an immediate reply and explanation. When the Lords Regent deferred and asked for time to speak to the king before making a response, two of them, William Slavata and Jaroslav Martinic, were thrown from the castle windows. Both men survived this undignified fate but the Second Defenestration of Prague, as the incident became known, marked the start of the Bohemian Revolt and led Europe stumbling into the Thirty Years' War.

In the dying months of November 1618, the name of Frederick of the Palatinate was first mentioned as a possible future king of Bohemia. His forces fought on the side of the Bohemian rebels, hastening the moment when the kingdom fell into Protestant hands. If he had thought King Ferdinand of Bohemia a worthy opponent, Frederick was to have another shock when on 20 March 1619, Matthias, Holy Roman Emperor, died. Ferdinand was named as his successor, meaning that the Bohemians who refused to recognise him as their king and those who had fought for the rebel cause were no longer facing the opposition of a monarch, but potentially the might of the entire Imperial army.

With war inevitable, the Bohemians hustled to appoint a new leader. Their first choice was John George I, Elector of Saxony, but he was in no mood to antagonise the newly enthroned emperor further, so quickly declined the offer. They now turned their attention to Frederick, who seemingly had no fears about incurring the wrath of the Holy Roman Empire. Years of unrest, plot and counter-plot came to a head on 26 August 1619 when Frederick was officially elected as the new King of Bohemia, just a few days before elections were held to formalise the identity of the next Holy Roman Emperor.

Only one man voted against Ferdinand II's appointment as emperor and that, of course, was Frederick. In doing so, he ignored the advice of his own family and that of England's King James I, all of whom urged him not to antagonise the mighty Holy Roman Empire.

Now Bohemia formally severed its ties with the Habsburgs, and Frederick accepted the dubious honour of being crowned king of Bohemia just days before the investiture of Ferdinand as the new Habsburg Holy Roman Emperor. Ferdinand and his powerful supporters still thought of him as the king of Bohemia whatever the Bohemian Confederation might wish. With neither side in any hurry to back down, conflict was inevitable.

Frederick was crowned at St Vitus Cathedral on 4 November 1619 and across his new kingdom, the people celebrated. Around them the land was devastated but still they rejoiced in the arrival of their new Protestant king, perhaps hopeful for what the future might bring. Sadly as time went by, it became apparent that the new king and queen were not as welcome in Bohemia as they might have hoped to be. Elizabeth in particular was regarded as somewhat peculiar. The language of the court was German, which Elizabeth didn't speak and although she was fluent in French, her new courtiers knew little of that tongue. Her menagerie of dogs and monkeys was at odds with what Bohemia expected from its rulers too. The strict religious observances of the new king and queen shook a populace that might not have wanted Catholics, but didn't want strict Calvinists either.

Frederick inherited an administration riven with division and debt. Facing aggressive opposition from the Holy Roman Empire his future was uncertain, and James I's dreams of one day brokering peace between the continent's Catholic and Protestant factions lay in tatters. The Bohemian crown was a bejewelled white elephant and it brought nothing but misery for Frederick.

Ferdinand, the Holy Roman Emperor, issued an ultimatum to Frederick, telling him to vacate his new throne by 1 June 1620, or face armed opposition. When Frederick called on James I to send troops, his father-in-law declined; hopelessly outgunned, the beleaguered King of Bohemia must have known that his days were numbered.

In November 1620, Frederick's reign in Bohemia ended. The Palatinate found itself besieged by Catholic troops and when Frederick's forces met their opponents at the battle of the White Mountain, just outside Prague, he was comprehensively defeated. His period on the throne had been so brief that Frederick became known as *the Winter King*. The pejorative nickname was coined by the Holy Roman Emperor, who prophesied that Frederick would be 'gone with the winter snow.'

How right he was.

With his territories now under occupation and his military forces decimated, the Winter King had no choice but to pack up his family, grab the crown jewels of Bohemia and flee for sanctuary in Breslau. He left in such a hurry that he forgot to take his garter, which he had been awarded in England when he was inducted into the Order of the Garter just before his marriage.

Those had been happier times, of course.

The Habsburgs reclaimed Bohemia and held it for nearly three centuries whilst from Frederick, they took everything. His lands and titles were confiscated and he was accused of treason in his absence. Once a powerful elector, he was now an exile.

Yet one cannot help but feel that he could be his own worst enemy. When Ferdinand looked as though he might be willing to enter into a truce, Frederick foolishly set the highest price possible. He wanted his titles and territories restored and the emperor would not agree to such terms. Yet life wasn't so bad for Frederick. He lived in a magnificent palace in Rhenen and enjoyed the best of everything thanks to supporters who were happy to fund his lifestyle. They stopped short of offering military support and Frederick found precious few allies when it came to his wishes to reclaim his lands by force. Fate was about to take a turn that would leave the Winter King in turmoil.

In 1629 the family's eldest son, 15-year-old Prince Henry Frederick, joined his father on a voyage across the Haarlemmermeer, a body of water outside Amsterdam. They were on their way to view a Spanish galleon which had been captured by the Dutch West India Company, an organisation in which Elizabeth held shares. The galleon had been loaded with plate worth nearly £900,000 and had been brought to anchor in the Zuiderzee. Keen to collect Elizabeth's share of the booty, father and son set out on their fateful journey.

The weather was dreadful and thick fog made visibility virtually nil on the treacherous journey. In these terrible conditions, the vessel carrying the pair was rammed by a far larger craft. Though Frederick was saved by another boat, the last glimpse he caught of his son was when he saw him clinging to the mast of the stricken vessel, screaming for his father's help. Frederick tried to dive into the freezing waves to save his child but was forcibly restrained from entering the water. He returned that same day but could find no trace of the sunken vessel or his lost son.

Frederick couldn't rest and was tormented by the sound of Henry Frederick's dying screams. When dawn broke, he was at the edge of the water again. Later that freezing morning, the wreckage was located. There, his cheek frozen against the mast to which he had been clinging, was the body of Henry Frederick.

It was a blow from which Frederick never truly recovered. His already fragile spirit was shattered and Elizabeth, usually so strong in adversity, crumbled. For a time, there were fears for her life, but when she learned she was pregnant yet again she knew that she had no choice but to rally. This was her duty, after all, and she must fulfil it. The beaten Frederick, meanwhile, desperately tried to rebuild his broken realms. He finally swallowed his pride and admitted that he had been wrong to accept the crown of Bohemia. Beaten and grieving, Frederick asked the emperor for official forgiveness.

It was not forthcoming.

Two Visits to Church

> 'In this year, 1630, and within a few months of each other, two children, a boy and a girl, were born to the brother and sister, Charles of England and Elizabeth of Bohemia. The English prince came into the world as the heir of three kingdoms; and his birth was the occasion of general gratulation. […]
>
> Elizabeth's infant was a girl, the twelfth child of a family already too numerous to be supported by the dependent parents, who required all the elasticity of parental affection to enable them to welcome into the world one after another, a tribe of helpless children, without home and without possessions.'[13]

Elizabeth, deposed Queen of Bohemia, gave birth to her daughter in The Hague on 14 October 1630. Just two weeks earlier the doughty queen had returned from a restful hunting trip to Utrecht, but despite the journey of forty miles, her physical fatigue was easily outdone by her emotional exhaustion and the Winter Queen was still tormented by the fate of her eldest son. Her husband, Frederick, was no more robust and remained mired in the unhappiness from which he no longer seemed able to escape. At their home of the Wassenaer Hof in The Hague he felt like yesterday's man, constantly subject to the whims of his father-in-law, whose envoys seemed to be around every corner. Always melancholic, his mood dipped ever deeper and when his 2-year-old daughter, Charlotte, fell ill in early 1631, Frederick sank lower than ever into misery.

With so many children to care for, a newborn princess had long since ceased to be a novelty. Having used every hereditary monicker they could muster, Elizabeth and Frederick even had trouble choosing a name for their daughter. They eventually resolved the matter by writing their favourites on slips of paper and drawing one from a hat. They chose *Sophia*. The name honoured Elizabeth's late sister, who had lived for just one day following her birth in June 1606. She had been laid to rest in Westminster Abbey but now her name lived again, embodied by the little girl who would *almost* rule a kingdom.

With the small matter of Sophia's name settled, the next issue to face was that of godparents. Just as the couple felt they had exhausted the most illustrious names, so too had they already made use of the most illustrious candidates for the role of godparents. All of these concerns paled into nothing in January 1631 when Charlotte of the Palatine, the newborn Sophia's sister, died. Any happiness that Sophia's birth had brought to the already stretched household was extinguished and Frederick and Elizabeth were left to ruminate on the christening of one child even as they planned the funeral of another.

Charlotte's tragic death and funeral delayed Sophia's baptism until 30 January 1631. In a pleasing twist of fate, when Sophia was finally christened in the Klosterkirk only a couple of days after Charlotte's funeral, two of the godmothers were, in true girl band style, also named Sophia[14].

The lucky ladies were the Countesses of Hohenlohe, Culenbourg and Nassau-Dietz, whilst the States of Friesland and Groningen and the Prince Palatine of Neuburg filled the role of godfathers.

Just under a year later, the family welcomed another new arrival. This time it was a son, Gustavus Adolphus, but the mood remained somber.

Yet Frederick had reason to believe that there would soon be much to celebrate. There was a new Protestant hope on the horizon and Frederick prayed that the end of his exile might finally be in sight. Once a contender for Elizabeth's hand, Gustavus Adolphus of Sweden had already given his name to Frederick and Elizabeth's youngest child, and he gave the Winter King and Queen hope too.

Nicknamed *the Lion of the North*, Gustavus Adolphus had coffers that were overflowing with French gold and when he entered Germany in late 1629, his sights were set not only on expanding Sweden's territory, but also on flying the banner for Protestantism against the Holy Roman Empire. His armies were strong and his successes decisive and in him, Frederick found a friend and ally. After misfortune and tragedy, the Winter King dared to hope that his luck had finally changed and that, in a territory redrawn by the seemingly unstoppable Gustavus Adolphus, he would once again rule.

But this is Frederick we're talking about and bad luck stuck to him like treacle.

On 16 November 1632, the Swedish army claimed a victory at the Battle of Lützen, one of the most important engagements of the Thirty Years' War. The emperor's soldiers were routed and for the Protestant forces and their supporters, this was a triumph to be relished. Yet when the smoke cleared, one man was missing from the victory celebrations. *The Lion of the North*, the figurehead whose leadership had been so vital to the cause of Protestantism, was nowhere to be seen.

The discovery of Gustavus Adolphus' riderless, wounded horse wandering on the battlefield was the first indication that all was not well and when the casualties were counted, the name of the king was written among them. Separated from his men in the miasma of gun smoke and fog, Gustavus Adolphus had been lost during a cavalry charge. Thrown from his wounded horse behind enemy lines, his fate was brutal and Gustavus Adolphus was stabbed and shot multiple times, including once in the head[15]. His body was then stripped and all the time around him, the battle raged on.

The Swedish king's death sent shockwaves through the Protestant alliance for he had been a vital figurehead for the cause. Without him the impact of the victory was diminished and Frederick, his hopes dashed once more, could not find it within himself to recover. Frederick succumbed to the plague on 29 November 1632, leaving some of the more romantic commentators to pontificate that it was as a result of his ongoing misery at the death of his eldest son years earlier[16]. For Elizabeth, the death of Frederick was a body blow. She sank into a deep melancholy that was hardly helped by her perilous financial situation, which grew bleaker with each new report from England.

Sophia did not remember her father, for the disenfranchised Winter King died when she was just 2-years-old. As the years passed she and her sisters would come to regard their elder brother, Charles Louis, as their father, and it was a role he would fill to perfection.

Daughters and Doggy-Doo

Despite her enormous brood, Elizabeth had little interest in her children and was not an involved parent. As a baby, Sophia was nursed by Sybella de Ketler, who had cared for her father before her. When Frederick died, Elizabeth sent Sophia ten miles away to live in Leiden with her siblings at the Prinsenhof, as, 'preferring the sight of her monkeys and dogs to that of her offspring, Her Majesty had all her children raised well out of her sight.'[17] The Leiden home had once been a convent and it was as regimented now as it would have been then, though life was not unhappy for the little girl. Nor was she entirely kept from the company of her mother, and the children made regular sojourns to visit her.

Though Sophia and her sisters made multiple trips to The Hague and Elizabeth wrote to her children weekly, there was to be no maternal warmth from the exiled queen of Bohemia. In Leiden, the care of the royal children was entrusted to their governess, Madam von Pless, and her daughters. The elderly Madam von Pless had been governess to Sophia's father too and seemed impossibly old to the little girl; indeed, even her daughters seemed ancient. Writing later, Sophia made the arch observation that their 'conduct was equally upright towards God and man. I believe that they prayed to God, and never disturbed man, for their appearance was frightful enough to terrify little children.'

At the centre of Madam von Pless' programme of education was the importance of faith and hours were devoted to the little girl's religious upbringing every day. As her pupil studied, her tutor scrubbed obsessively at her teeth, leaving the little girl sickened by the grotesque grimaces her governess seemed to pull during her ablutions. Sophia was bewildered and bored by the mix of etiquette and ritual, by the daily routine of formal dinners, of curtsying to her brothers and her governess curtsying at her, of more curtsies when gloves were removed and even more when she washed her hands. On one occasion, Sophia recorded that she had to make nine curtsies before she could even sit down at the dinner table.

For an intelligent and inquisitive child such as Sophia, the routine was stifling. She rejoiced in her daily dancing lessons, a rare respite from a rigorous schedule that included multiple languages, history, maths and, of course, theology. She took enormous delight in outdoor pursuits, particularly gardening, and she spent many long hours tending the gardens of her home with her friend and companion, Anna Katharina von Offen. Later better known by her married name of von Harling[18], Katharina was to become a lifelong friend of Sophia and would eventually care for her children, as well as serving as Sophia's Mistress of the Robes when she was Electress of Hanover.

When the weather kept her from the gardens, Sophia took immense pleasure in the company of her drawing master, the Dutch Golden Age painter, Gerard von Honthorst, who taught her to draw. Add to this roster of teachers no less a man than René Descartes, a favourite of her sister,

Elisabeth, and there can be no doubt that this was a thorough education indeed. Descartes remained utterly enchanted by Sophia until his death in 1650 and he wrote to her:

> 'When angels vouchsafe to visit men, they can scarcely leave behind them traces of deeper admiration and respect than have been impressed upon my mind by the letter wherewith you have favoured me. I see by the same, that not only do your highness's features deserve comparison with angels, and to be preferred as a pattern for those painters who represent beauty celestial, but the charms of your mind are such that philosophers are compelled to confess their excellence.'

Sadly for Sophia not everyone was so complimentary and she learned early in life exactly what was expected of a little girl of royal birth. Her mother delighted in showing off the children as though they were pedigree show poodles and Sophia and Gustavus were duly trotted out to be admired by Lady Lettice Goring[19], who was visiting The Hague. Wrongly assuming that the little Winter Princess would not be able to understand if she conversed in English, Lady Goring cruelly dismissed her, saying, 'He is very handsome, but she is thin and ugly." As an afterthought she added, 'I hope that she does not understand English.'

Sophia *did* understand, however, and took the insult to heart. In lonely Leiden she watched as her siblings grew older and, one by one, were recalled to Elizabeth's side until only Sophia and Gustavus, the king and queen's youngest child, remained. Gustavus had been a weak boy from birth and ultimately died when he was just 8-years-old, his last days having been spent in agony. The little boy's autopsy revealed five bladder stones and an enormous kidney stone and the pain of his death affected Sophia greatly. She wondered at the care he had received in his lifetime too for many doctors had examined her ailing brother, and none had diagnosed or treated the condition that ultimately killed him.

With only Sophia left in Leiden, she had far too much time to dwell on the loss of her beloved little brother. So deep was her despair and loneliness that she soon became unwell and in reply, Elizabeth closed down the household and summoned her daughter home to The Hague. The governesses remained in Leiden, too old to begin anew elsewhere[20], and recommended instead the services of an elderly lady named Galen. Not only did Sophia loathe her on sight, but she found the move perplexing at first, separated in one fell swoop from all that had been familiar. Here the stifling protocol of Leiden had been replaced by such life and warmth that she hardly knew where to look first. The Hague was filled with various disenfranchised nobles from Bohemia and the Palatinate and Sophia was wide-eyed at the characters she met. With the sabres of the English Civil War rattling, there were soon to be even more visitors flocking to her mother's impoverished court.

Not all was light and happiness though. Though her brothers were away travelling and fighting, the girls were kept close to Elizabeth's bosom and given both their chronic lack of funds and ongoing rejection by the Holy Roman Empire, the future looked uncertain. Sophia provided future readers with a wonderful portrait of those sisters, vividly bringing them and their foibles to life for the generations to follow:

'My sister, who was called Mme Elisabeth [twelve years older than Sophia], had black hair, a dazzling complexion, brown sparkling eyes, a well-shaped forehead, beautiful cherry lips, and a sharp aquiline nose, which was rather apt to turn red.[21]

[…]

Louise [eight years older] was lively and unaffected; Elisabeth very learned - she knew every language and every science under the sun, and corresponded regularly with Descartes. This great learning, however, by making her rather absent-minded, often became the subject of our mirth. Princess Louise was not so handsome, but had, in my opinion, a more amiable disposition. She devoted herself to painting, and so strong was her talent for it that she could take likenesses without seeing the originals. While painting others she neglected herself sadly. One would have said that her clothes had been thrown on her.

[…]

My sister Henriette [four years older] bore no resemblance to the other two. She had fair flaxen hair, a complexion, without exaggeration, of lilies and roses, and a nose which, although well shaped, was able to resist the cold. She had soft eyes, black well-arched eyebrows, an admirable contour of face and forehead, a pretty mouth, and hands and arms as perfect as if they had been turned with a lathe. Of her feet and ankles I need say no more than that they resembled those of the rest of the family. Her talents, by which I chiefly profited, lay in the direction of needlework and preserve-making."

And what of Sophia, the youngest of these sisters, and the one in whose hand the descriptive pen was clutched? Of herself, she writes, 'I had light brown naturally curling hair, a gay and easy manner, a good though not very tall figure, and the bearing of a princess.'

Sophia was always proud of her birth and bearing, so much so that she playfully dismissed Lord Craven as 'le bon homme' in her writings. Craven might have eventually been a rich, titled man, but he began life as nothing more grand than a poor boy from North Yorkshire, something of which Sophia, who was acutely conscious of her rank, would have been very aware of.

Faced with these three mature, cultured and beautiful sisters, Sophia might have been expected to feel Lady Goring's insult more keenly than ever, but she did no such thing. She was still young and filled with mischief so decided, as many children often do, to become the joker in the pack. Her sisters possessed a beauty and composure that Sophia felt she couldn't match but her love of pranks and a ready wit soon began to pay dividends. One such prank involved an ongoing battle of wits with Sir Henry Vane, an envoy of Charles I who was stringently loyal to the late Frederick's cause. When he jokingly sent Sophia a letter claiming to be from a young admirer, she responded by sending him an ornate box that she claimed contained a ring to show her affection. It actually contained dog faeces!

Never afraid to get her hands dirty, she also drenched a playmate in the contents of her mother's chamber pot when his teasing became too much. Life really couldn't have been more different than it was in Leiden.

Just as Sophia wasn't above a little toilet humour when she thought it might win her some attention, nor was she above the most precocious behaviour of a little sister. When her siblings decided to put on a production of Pierre Corneille's *Médée* to entertain Elizabeth, Sophia was told that she was far too young to take part in such a play. The young princess was incensed and determined to teach her doubters a lesson. Not only did she then learn every single line of the play by heart, but she also employed the services of a professional actress to bring her performance up to scratch. In return she was given the role of Nérine and, teetering atop a pair of high chopines to give her some much-needed height on stage, she was a triumph. Sophia recalled later that she was rather proud of this achievement though she conceded that her siblings were right about one thing - she had no understanding whatsoever of the play, despite being able to repeat every word of it like a well-trained parrot!

For her family, it was a lesson well-learned. Sophia would never be the neglected little girl of the clan again and with Leiden a fast-fading memory, she was ready to jump headlong into this colourful new life.

Freed from the expectation of royal marriage and the crowded court of The Hague, little Sophia could come into her own. She became a clown to some and flattered herself that, whilst, 'clever people enjoyed the sport […] to others, I was an object of terror'!

Far from fading into the background at her mother's crowded court at the Wassenaer Hof, Sophia was soon standing out instead.

When Queen Henrietta Maria of England visited The Hague to seek financial assistance for her husband, Charles I, or at least a place to sell her jewels and raise some vital capital, she brought with her their daughter, Mary, Princess Royal. Mary was already engaged to William II, Prince of Orange[22], and Sophia was chosen out of all her sisters to be Mary's companion during the trip. Anticipating a beauty on a par with Helen of Troy, Sophia found herself sorely disappointed as harsh reality rather destroyed her expectations. Instead of the breathtaking figure immortalised in portraits, she found Henrietta Maria somewhat wizened and boney, whilst her questionable dental work left a lot to be desired. Of course, the young lady was still smarting from Lady Goring's comments on her physical attributes so when Henrietta Maria complimented Sophia on her pretty looks and compared her favourably to the Princess Royal, she swiftly changed her appraisal. With Henrietta Maria's compliments still ringing in her ears Sophia decided that the queen was actually quite beautiful too!

Whilst Sophia was busy learning her lines and playing pranks, the Princess Royal's fate was a rather different one. Though Charles Louis, Sophia's brother, quite fancied the idea of one day being married to this well-connected cousin and reaping the benefits of being on such good terms with the English crown, he had left it too late. She was already betrothed to William, son of Prince Frederick Henry of Orange and Amalia of Solms-Braunfels. He was five years her senior and when the bride was just 9-years-old, the couple was married. Due to her age, the marriage was unconsummated for a number of years and in the event it was short too, for William died in 1650, leaving Mary a widow before she was even 20-years-old.

Charles Louis likewise never made the connection with his English relatives that he hoped for, despite taking up temporary residence in his mother's homeland. His brother, Rupert, became a fearsome and dedicated Royalist who devoted himself to his uncle but Charles Louis didn't have the stomach to nail his political colours to the mast so wholeheartedly. Charles I repaid what he considered a lack of loyalty with angry disdain and when Charles Louis realised that he was on a hiding to nothing at the doomed king's court, he wisely packed his bags and left England behind!

To Wed a Prince

Marriages, for better or for worse, were to be troubling affairs for the Palatine family. The first rumblings of unrest thanks to a so-called unsuitable match came in 1645 when Sophia's brother, Edward, who had established himself in Paris, converted to Catholicism and married Anna Gonzaga. Anna's story is a particularly fascinating one, for she could trace her bloodline all the way to the French royal family, and her sister was to become Queen of Poland twice, first as the wife of Władysław IV Vasa. Just twelve months after his death she married his half-brother, John II Casimir Vasa, to become queen once more!

Anna was not destined to be a queen of anywhere, but scandal followed her around thanks to an affair with her second cousin, Henry II, Duke of Guise. It was a passionate and fiery relationship but it was not to last, despite Anna firmly believing that the couple had undergone a legally-binding marriage, something that Henry always denied. With her reputation looking rather ragged and doors closing left, right and centre, Anna needed a husband and she needed one quick. Edward, meanwhile, just needed money so the couple agreed that if they pooled resources, each could give the other exactly what they wanted. Officially, of course, Edward told his friends and family that he had converted not out of expediency but because he had experienced a divine intervention and been seized by the certainty that Roman Catholicism was the one true faith. Perhaps that's true, but it's more likely that what tempted him was the glamour of France and the coffers of his wife rather than heavenly rewards in the next world!

Once Edward's conversion was complete the couple was married and when word reached Elizabeth in The Hague, she was devastated. Although her decision to disown Edward didn't last, it was a lesson that Sophia took firmly on board. When she had children of her own she chose not to raise her daughter in any particular faith, thus making her a tempting marriage prospect regardless of a gentleman's religious persuasion. It also meant that, unlike Elizabeth, Sophia would never be forced to choose between family and religion. Yet Elizabeth's estrangement from her son was largely self-inflicted. Of course, given the era and Elizabeth's own upbringing and background it's hardly surprising that she acted as she did, but Sophia's burgeoning interest in philosophy led her along a very different religious path to her devout Protestant mother.

There was more drama to come for the Winter children.

Elizabeth decided to take matters in hand when it came to her daughters, determined to get them a good start on the social ladder. First on the list was finding a husband for her youngest daughter and she knew just where to look.

Sophia, for all Lady Goring's less than effusive praise about her looks, had grown into an accomplished and good-natured young woman. Accompanied by her constant companions, Mary and Anne Carey[23], she was soon an old hand at dealing with the machinations of life at the Wassenaer Hof. It would prove a valuable education. Once she was ready to enter the seething dynastic wrangling of the royal marriage mart, Sophia would need all the chutzpah she could muster.

It's fair to say that the marriage of Elizabeth Stuart, daughter of James I, sister of Charles I and aunt of Charles II, had not necessarily gone to plan. Without any real supporting evidence to back up their assertions, her critics painted her as a woman who had sacrificed her husband to her own ruthless ambitions. They claimed that it was she who had urged him to take the Bohemian crown that marked the start of his swift downfall and who set him on the road to exile and misery.

In fact, Elizabeth had had little interest in politics at that point of her reign and as her niece, the Duchess of Orleans, later recalled, she cared for nothing but 'plays, masquerades, and the reading of romances.' Yet The princess had been thrust from her London life into a very different world indeed and had adapted admirably well. Now she was no longer a young woman, but she had been through an unexpected invasion and exile where perhaps she had envisioned a rather more uneventful life as the Electress Palatine.

For now, Elizabeth's time was occupied with the matter of finding a suitable husband for her daughter, Sophia, and she was determined that the choice would be a considered one. No doubt recalling her own mother's wish for her to marry a man of prospects and impeccable credentials, Elizabeth's favoured candidate was her nephew, Charles, Prince of Wales, who was later to rule as King Charles II of England. Charles was bound for The Hague and Elizabeth was determined that he would find a willing prospective bride waiting to receive him.

Elizabeth's domestic situation was no happier than her political one. Her children were busy converting to Catholicism, going into battle or sending parcels of dog poo to courtiers. Though outward appearances were good, the household's coffers were becoming more depleted with every passing day until Sophia commented that there was often 'nothing to eat at our court but pearls and diamonds'. Elizabeth pinned her hopes of a financial bailout on finding a good marriage for her youngest daughter. Sophia knew that she had no say in any of this, but still went along for the ride. She found an unlikely ally in William Craven, at the time Baron Craven and later to be 1st Earl of Craven[24], who was a lifelong supporter of the exiled king and queen of Bohemia. In fact, some claimed that Craven and Elizabeth were lovers after the death of her husband. It's outside the scope of this book to delve into that but years later, when Elizabeth finally returned to England at the invitation of Charles II, it was to Craven's opulent home that she hastened.

Craven was a staunch and committed royalist, so the thought that the daughter of the woman he adored, whether platonically or otherwise, might be united with the prince whose cause he supported with every fibre of his being, lit a fire in his blood. He encouraged the match wholeheartedly but there were other hands in play, and behind the scenes gossip was swirling.

Amalia of Solms-Braunfels, Princess of Orange, and former lady-in-waiting to Elizabeth, rather fancied snatching the hand of Charles for her own daughter, Louise Henriette[25]. With little to choose between the girls in terms of who might make the better wife, Amalia resorted to underhand methods. She employed her son, William, to compromise Sophia, despite the fact that he had recently married Mary, Princess Royal.

The plan was simple. The suave and worldly William would seduce Sophia with his good looks and charm, leaving her reputation in ruins. Luckily for our hapless heroine, a German valet by the improbable name of Fritz found out about the plot and told Streithagen, the chaplain of Sophia's brother, Charles Louis[26]. With the elector now on notice for any inappropriate behaviour from William towards his sister, Streithagen saw with his own eyes that the prince visited Elizabeth's chambers every night when he knew Sophia would be present, just as his mother had instructed him to do. However, the intrigue was doomed to fail for as soon as William made his nightly entrance, Sophia left. Night after night this went on, regular as clockwork, with the young princess merrily leading her would-be corrupter a merry dance.

Amalia wasn't about to be deterred in her scheme to ruin the reputation of Sophia before the Prince of Wales could arrive in The Hague and be won over by her good looks and sparky character. With all efforts to get William and Sophia alone together frustrated, the House of Orange-Nassau instead decided to stage a ballet in which Sophia's brother, Prince Philip, would play a key role. It might sound like a bizarre plan but strict protocol meant that if Philip agreed to take part, then the rehearsals should be held in his own apartments rather than at the Orange court. This would also guarantee Amalia's son relatively unfettered access behind the scenes at the Wassenaer Hof and provide him with plenty of opportunities to stoke gossip. Forewarned by Charles Louis, Philip saw through the plan straight away. He kiboshed the scheme before anybody could dance so much as a step by simply declaring that his apartments were far too small for ballet rehearsals, regardless of protocol.

Imagine Amalia's frustration as her farcical attempts at romantic subterfuge were thwarted time after time by our plucky heroine. All of this comical scheming by Amalia provided a somewhat ridiculous counterpoint to the situation currently being faced by the Prince of Wales. After all, every royal mother seemed rather keen on snaring the man whom Sophia herself referred to as the most tempting prize in Europe for her daughter.

In late June 1646, the ballet was forgotten as Prince Philip Frederick of the Palatinate made a split second decision that changed his life and ended another. Lieutenant Colonel Jacques de l'Epinay was a French exile in The Hague with a penchant for women and gossip and he loved to be the centre of attention. During an argument with Philip Frederick, de l'Epinay claimed that he had bedded not only Philip Frederick's sister, Louise, but his mother too. The hot-headed prince reacted in precisely the way you might expect and challenged the would-be Casanova to a duel. Philip Frederick claimed the victory and killed his opponent, but he was left with no choice but to flee The Hague.

The Prince of Wales had other things on his mind besides the family dramas of the Winter children. By the time he reached The Hague his father, Charles I, was being held captive on the Isle of Wight[27] and he had more than ballet rehearsals and backstairs chitchat to contend with. The thought of a marriage between Charles and Sophia was one that his allies fully supported. For Charles, however, marriage plans weren't at the forefront of his mind. He arrived in The Hague in 1648 seeking the aid of his sister, Mary, and her husband, William II, Prince of Orange, the chap who had singularly failed to ruin Sophia's reputation at his ambitious mother's command. Money, not marriage, was the focal point of his journey.

For all Elizabeth's lofty dreams of a royal wedding, it was not to be. Charles was simply not interested[28] in courting *anyone*, though he wasn't above a little flirtation to secure funds and besides, Amalia was still planting the seeds of doubt in Sophia's mind. Seeing that Charles and Sophia frequently attended Common Prayer together, she canvassed the Presbyterian factions at court to reject Sophia as a suitable bride. She needn't have bothered. In the event it was ultimately Charles himself who showed Sophia that there was no future for them.

During a walk with Sophia, the Prince of Wales innocently told her that she was far prettier than his mistress, Lucy Walter[29], and mooted the idea that she might one day like to visit him in England. Far from being pleasantly surprised by the 18-year-old prince's overture, Sophia was somewhat taken aback. A compliment was one thing but to be held in comparison to a mistress was quite another. Still processing his comments, Sophia swiftly discovered the real reason for his interest. Far from being bewitched by the princess' beauty, Charles hoped that he might be able to charm Sophia into approaching Lord Craven, the wealthy benefactor of the Winter Queen, for money on his behalf.

Sophia was bitterly disappointed by the revelation that it was Craven's purse and not her wit and beauty that had attracted the heir to the English throne. Feigning discomfort from a corn on her foot, she avoided the prince the following evening and earned her mother's anger at her lack of cooperation. After all, the reason for the attention wasn't important to Elizabeth, it was enough that it was Sophia whom Charles wished to stroll with, regardless of his reasons for doing so. The young princess was rather more realistic than her mother when it came to such things and realised that 'the marriages of great kings are not made up by such means.'

It was a political lesson well-learned for the girl who would grow into a self-possessed electress, capable of more than a little politicking herself. As long as Sophia held the prince's attention she was flavour of the month among courtiers and they jostled to be her new best friend, yet she knew that as soon as the Prince of Wales set his sights elsewhere, she would be yesterday's news. As she recalled with the wisdom of years, she saw many signs of weakness in him, but even at this tender age Sophia was watchful, weary of surrendering heart and head. When reading her memoirs though one struggles to accept that she was as unaffected by the whole experience as her recollections might apparently suggest.

Sophia had come close - not terribly close - but close, to escaping the chaotic court at the Wassenaer Hof, where the financial straits were dire indeed. The benevolent Craven's royalist sympathies saw his vast estates and wealth seized by Parliament and with it, Elizabeth's last means of guaranteed financial support dried up.

Her next victory was to be a pyrrhic one.

The Elector Restored

Elizabeth had entered into marriage with every expectation that her life would be one of power and privilege. Instead she had been thrust into exile and forced to learn swiftly how to wheel and deal in the world of continental politics. Frederick's death left his widow bereft. She was utterly heartbroken by her loss and in the years that followed, she became consumed by the battle to win back the Palatinate.

Having seen her husband die without ever achieving his ambition of restoring the Palatinate to his rule, Elizabeth was tireless once she took up the cudgels on behalf of her son, Charles Louis. In 1648 all of that toil was rewarded and Charles Louis finally assumed the title and role of Elector Palatinate, ruler of a land in ruins and territories in crisis. Though the Rhine Palatinate was restored to him, the Upper Palatinate, which had land borders with Bohemia, was not. Elizabeth couldn't rest with only a partial restoration and she begged her son not to accept the compromise, urging him to fight on for all of his rightful inheritance or accept none of it. In this at least Charles Louis was a realist and he accepted what was offered, surrendering the Upper Palatinate.

It was the best that anyone could hope for.

Now that her son was the elector and her ambitions had been realised, Elizabeth was ready to go home to the Palatinate, but the Palatinate was not ready to receive her. She was utterly penniless and informed Charles Louis that there was neither food in the kitchen nor money to buy any. Had she not given everything for him, devoted herself to his own restoration, she asked? What might she expect in return?

What Elizabeth expected was that Charles Louis would satisfy her many creditors in The Hague so that she could finally leave her exile and return to the Palatinate. Of course, we already know that Elizabeth and her children weren't particularly close thanks to the time she lavished on her dogs and monkeys, and it's probably no surprise to learn that Charles Louis wasn't at all fond of this idea.

In fact, Charles Louis was having none of it. Regardless of what his mother had done to restore him, he baulked at the idea of Elizabeth riding triumphant into what remained of the Palatinate, expecting the red carpet to be rolled out before her. Charles Louis cannily made no mention of the nicely appointed quarters available at Heidelberg and instead offered to lodge her in the draughty old rooms of the Schafforet at Frankenthal. The women there were dull, the men boring and the whole place, he assured her, was quite, quite insufferable.

Knowing that Elizabeth couldn't leave The Hague as long as she was so heavily in debt, Charles Louis hoped that his assertion that there was no money to spare might hold back the tide, yet she was as determined as ever. She asked the ruling States-General for permission to leave The Hague despite her debts, explaining that she had satisfied the most pressing creditors and would settle every outstanding claim if she could but return to the Palatinate. The walls seemed to be closing on her and though the States-General could see the sense in this request, it was not in their interests to see her gone. An unnamed commentator wrote of her desire to leave:

> 'Some desires have been made by the Lady Elizabeth, but she is a trouble both to them [the States] and the people; she hath contracted large debts, and the people do mutter much at her; many wish she were gone, but then some would lose considerable sums which she owes, and is not like to receive for anything I see, if she stays.'[30]

For obvious reasons, Elizabeth would not approach Oliver Cromwell and the English Parliament for assistance but the States-General *did*. Unsurprisingly the answer came back as a firm *no*. There would be no financial assistance for Elizabeth from the administration that had executed her brother and on top of that, her pension was stopped. Keen to keep in the Protectorate's good books, no further representations were made by Elizabeth's place of exile on her behalf.

Despite all of this she remained determined to go to Heidelberg and eventually Charles Louis dropped his pretence at reason. Instead he argued that his mother had shown little interest in his affairs until she needed money and suggested that, if she had, something might have been done to resolve her debts long ago.

Think how keenly that must have stung.

There was an even harsher sting to come.

A Trip to Heidelberg

Charles Louis, the son who resisted all his mother's efforts to gain an invitation to Heidelberg, did not seem nearly so reticent when it came to his younger sister. Having realised that there was no realistic chance of a marriage to the Prince of Wales, Sophia was well aware that the courtiers who simpered at the hem of her skirts would soon transfer their affections once it became known that there was to be no royal wedding. Though Charles Louis had no interest in a visit from his mother, when it came to his sister it was a very different matter indeed.

At thirteen years Sophia's senior, Charles Louis became a father figure to the girl whose own father had died when she was still in infancy, and it was he who now held out the hand of friendship to Sophia. When he heard of the situation with the Prince of Wales, he invited his now 20-year-old sibling to visit Heidelberg and remain for as long as she wished. Accompanied by the Carey sisters, with Lord Craven charged with ensuring that the party didn't get into any mischief, Sophia couldn't wait to travel. In the event, she stayed with her brother for eight years and left only when she married.

Elizabeth was furious and wrote a letter to her son that is a masterpiece of passive aggressive mothering. She didn't care what Sophia did, she declared, for why on earth would she want to keep company with someone who had no wish to keep company with *her*?

> 'As for Sophies journey, I uill neuer keep anie that has a mind to leaue me, for I shall neuer care for anie bodies companie that doth not care for mine.'[31]

Sophia was not a particularly well-travelled young lady and it was with trepidation that she began the long journey up the Rhine in a borrowed pinnace in the company of the gentlemanly Lord Craven, who had bankrolled the journey from the few assets that had escaped Parliament's confiscation. History almost took an interesting swerve during this trip when Sophia visited a convent in the company of the elderly Wolfgang Wilhelm, Count Palatine of Neuburg, the man who had almost been her father's Regent all those years ago. She found the convent so peaceful and the novices there so happy that she briefly contemplated the possibility of abandoning her trip and leaving mothers and marriages behind to take holy orders, as more than one of her sisters eventually did[32].

Clearly Wolfgang Wilhelm thought he had a keeper here and, seeing how keen Sophia was on the convent, he decided to withdraw his escort and allow her to make the decision as her conscience dictated. He would not walk out of the convent with Sophia, he declared, and if she wished to leave then it would be without his accompaniment. Had she opted to remain, who knows what the British monarchy would look like today, but the promise of a new life in Heidelberg overcame the lure of holy orders. Sophia left the convent in accordance with her original plans and rejoined Wolfgang Wilhelm at dinner that night, before continuing on her journey towards the Palatinate and the care of her devoted brother.

Sophia's first uninspiring steps on Palatinate soil were in Oppenheim, where she found herself paddling through mud and having to undertake part of her journey in a carriage that didn't even have any seats. She made do, displaying a little of the fortitude she had inherited from her exiled mother and would later bring to bear during her years in Hanover, when perching on a cushion in a dilapidated carriage was naught but a distant memory.

The sun was setting when Sophia arrived at Heidelberg and she was taken to her new home at the Kommissariat, formerly a government building. The Thirty Years' War had decimated the ancestral castle and the elector and electress had made their home in what had once been the offices of the finance commission. It was a court unlike any Sophia had ever experienced, filled with passion and intrigues. There can be no question that she adored her brother but her sister-in-law figured less highly in her estimation. In fact, Sophia dismissed her fairly swiftly as 'very stupid'. The electress was a fine looking woman with a striking figure - a beautiful bosom, according to Sophia - but the overall impact was rather spoiled by her eyebrows which, despite her blonde hair, she had chosen to die jet black.

One can't help but picture a seventeenth century Joan Crawford.

The possessor of that bosom and those eyebrows was Charlotte, Landgravine of Hesse-Kassel, daughter of William V, Landgrave of Hesse-Kassel, and Amalie Elisabeth of Hanau-Münzenberg. Charlotte was a beauty and her remarkable good looks were matched only by her remarkable bad temper. She was prone to violent rages but despite that, Charles Louis was entranced. After the couple was married in 1650, his fascination with his mercurial bride only deepened, occasionally tipping into furious jealousy. He was utterly obsessed with Charlotte and could often be found supplicated on his hands and knees before her, begging for her favour. Should she dismiss him or happen to let her gaze wander to another gentleman, no matter how innocently, he was consumed by furious envy, which he couldn't help but give vent to. Their bitter and very public arguments were eclipsed only by the even louder cries as they made up behind their closed bedroom door at sunset!

As she was only three years older than Sophia it was hoped that Charlotte would become a friend, but so swift was Sophia's damning conclusion about her sister-in-law that such a friendship stood no chance. On the day after she arrived in Heidelberg, Sophia was charged with accompanying Charlotte to church but instead of idle small talk she found herself on the receiving end of a confession. She hadn't wanted to marry Charles Louis at all, Charlotte confided, but had been forced to do so by her mother. Indeed, said Charlotte, a parade of dukes had lined up to ask for her hand and among them were George William and Ernest Augustus of Brunswick-Lüneburg, both of whom will become important figures later in our tale. As Charlotte droned on and on and on about herself and her many impressive qualities, showing off her gowns and jewels, telling tales of the men who had vied for her heart, Sophia indulged in a little bit of good, honest looking down her nose. Charlotte was gauche and ill-bred, she decided, and the two had simply nothing in common.

Now, perhaps Sophia really *was* motivated to dislike Charlotte by this combination of egotism, lack of self-knowledge and sheer arrogance but at the heart of her rejection of her sister-in-law is, I think, something more personal. She was devoted to her brother and considered him a father, so to hear his own wife waxing lyrical on the supposedly better men she could have married was beyond the pale. Once Charlotte had done that, there was no way she could win back Sophia's favour, not that she ever seemed to try. One had class, Sophia likely thought, one had flash, and they were never going to get along.

Sophia, young, smart and a girl who knew all about playing her cards close to her chest, quickly discovered that it wasn't only her sister-in-law who was miserable. Her brother might have been absolutely besotted by his wife and given to dramatic and eyebrow-raising displays of affection, but he found her notorious temper increasingly difficult to deal with. With her love of the spotlight and his penchant for jealousy, it was a recipe for marital discord from the very beginning. The more attention Charlotte got, the more she revelled in it and the more she courted whilst all the time her husband looked on, mistaking her love of the limelight for serious flirtation. They clashed regularly and after each clash and each noisy *making up* session, they clashed again as soon as the sun rose.

Families at War

Prince Philip Frederick of the Palatinate, the brother who had fled The Hague as a wanted man after killing Lieutenant Colonel Jacques de l'Epinay, met an enemy that he couldn't outrun in 1650. Following his escape from justice he had pursued a military career in the service of the Duke of Lorraine but that came to a shuddering halt when he died during the Fronde[33], fighting in the Battle of Rethel on 16 December 1650. In her new Heidelberg home, Sophia received the news with sadness. Her family was fractured and was now diminishing at a rapid rate, it seemed, whilst she had yet to even start out as a woman in her own right.

Though things in the electorate took a happy turn with the birth of Charles, the first son of Charlotte and Charles Louis, the happiness didn't last. Sophia swiftly discovered that life in Heidelberg wasn't that much more enjoyable than life in The Hague. Charlotte's foul temper meant that she had to control everything and everyone and her word at court was law. The young princess grew so disenchanted with her new life that she begged Charles Louis for permission to invite their sister, Princess Elisabeth, to join her and he agreed, well aware of how unsatisfied Sophia had been since her move.

Unfortunately what should have been a happy family reunion was destined to be anything but thanks to a bit of matchmaking that Elisabeth had indulged in before she left The Hague. She had played a pivotal role in arranging the marriage of her sister, Henriette Marie[34], to Sigismund Rákóczi, Prince of Transylvania. Though Charles Louis had reluctantly given his consent to the marriage, he had a change of heart at the last moment. Unable to find a way to extricate Henriette Marie from the Transylvanian marriage, Charles Louis was left fuming and placed the blame firmly at Elisabeth's feet. Sigmund had money to spare but as far as the elector was concerned, that was all he had going for him and he bitterly regretted allowing the marriage to take place. Poor Elisabeth was at her wit's end. She had consulted Charles Louis through the betrothal process at the request of their mother and had happily thought that all was proceeding grandly until his change of heart. Added to that, the death of Philip was the final straw for Elisabeth. With brothers seemingly dying at a rate of knots and lining up to tear strips off her on either side, she simply wished to be left alone.

Sophia would not allow her beloved sister to retreat into grief and misery though and pressed for the invitation to Heidelberg to be issued despite her brother's annoyance at Elisabeth's part in the Transylvanian marriage. Recognising that perhaps both of the women might benefit from spending some time in each other's company, he agreed. Given all that had happened with Henriette Marie this was not a particularly happy reunion and when Princess Elisabeth arrived in Heidelberg at the same time as a visit from their brother, Edward, she walked into a less than welcoming atmosphere. Charles Louis still resented her matchmaking of their sister and Sophia found that the sibling whom she had longed to see again had changed somewhat during their separation. Her bright nature and wit had vanished and in their place she had adopted a combination of self-righteousness and self-pity, never a happy mix.

Sophia, one might assume, was starting to get rather tired of these dramas in which she was never more than a supporting player, subject to everyone else's whims and fancies. With Elisabeth and Charles Louis engaged in a quiet war of attrition, this was one more domestic quarrel just waiting to happen. It wasn't helped when the electress immediately decided that she and Elisabeth were to be enemies but she wasn't about to let it show. Instead she took the opposite approach and encouraged Elisabeth's friendship, simply to antagonise Charles Louis and Sophia. What fun it must have been to be at the Heidelberg court!

There was a brief ceasefire with the birth of Elizabeth Charlotte in the spring of 1652. Known as *Liselotte*, she was to become the apple of Sophia's eye and adored her aunt in turn. With her arrival came some faces from the past as those old ladies who had cared for Sophia at Leiden were suddenly on the scene once more. Though the von Pless women had been too advanced in age to join Sophia in The Hague more than a decade earlier they were still alive and very much kicking and more than ready to keep royal children on the straight and narrow.

The atmosphere grew tenser still when news was received that Maurice of the Palatinate, who had been sailing as part of his brother Rupert's fleet, had been lost at sea. His ship, *HMS Defiance*, went down in a hurricane in the West Indies. It was something that Sophia, who once wrote, 'it is such a long time since I have heard of him that I do not know if he is still alive'[35], had long dreaded. He was the seventh child of the Winter monarchs to die.

Sophia's grief at her brother's death was eased somewhat by the companionship of Anne Carey, who had elected to join her friend in her new home. It was a plan that did little to impress Elizabeth. After all, she thought Sophia was more than capable of taking care of herself, and that she certainly didn't need a friend there to hold her hand.

> '[If Anne claims] she went uith Sophie by my order she is much in the wrong, for she knows when she asked me leaue to goe with Sophie, I tolde her I woulde not refuse her but I did not take it for an obligation from anie that did goe with her, for to tell you the truth, I was not verie well satisfied with Sophie going, neither did I ever committ anie charge to her of Sophie for I think Sophie has as much uitt as she to gouuerne her self, this is most true upon my faith and worde and if Cary [sic] say other uise she doth not say true.'[36]

Life was proving rather challenging for our plucky heroine, but it was about to get even worse. Charlotte, looking for a quarrel as was so often her way, soon began once more to question why Sophia and her brother spent so much time together. At first she decided that Charles Louis was using Sophia as cover for his own infatuation with her friend, Anne Carey, but that was just for starters.

In fact, Charles Louis took refuge in Sophia's chambers for the simple reason that he was finding it increasingly difficult to spend any time whatsoever with the wife he adored to jealous distraction. With her bad temper and constant paranoia that he might be in love with someone, *anyone* else, he found the company of his sister much easier in the face of such outright hostility. In Charlotte's fevered mind, this sibling devotion became something far more sinister and she began to fear that the bond was an incestuous one.

Charlotte decided to teach her husband a lesson by befriending his *other* sister and, as the husband complained to Sophia, the wife complained to Elisabeth. She spun stories of Charles Louis and Sophia being thick as thieves and eventually succeeded in making Elisabeth envious too, seeing herself very much as sidelined in favour of the younger sibling.

The situation reached such a head that Charlotte eventually demanded that the brother and sister stop spending time together. In reply, Charles

Louis spent more time with Sophia than ever and worse still, began taking the entire court to Sophia's chambers to pay their respects. If that didn't make an already awkward situation worse, it was left to Charlotte to twist the knife and she took up her pen, writing letters to all and sundry claiming that Charles Louis loved his sister, and not in the sibling sense of the word. Sophia was a minx, she claimed, and happily simpered along in return for gifts and favours. It was a shocking lie and one that pushed Sophia's patience to her limits, for nothing was more important to her than her reputation. She longed to escape this strange, angry place and more than anything, she longed to say goodbye to the strange, angry electress who she had found there.

Sophia was ready for a leading role of her own.

Reputation and Ruin

Sophia knew that she was marriageable material and she was keen if not to be a bride, then not to be in thrall to the whims of her family anymore. This was, after all, the young lady who had once been touted as a match for the Prince of Wales, so surely the man who eventually became her husband would be of fine blood indeed. It was a shame that every eligible court in Europe knew of her mother's empty coffers. There was a dowry though, so all hope wasn't entirely lost for Sophia's marriage.

The Winter Princess was keenly aware of her appeal to the opposite sex and thought it as amusing as it was pleasing though of course, she remained above it all. On a family trip to Stuttgart she met a prince of Holstein who took an immediate shine to her, despite the presence of plenty of other princesses and ladies of rank to charm him. He drank Sophia's health and took such an almighty gulp of wine that he immediately choked and threw the whole lot back up again. Aiming to impress the young lady, the prince downed the regurgitated booze all over again in one almighty gulp. Sophia encouraged him in his silliness and revelled in the envious looks of the other princesses, even though she had no interest in the gentleman beyond that of a jester.

Two years after her arrival in Heidelberg, Sophia fell victim to smallpox. Thankfully she survived the infection - or this would be a short book indeed - but the illness left disfiguring scars on her face. Sophia, however, wasn't about to let that ruin her ambitions to make a good marriage and she rejected out of hand any suggestion that she might be wed to Raimundo de Lencastre, the Duke of Aveiro, for he was nowhere *near* a king. After all, as Sophia herself wrote, smallpox scars might now mar her beauty somewhat but, having considered marrying a king, she could not allow herself to even entertain the idea of being the wife of a mere subject.

Ouch.

It was as Sophia was considering these weighty matters that Duke Ernest Augustus of Brunswick-Lüneburg happened into Heidelberg. Though Sophia and Ernest Augustus had met in passing when they were very young, he had made virtually no impact on the little girl. Now she was a child no longer and Ernest Augustus had grown into quite the catch.

Ernest Augustus might have had good looks to spare but as the youngest of four brothers, his prospects of climbing the dynastic ranks weren't high. Sophia, however, took something of a shine to the young duke, who was just a year her junior. Both in their early twenties, the couple got along swimmingly and shared a love of music, in particular the guitar. In fact, these two axe gods struck up a correspondence on the matter of music, with Ernest Augustus sending Sophia some practice pieces that he had particularly enjoyed and thought might appeal to her. The young lady was flattered and rather charmed but eventually broke off the correspondence when some, including her elector brother, suggested that their friendship might be misconstrued as something more. As innocent as she was apparently guileless, Sophia apologised to Charles Louis but assured him that her letters to Ernest Augustus had been sent only to thank him for the musical pieces he sent her. It was good manners that motivated them, she swore, and there was nothing more to it than that.

She *was* a princess, after all.

Sophia attached a huge amount of importance to her character and reputation and the thought of anything smearing her good name left her in spasms of horror. This was the young lady, let us not forget, who had fled The Hague to escape the self-interested attentions of the Prince of Wales, who had endured her sister-in-law's claims of all sorts of bad behaviour with her own brother and who now cut off correspondence with Ernest Augustus for fear that their friendship might be misconstrued. Living in the pot boiling atmosphere of Heidelberg, where passion and violence were par for the course, she was determined to remain the very model of calm and protocol. In a world in which Charlotte brandished knives at her husband and Charles Louis hit his wife with such force that he almost broke her nose, Sophia was a ship sailing a steady course through a storm-lashed sea. The more that drama errupted around her, the more determined she became to escape and for a young lady at court, escape meant marriage.

When Charles Louis was invited to a meeting with the Holy Roman Emperor at the White Mountain, where his father had lost so much, it was a moment of great triumph for the family. This time he rode at the head of a grand and celebratory procession to be awarded the rank of Imperial Arch-Treasurer. The Palatinate was welcomed back with wide open arms into the empire that had once forsaken it. Once again, a member of the family would sit at the table of power and once again, Sophia could enjoy a glimpse of the highest of high lives.

As a mark of respect the heavily pregnant Charlotte was allowed to sit in an armchair by the empress, which was a rarely bestowed honour, and the festivities seemed unending. For Charlotte, of course, who was never without complaints, the whole thing was a disaster, armchair or not. Her fashionable, expensive French gowns wouldn't fasten around her growing bump. Not only that but Sophia was still at her brother's side far too much for her liking and she complained of it to anyone who would listen, sharing scandalous stories of her imagined betrayal at the hands of her own sister-in-law. Thanks to this jealousy and despite their professional triumphs, the marriage of the elector and electress went from bad to worse. With Charlotte still accusing both Charles Louis and Sophia of romantic and incestuous intrigues, her jealous fears were about to come true after a fashion. Happily for our story, however, the woman who caught the elector's eye wasn't his own sister but a young lady named Marie Luise von Degenfeld, better known as Luise.

Luise was just 16 when she became a lady-in-waiting to Charlotte and the first time Charles Louis clapped eyes on her, he was bowled over. Though she didn't quite share Charlotte's dazzling beauty, she also lacked her bad temper and combined an unassuming prettiness with intelligence and good humour. She also possessed an unimpeachable character and for three years the determined lady valiantly resisted Charles Louis' efforts to make her his mistress. Charles Louis wasn't the only man who was enchanted by the young lady and soon the very married elector found himself in competition for Luise's favour.

Charles Louis had invited his dashing brother, Prince Rupert, to Heidelberg and the two men set about trying to reach an agreement on territory that would suit them both. Whilst agreement eluded them, one thing that they certainly shared was a taste in women and Rupert fell hard for Luise, determined to make her his mistress. When Luise rejected Rupert's attentions, he wrote to her asking why she wouldn't let him court her but the unaddressed letter fell into Charlotte's hands and the electress immediately assumed that it was intended for *her* eyes and that her brother-in-law was getting rather above himself. She asked Rupert what the meaning of it was and why he had ambitions to court her. When she learned that he had intended the letter for her lady-in-waiting, Charlotte was seized by bitter jealousy. Things went from bad to worse when Luise finally capitulated and became the mistress of Charles Louis, a situation that Charlotte had simply not been expecting.

When Charlotte caught her husband and the young woman in bed together, she flew into a rage that she directed straight at her rival. During the confrontation that followed her discovery, the electress tore out clumps of Luise's hair and even managed to catch her finger and bite it down to the bone before she was dragged away from the bloodied, battered mistress. Now the household was divided into two camps. On one side were the supporters of the electress, including Sophia's sister, Elisabeth, and on the other were the supporters of the elector including, of course, our heroine.

The household was in constant conflict. Charles Louis gave his wife's jewels to his mistress and moved Luise into a room above his own, which was accessible only by a trapdoor and ladder. Of course Charlotte soon discovered this ruse and was found attempting to climb up to deal with her rival once and for all. This time she was going to rely on more than her teeth and went armed with a sharpened blade. Fearing for their safety, Charles Louis and Luise left Heidelberg and moved to Frankenthal, where the determined elector began to search for some means to escape the wife he had once adored and now hated. He was determined to get his divorce and marry Luise, no matter how arcane the law he might have to invoke.

Meanwhile, the one-time Queen Elizabeth of Bohemia, daughter of James I, sister of Charles I, aunt of Charles II, had big plans for her youngest daughter. She wanted her to marry if not the most well-known and famed of husbands, then one who could at least bestow on his bride the title of *queen*. The current incumbent of the troublesome throne of Bohemia was Ferdinand IV, who shared responsibility for the territory with his father, Ferdinand III, the Holy Roman Emperor. Ferdinand IV was three years Sophia's junior and had an impressive roster of other titles to boast of too, including King of Hungary and Croatia, and King of the Romans. His father fully intended his son to succeed him as Holy Roman Emperor when the time came, so he was certainly a young man who was destined for the greatest things.

He was *vastly* eligible.

He was also a Roman Catholic.

When the much sought after Ferdinand IV arrived in Heidelberg and set his eyes on Sophia, he was bowled over. The religious issue might well prove to be an obstacle but for Ferdinand, it was one he was willing to try and overcome, for he longed to make Sophia his wife. What more might Elizabeth wish for her youngest child - other than the Catholic part, of course - than for her to marry the heir to the Holy Roman Empire?

Sadly for everyone, but saddest of all for Ferdinand, it was not to be. The young king died of smallpox in 1654 and at the moment of his death, an enormous earthquake shook all of Vienna. It seemed to those who admired him that the earth itself was crying out in anguish at his loss.

Suitors Fit for a Princess

The portrait of the unfortunate Ferdinand IV was still hanging in pride of place in Heidelberg when a new visitor, Adolph John I, Count of Zweibrücken-Kleeburg, rode into the city. He brought with him more than just his good wishes. Sophia was rather put off by his 'long pointed chin like a shoehorn' but as the younger brother of the heir to the Swedish throne[37], his prospects were better than his looks. Adolph John, on the other hand, found nothing to dislike about Sophia whatsoever and Charlotte, once her hated sister-in-law's loudest critic, now became her greatest champion. In Adolph John she saw the opportunity to be rid of Sophia once and for all and she wasn't going to let it slip away.

Though he was only one year older than Sophia, Adolph John was already a widower[38]. His first wife, Elizabeth Beatrice Brahe, died in early 1653 and with a year having passed, he was keen to marry again.

Yet the spectre of that first marriage followed him around, for it had been famously dire. The duke was notorious for his neglect and ill-treatment of his late wife, whom he was known to physically abuse, but none of that mattered to Charlotte. Instead she encouraged Adolph John to pursue Sophia's hand in marriage, spying an unmissable chance to pack her off for good. She stressed his supposed virtues to Charles Louis too, pointing out not his cloudy past, but his potentially promising future. With Adolph John's childless brother weakened by ill health and weight, it was fully expected that he would one day become the king of Sweden. He was determined to do so with a whole brood of heirs and spares to his name who would carry on his line through the ages. Though his short first marriage had resulted in a son, that child had died within six months, so there was no time to lose[39].

So far, so scheming.

Adolph John's motives weren't as well-hidden as he might hope and his plans for dynastic takeover might have repercussions for far more parties than those in Sweden and Heidelberg. Hearing of the news and well aware of the possible implications for Britain, John Thurloe[40] wrote:

> 'I forgott to tell you of a storie I heard from the elector Palatine's court, which is, that the king of Sweedland's [sic] onlie brother shall be married to the elector's sister, called Sophia, which is here much spoken of; and that this kinge of Swedland [sic] will never gett a childe, being so corpulent, fat, and grosse a man; and therefore the brother beinge heir, and like to gett children, will in tyme strengthen R. C.[41] and his party, &c.'[42]

Adolph John approached Charles Louis and asked for his consent to marry Sophia. The elector had always been close to the Swedish king and now, faced with this request from the monarch's brother, he felt that he had no choice but to accept. He attached a condition to this though and made it clear that the betrothal could not go ahead without the consent of King Charles X Gustav. An envoy was dispatched for Sweden and Charles Louis wrote to his mother to appraise her of the situation.

Elizabeth was characteristically underwhelmed and sent the written equivalent of a disinterested shrug, saying only, 'I cannot be against [the marriage], considering the condition wee are all in'[43]. As the court waited with bated breath to receive word from Sweden, Sophia must have considered it a done deal and she was miserable at the thought of it. Her brother said yes, her mother said *whatever* and she… well, that didn't matter. She was a princess and her duty was to behave like one; that included getting married when the time came, whether she liked the groom or not.

Though her response was less than enthusiastic, Elizabeth's own marriage treaty forbade her from approving a betrothal for her daughter without the consent of her nephew, Charles. So she took up her pen and wrote to him via his secretary to make that official request.

> 'I send you here a letter for the King [Charles II]; it is about a match betwixt Prince Adolphe, the King of Sweden's brother, and Sophie. He has desired it very handsomely. My son [the Elector] has consented to it, *reservings* the King of Sweden's consent and mine, who am to acquaint the King with it. I do it now, and send you the copy of Prince Adolphe's letter. I pray get an answer from the King [Charles II] as soon as you can. I have no more to say but am ever your most affectionate friend.'[44]

The request was accepted and gossip on the continent grew louder than ever. Despite the promise of secrecy Adolph John started flashing Sophia's portrait around and telling everyone that she would soon be his wife. Thurloe recorded, 'Adolph John hath concluded a match with the princess Sophia. 'Tis thought he speedily returns, and then the marriage is to be.'[45]

As the saying doesn't quite go, *'tis thought wrong*.

A Hanoverian Overture

In Hanover, meanwhile, there was suddenly a duke in reluctant search of a bride. This wasn't Ernest Augustus, however, with whom Sophia had spent many happy hours strumming the guitar. It was his brother, George William.

George William liked to have a good time and to have a good time, George William needed money. Now, he had *some* money, but it wasn't enough to meet his lavish needs and he was told by those holding the purse strings that, if those strings were to be loosened, then a compromise must be agreed. If the duke were to take a bride, he would be given a larger allowance; but no bride, no payout.

The duke put his thinking cap on. He began to consider all of the likely candidates he knew of, but few of them seemed particularly appealing. Eventually he settled on the idea of Sophia, but he had heard about the supposedly secret Swedish request for her hand, as had virtually every noble house on the continent. By then no reply had been received from the king of Sweden though, so as far as he was concerned, Sophia was still up for grabs.

With no time to lose, George William sent an envoy[46] to Heidelberg to ascertain the situation regarding Sophia and her shoehorn-chinned suitor. Upon learning that the Swedish sovereign's permission was still outstanding he swung into action and asked Charles Louis if he might be permitted to marry Sophia. The young princess was thrilled by this turn of events, for she was fond of George William and next to the shoehorn-faced, bad-tempered Adolph John, he was certainly the better choice. As she later recalled, 'my answer was not that of a heroine of romance, for I unhesitatingly said "Yes"!'

Was there more to the breaking off of the engagement than this breathless procession of romantic twists and turns might suggest? Why *was* Charles X Gustav of Sweden dragging his feet on giving his consent and could it be related to events in England, where Oliver Cromwell now sat in power as Lord Protector? Charles X Gustav was engaged in very delicate negotiations with Cromwell, whom he saw as a man worth keeping on side, and he was very well aware of how a marriage between his own brother and the niece of the late, executed king, might go down.

The *State Papers of John Thurloe* from 1655 give an insight into exactly what was going on behind the scenes and the implication is clear. Cromwell and Charles X Gustav had reached an accord since the former assumed power in England. For Charles X Gustav, this made the prospect of a marriage between his brother and the cousin of the deposed Charles II very awkward indeed. Might this be the cause of the delay in the Swedish monarch's agreement to the betrothal?

> '[Moore, Prince Adolph's envoy visited Thurloe] to sound and enquier of mee, how his highnesse [Charles X Gustav] liked of his suite to the lady Sophia daughter to the queen

of Bohemia; but the said Moore having first spoken of it to the king, he fell into a great passion, and told coll. Moore, that if his brother should thinke of that match, or endeavour any longer to seeke soe near allyance as by marriage with those, that were enemyes to his highnesse, with whome he had already made a peace, and att this time was contracting a more close and feirmer league of amity and allyance (being a thing he more desired then with all the princes of Europe) he would discountenance him, and never see his face more.'[47]

Things were progressing apace. Wedding outfits were ordered in Paris and got as far as completion, even without the Swedish crown's blessing. Happily for all the parties concerned other than Adolph John, the wish to escape from the betrothal was mutual. Sophia wished to marry George William, George William wished to marry her - for now - and in Sweden, the king was anything but keen. Rather than be placed in the awkward position of denying Charles Louis' request for his consent to the marriage, Charles X Gustav simply dragged his heels and delayed matters for as long as he possibly could. It was just long enough to ensure that word got out. Intriguingly though, it wasn't Sophia who was held responsible.

'The Electoral Court at Heidelburgh is much discontented at the retraction of the Match intended between the Prince *Adolph* the King of *Swedens* Brother, and the Princess *Sophia*, Sister to the Elector. Prince *Rupert*, taking a snuff at the abandoning of his Sister, is gone to the Emperour, who gave him a command.'[48]

Sophia's request to her brother that she be allowed to marry George William instead was, therefore, a God-send. As soon as the elector saw how keen his sister was for the match, he said yes. Charles Louis was determined not to cause any further diplomatic upset in resolving the matter and, wary of the delicacy with which it would be necessary to break the news to the jilted Swede, it was agreed that the engagement to George William would remain a secret until Charles X Gustav had been informed. This suited George William, who wished to be able to drive a bargain with the Estates regarding his allowance and if they learned he was already betrothed, then that plan would be dead in the water before it even began. Instead he intended to negotiate an increase in his allowance and only reveal that he already had a bride to be when he was happy with the payout on offer.

Luckily for the Palatinate contingent, as we have already learned, the Swedish monarch was far from convinced that the marriage between Sophia and Adolphus John would be a good idea. Even without the political considerations Charles X Gustav knew his brother better than anyone. It didn't matter how charming and accomplished the ladies might be, he had his reservations about whether *anybody* deserved the fate of being married to his sibling. With a combination of doubt about the suitability of his brother as a husband and Cromwell rattling his sabre over in England, an end to the engagement was the best possible outcome that the Swedish sovereign could have hoped for.

Despite the secrecy, one person who was entrusted with knowledge of the clandestine betrothal was George William's best friend, confidante and brother, Ernest Augustus. He was with George William when he arrived in Heidelberg to negotiate the marriage and when that business was concluded, the two siblings travelled on to Venice.

They were not the only ones.

Upon their arrival in Italy, the worst coincidence imaginable occurred and, horror of horrors, George William and Ernest Augustus found themselves caught in an encounter with Adolphus John. The hopeful duke was full of excitement at his forthcoming nuptials and he loved cornering people and showing them a miniature of Sophia, the woman he was by now confident he would marry. As soon as Charles Louis heard this he called Adolphus John's envoy, Lasalle, to request his presence to discuss the delicate matter. One does not become a trusted member of the royal household without being a shrewd operator and as soon as Lasalle saw a portrait of George William being hung in the palace he immediately put two and two together. The canny Lasalle dropped into a courtly bow and declared that he was and would always be George William's most devoted servant.

That's social climbing.

When Lasalle left Heidelberg to break the bad news to the unfortunate Adolph John, he was armed with the finest gifts imaginable courtesy of Charles Louis. Whatever conversation occurred we can only guess but the rejected duke flew into a fury, offering a glimpse of his legendary bad temper. He declared himself to be a man wronged, and wronged by a woman who should know better. When his tantrum achieved nothing, he went to his brother, the king of Sweden, and demanded that he force the union. Unfortunately for Adolph John, Charles X Gustav was rather preoccupied with fighting a war and if the elector and his family didn't want the marriage to happen, then he wasn't about to tell them it must be otherwise.

Adolph John ranted and raved and even wrote to Sophia's mother protesting against his abandonment. It was all to no avail, he had lost his princess to another.

Little did Sophia know that she too was about to lose her fiancé as a clandestine liaison in Venice set in place a chain of events that changed the course of royal history forever.

Breaking the Engagement

Absence does not always make the heart grow fonder and in the case of George William, it did quite the opposite. Safely in Venice and with the matter of the marriage settled, he resumed his partying lifestyle and promptly acquired a rather unpleasant souvenir of his travels. This wasn't a cheeky t-shirt or a colourful fridge magnet but a nasty case of venereal disease. This itchy issue bothered the duke less than the knowledge that he had thrown away his bachelor lifestyle and when his allowance was increased *without* any further demands for a wedding from the Estates, he realised that he had jumped the gun somewhat. If only he had waited, George William wailed, he might have had his money *and* his freedom.

He wanted out.

George William's letters to Sophia grew more infrequent and a long-planned visit to Heidelberg was called off at the duke's say-so, leaving his intended in no doubt that she was no longer the apple of his eye.

She wasn't even the shoehorn.

From this distance, given the intricate dance of the dynastic marriage mart it's all too easy to forget that these were the lives of real people under discussion. Sophia was rapidly approaching 30 and as far as the eligible bachelors were concerned, her all-important heir and spare producing years were dwindling. She herself was all too aware of the scars smallpox had left on her face and to be publicly slighted by a suitor who simply didn't turn up when expected must have hurt Sophia keenly.

Sophia knew how to give the impression of confidence even if inside she must have been at the very least annoyed. From the Winter Queen, the princess had inherited a pragmatic nature that might have made her a queen to be reckoned with and her engagement to George William was to test that to its limits. For now though, she was still learning how best to play the diplomat, but she knew that the only thing she had that she could bargain with was her hand in marriage. Ultimately the decision of who Sophia would and wouldn't marry would be made by her brother, Charles Louis, but he adored her and after the Swedish debacle was willing to follow his sister's lead in a way that many young women found that their families were not. Sophia wasn't about to sit at home and pine for George William so when she heard that Ranuccio Il Farnese, Duke of Parma[49], had also taken a fancy to her, she revelled in it.

Of course, Sophia had no intention of marrying the Duke of Parma, and she would have had to convert to Catholicism to do so, which was even more unlikely, but if she hoped that she might make George William jealous, she was to be sorely mistaken. Little known to Sophia, he was already making arrangements of his own, and they were to involve his brother.

George William remembered all too well those shared guitar strumming sessions between Ernest Augustus and Sophia of the Palatinate back in Heidelberg, and he knew that his brother thought back fondly on them too. Ernest Augustus was still unmarried and as neither of them was the eldest brother of the family, there was little to choose between the two dukes. In fact, there were two other brothers making up the family group and they were Christian Louis, the eldest son and heir, and John Frederick, whose most remarkable - and remarked upon - feature was his immense weight. Hanover was not yet an electorate, but the family ambitions were high and whilst the childless Christian Louis was being prepared to fulfil them, the younger brothers must each make a marriage of their own.

George William asked Ernest Augustus if he would like to marry Sophia, the girl to whom he had once sent guitar tunes to practice at home. Ernest Augustus, showing a little of the negotiating skill that would later serve him well as an elector, said that he would happily consider it, but he had a couple of caveats before he gave his final agreement. George William had a bit of a wait to find out what those caveats were though, for Ernest Augustus was enjoying a stay in Venice, so his correspondence was just a tad delayed.

The delay went on. And on. What George William didn't know was that his brother wasn't stalling for time, but had been taken dangerously ill. There is, I think, no better example of George William's emotional, reactive manner than something that occurred at this point in the story. He received a letter from Venice that explained that Ernest Augustus had been near death but had happily survived. George William saw only the words *Ernest Augustus* and *death* and assumed that his beloved brother had passed away. In a fit of grief he tore the letter to shreds and threw it into the fire. Only when a quick-thinking attendant grabbed the pieces and reassembled the letter for him to read did he realise his mistake. This wasn't a man who was given to considered thinking.

Amongst the conditions that Ernest Augustus wanted George William to satisfy were two of particular importance. Firstly, Ernest Augustus wanted his brother to hand Lüneburg over to him if he agreed to marry Sophia. Always a savvy sort, Ernest Augustus would prove adept indeed at acquiring territory. Secondly, he wanted George William to give his word that he would never pursue a future marriage. This might seem like an odd condition but the reasoning behind it was sound. As Ernest Augustus' older brother, should George William later become a father, any heir might challenge Ernest Augustus for the return of Lüneburg and that would never do.

No heir, no challenge.

Now, let us keep in mind that George William didn't have great form when it came to making reasoned decisions and fully considering their future implications. Upon hearing his brother's conditions he happily accepted in principle but suggested that they had better run the idea past John Frederick, the third brother of the four, first. They assured their brother that, should Ernest Augustus die first, then the surrendered territories would be inherited by John Frederick as the next brother in line. This wasn't good enough for John Frederick though, who failed to see how it was that Ernest Augustus, the youngest brother of all, seemed to have jumped ahead of him when it came to marriage discussions. He knew that it wasn't only Sophia's hand that was at stake, but the territory of Lüneburg too, and he wanted both.

The more John Frederick thought about it, the more furious he became. He demanded to know why Ernest Augustus had been given first refusal on Sophia and Lüneburg and in an angry confrontation, lunged at Ernest Augustus and attempted to tear the agreement from his hand. George William was present at this undignified scuffle and as the two brothers struggled over the paperwork, he stood by and laughed. For Ernest Augustus and John Frederick, there was little cause for humour. The pair had never been close and now they grew more distant than ever but the plan, once in motion, was not to be stopped.

What a thing it was for Sophia, a proud and intelligent woman, to be passed around like this. She might have claimed that 'a good establishment was all I cared for, and that, if this was secured to me by the younger brother, the exchange would be to me a matter of indifference,' but can we really take her at her word? All her value was tied up in her prospects of marriage and with her thirtieth birthday on the horizon, her offers were not exactly plentiful. Her choices if she didn't marry were limited indeed and life at the elector's court was anything but welcoming.

In Heidelberg, there was another conflict between brothers as Rupert, who had not been able to come to an agreement on territory with Charles Louis, was banished from the city. Charles Louis couldn't stay in Frankenthal forever and behind the walls of the former Kommisariat things between the elector and his wife were worse than ever, as what had once been a fiery relationship had descended into all-out war. Charlotte's physical attacks on her husband's mistress and her own attendants were as frequent as they were frightening, and the smallest thing could provoke her into a rage. From the finger she nearly bit off to the regular violent beatings, life was rarely peaceful. Though we only have Sophia's word on these attacks, there can be little doubt that things in Heidelberg had deteriorated. At best, the elector was jealous and the electress bad-tempered, at worst they were at daggers drawn and Charles Louis began to find as many excuses as he could to flee the company of his wife, regularly taking refuge in the safe distance provided by Frankenthal. It's only natural, therefore, that Sophia was also keen to escape.

It was to Frankenthal that Ernest Augustus sent his advisor, George Christopher von Hammerstein, where he was charged with selling the idea of the change of groom to Charles Louis. Hammerstein was at pains to point out that the only thing that would be different was the identity of the groom and that Sophia could expect a life of comfort as the wife of Ernest Augustus, who was to be appointed Bishop of Osnabrück. Of the remaining three brothers George William was willing to sign away his right to marry, Christian Louis looked unlikely to produce an heir after several years of marriage whilst John Frederick was single, though he would not remain so, and was believed to be impotent due to his corpulence[50]. All of this meant that Ernest Augustus and subsequently his heirs - and Sophia's too, should she consent to be his bride - would eventually inherit all that was currently split four ways in Brunswick-Lüneburg. Should there be any doubt about George William keeping his promise not to marry and have children of his own, Hammerstein assured the elector that George William's brush with venereal disease in Venice had left him unable to father a child. On this matter he would prove to be gravely mistaken.

For a young lady who was acutely aware of her Stuart birthright, there was something even more important on the table: heritage and breeding. Ernest Augustus could trace his line back to Henry the Lion, an immensely powerful German prince of the twelfth century. Henry's House of Welf had diminished somewhat over the centuries but blood was blood and in Ernest Augustus' veins, the blood of the Lion flowed.

The elector listened to these entreaties carefully and informed Hammerstein that, though he would be happy to agree to the change of plan, the decision ultimately rested with Sophia. She in turn agreed to the suggestion, assuring her brother that she trusted his judgment implicitly. Besides, what she cared most for was a good marriage and security and she knew she could look forward to both with Ernest Augustus. Of all the four brothers, only Ernest Augustus now seemed likely to father an heir and that meant that all the territories that were currently split four ways might, unless the familial situation of any of his brothers changed, eventually fall into his hands or at least those of his heirs. Though the Treaty of Westphalia[51] already assured Ernest Augustus and the House of Brunswick-Lüneburg the position of the next Bishop of Osnabrück, this was just a stepping stone. It's not unreasonable to assume that Ernest Augustus was already considering his claim for the electoral cap of Hanover, once his position was established.

Sophia, for now, had no such ambitions. Her brother had teased her about the lofty aims of her husband's family, asking how four brothers might share an electoral cap. Perhaps, he ventured, they might also like to revisit their family crest, which showed a Saxon horse. It would have to be a strong horse, he teased, if it were to carry four strapping dukes all at once. Of course they could always take turns with the cap, Charles Louis mused, for how else could such a role possibly be divided between four frequently argumentative and ambitious siblings?

All of this seemed like very silly talk indeed to Sophia. All she was interested in for now was gaining her freedom and an establishment of her own, and she finally stood on the cusp of achieving that ambition.

In order to ensure that all the parties were clear on exactly what they were getting, George William agreed to sign a Renunciation of Marriage. In it, he set out the terms and conditions under which the agreement was made.

'Having perceived the urgent necessity of taking into consideration how our House of this line may best be provided with heirs and be perpetuated in the future; yet having been and remaining up to the present date both unable and unwilling in my own person to engage in any marriage contract, I have rather induced my brother, Ernest Augustus, to declare that, on condition of receiving from me a renunciation of marriage for myself, written and signed with my own hand, in favour of himself and his heirs male, he is prepared forthwith and without delay to enter into holy matrimony, and, as may be hoped, soon to bestow the blessing of heirs on people and country, as has been agreed and settled between him and myself; and where whereas my brother, Ernest Augustus, for reasons before mentioned, has entered into a marriage contract with her Highness Princess Sophia, which contract he purposes shortly to fulfil, so I, on my side, not only on account of my word given to and pledged, but also of my own free will and consent, desire to ratify and confirm the aforesaid conditions to my before mentioned brother, and promise, so long as the said Princess and my brother continue in life and in the bonds of matrimony, or after their decease leave heirs male, that I neither will nor shall on any account enter into, much less carry out, any marriage on tract with any person, and with nothing else than to spend what remains to me of life entirely *in celibatu*, to the extent that the heirs male if the before-mentioned Princess and of my brother, in whose favour this renunciation is made, may attain and succeed to the sovereignty over one or both of these our principalities. For the safer and truer assurance of all which conditions I have, with my own hand, written and signed this renunciation and sealed it with my seal, and thereafter handed it over with all due care to my brother's own charge and keeping. So done at Hanover.'

So done, indeed.

A Divorce and a Marriage

By this point, Sophia was 27 and a girl no longer. Keen to get the show on the road, Ernest Augustus asked Sophia to come to Hanover to be married there in a low-key ceremony but Charles Louis wouldn't hear of it. The elector had always been inordinately fond of his younger sister and there was no question of his letting her go to Hanover as an unmarried woman. Let the duke come to Heidelberg, he said, and be married there. Only then would Sophia leave for her new home.

All of these discussions were carried out in secret, for Sophia's marriage plans had been disrupted enough times. Even her mother, Elizabeth, knew nothing of what was happening between her children, busy as she no doubt was with her monkeys and dogs!

There was just one thing that everyone had forgotten.

In Heidelberg, a monk named Father Manari waited patiently for word from his own patron, the Duke of Parma. As far as Manari was concerned, Parma's hopes for the hand of Sophia were still alive and as soon as he received the go ahead, the monk was ready to start negotiating. When no message was received from the duke, Manari began to grow more and more convinced that his employer had forgotten his plans to wed Sophia and with them, forgotten Manari too. Imagine Manari's horror when he saw an unfounded rumour in a scandal sheet that Parma had already married another, which meant that he had forgotten his faithful servant and quite abandoned his loyal clerical envoy in Heidelberg.

The distraught Manari was found dead. He had drowned and one can only wonder whether it was self-inflicted. Only when the Duke of Parma heard this sad news did he send a representative to continue the marriage negotiations. Upon discovering that Sophia was now betrothed to another, the matter was left, much to the relief of all concerned.

Only now did anyone think to tell Elizabeth that her daughter was to be married to Ernest Augustus. She reacted with precisely the enthusiasm you might expect. Perhaps it was family loyalty that kept her from congratulating the couple for her nephew, Charles II, had of course been her own preferred candidate. Indeed, had she not hoped that Sophia might one day be able to call herself a queen? Instead her daughter was about to marry a man who, as the younger son of Hanover, could not expect to ever amount to anything particularly illustrious. Ever the mistress of the passive aggressive family missive, she wrote:

> 'I easilie beleeue you haue business enough at this time to hinder your writing to me often, but I uill not dissemble uith you that I wonder you did not lett me know of the change of Sophies mariage. You trusted me with the first secret[52], where I assure you that I kept my worde, for by me none knew of it, though Poletandre has gott the knowledge of it, which I ame verie innocent off, he has gott it but uithin these seauen or eight weekes, yett he neuer saide anie thing of it to me nor I to him, still now the other is knowen and I did not mention it to him till he begane to me; as for this great secret of Duke Ernest Augustus it was onlie a secret to me, for all at Cassel and euerie where it was known before I knew it, and did positiuelie denie when it was known before I knew it, and did positiuelie denie when I was asked the question. I doe not at all dislike the match concerning the person, being no exceptions against him for whome I haue a great esteeme, which is all I uill answere, since neither my opinion nor consent hath bene asked, I haue no more to say, but uish that it may proud for Sophies content and hapiness, I shall be verie glade to see her, and uish it may be speedilie, and that the business may not too long a doing.'[53]

It was as effusive as Elizabeth was ever going to get. Besides, she was rather enjoying revelling in her own drama, for she had recently been abandoned herself. Louise Hollandine, who had always seemed so meek and loyal, had done the unthinkable and absconded from The Hague.

On the day of her disappearance she missed lunch with her mother but this in itself hadn't been taken as anything unusual, for she had mused on the possibility of spending the day paying visits and she was often too occupied in her artwork to emerge from her rooms. When Louise Hollandine failed to materialise even as the night drew in, a search of the building revealed no sign of her other than a note in which she informed Elizabeth that she had left The Hague for a new life as - cue dramatic drumroll - a Catholic nun.

It was later discovered that Louise Hollandine, tired of being condemned to remain forever in her mother's home, had been planning her escape for months and had left before dawn. She travelled alone through the country until she arrived at a rendez-vous with friends who took her on to Paris where she was granted the protection of the exiled Queen Henrietta Maria, wife of Charles I, and the entire French court. Though rumours soon spread that she had fled to conceal an illegitimate pregnancy there was no truth in this. She went on to lead a long and happy life in her new land, devoted to her faith and convent.

Of more immediate concern to Charles Louis was the small matter of his sister's dowry and the expense of her marriage. Happily for Charles Louis, the rather reduced Elector Palatine, a third of this expense was borne by the Holy Roman Emperor and not his own treasury. The wedding itself was eye-wateringly expensive even without having to meet the full costs of the dowry. He wrote to his mother to inform her that he was going to have to tighten the purse strings a little further, for this was an expense that must take precedence above all other.

> 'The expences about my sister's marriage (not for the ceremonies or pomp, but for the realities fit for her) to which I am obliged, render me uncapable of what your Majesty is pleased to require of me, concerning the 4,000 rix; for, besides her due, which I must advance, I am bound to an extraordinary, more especially for the friendship she always shewed me, and because nobody else hath done anything for her.'[54]

And in many ways, he was right. The dethroned Queen of Bohemia had no maternal instinct when it came to her children though for her animals, she had it to spare. Elizabeth's marriage hadn't gone to plan and the flaxen-haired beauty who had once had the world at her feet had not lived the life she might have hoped for. She had loved her late husband but his mental state had often been fragile and when Frederick had accepted the crown of Bohemia, the blame for this ambitious, mistaken move had all too often been laid at Elizabeth's door. She was criticised as a woman of rampant ambition and influence, an arrogant social climber who was reckless when it came to achieving her dreams, and who was so blinded by the supposed splendour of the Bohemian throne that she had sacrificed the stability and future of the Palatinate to get at it.

Instead Elizabeth was in exile. She was still surrounded by admirers, of course, but this was not where a woman with Stuart blood in her veins might have expected to end up. She never gave up her political interests and always battled for the dynastic cause of her marital house but in reality she was isolated from her homeland thanks to her lobbying for English assistance in the Palatinate and the subsequent overthrow of the monarchy. Her relationship with her children was strained at best and she held little influence over them, despite her occasional passive aggressive salvos from exile.

Ultimately, Sophia's life in The Hague had come to an end with the unfortunate episode of the clumsy approaches of the Prince of Wales, one day to become Charles II. This would have been the time for Elizabeth to step in and support her daughter, who had inherited her mother's political sense and knew an angle when she saw one. Instead she had chastised Sophia for not playing up to Charles' attentions, for not putting prince ahead of pride. After that, Sophia couldn't wait to get away and in all likelihood she was as keen to escape Elizabeth as she was to leave The Hague.

Life in Heidelberg might have been more glittering and though there wasn't exactly much money to splash around, thanks to the violent marriage between elector and electress, there was drama to spare instead. Having long since ceased to love his wife and her eyebrows Charles Louis got the divorce he longed for in 1658 when he announced that he and Charlotte were no longer married, citing her 'unpleasant, disobedient, obstinate, insupportable and recalcitrant behaviour.' That same year, he married Luise.

Despite his wife's fury, Charles Louis offered Charlotte an olive branch following the divorce. Should she consent to treat his new wife with respect, he would agree to repay her with half of the Heidelberg castle as well as a regular annuity to keep her in the manner to which she had become accustomed. There was no point in arguing for the decision was made, but it was hardly conducive to a happy home life[55]. Of course the furious Charlotte couldn't behave civilly to Luise and in the end, she had to be removed from Heidelberg and bundled home to Hesse.

In her brother's custody, Sophia saw a side of life that she had never experienced at Elizabeth's court, from the furious electress to the romantic intrigues of her potential suitors. Here she grew into a woman and here, with Charles Louis becoming the father she had lost in infancy, Sophia wrote the next chapter of her life.

Act Two

Duchess

'I, being resolved to love him, was delighted to find how amiable he was.'

A Married Woman

On 30 September 1658, Sophia of the Palatinate married Ernest Augustus, Duke of Brunswick-Lüneburg. The wedding took place, as her brother was dead set that it would, in Heidelberg. Sophia had waited a long time to reach this day and she was determined to make a splash. It took so long for Miss Carey to adorn her friend in a gown of silver brocade and dress her loose hair with a diamond crown that the ceremony, scheduled for 6.00 pm, didn't take place until 9.00 pm. Four ladies-in-waiting bore the bride's immense train and not one but two brothers escorted her to the altar, for the elector was joined by the Roman Catholic Edward, who had travelled from his home in Paris to see his little sister get married. Her mother, still smarting from Charles Louis' rejection of her requests for financial help and unable to leave her creditors in The Hague, did not attend. She did, however, write to Charles II and request that her new son-in-law be granted the Order of the Garter. The request was duly granted.

A sobbing and abandoned Electress Charlotte was likewise absent, watching the festivities from a secluded spot out of sight of the other attendees. Perhaps unsurprisingly, none of Ernest Augustus' family was in attendance. George William could hardly occupy a front row seat at the wedding of the girl he had abandoned and John Frederick, still sour from not being offered his own chance to woo Sophia, wouldn't even consider attending.

Though Ernest Augustus had been keen for a smallish wedding, in the event it turned out to be anything but. Sophia herself looked back on the ceremony with obvious pride, for this was the day that she finally graduated from supporting player to lead.

'Twenty-four gentleman marched before us, bearing lighted torches, adorned with ribbons in our armorial colours, (blue and white for me, red and yellow for the Duke). Cannon were fired at the moment when the clergyman united us. We were then placed opposite to each other, under a canopy, the Elector also having one apart for himself, while the *Te Deum* was sung. After the ceremony we returned to our apartments, where I renounced all claim to the Palatinate.'

Just as George William had renounced his rights to wed, so now did Sophia renounce her territory. The difference was, only one of them would keep the promise they made.

After an opulent wedding feast that began at 11.00 pm, the couple finally retired to bed at 6.00 am. Though what happened behind those closed doors must remain a secret shared only by those who were present, there can be little doubt from Sophia's recollections that she was delighted with her husband and that he was equally smitten with her. The newlyweds didn't emerge from their chambers until the following afternoon and by this time, Sophia and Ernest Augustus might reasonably be expected to have done rather more than practise their guitar chords.

The festivities were followed by a parting, as Ernest Augustus had official business that kept him from accompanying his new bride to Hanover. As the couple parted, Charles Louis finally made his secret divorce a matter of public knowledge. Sophia was too busy being dazzled by her dashing duke to bother with any domestic drama. Instead she was determined to fall in love. Not for her the misery of the Elector and Electress Palatine, their relationship marked and marred by mutual combat and a love that had long since turned to loathing. In some ways, to fall in love in such circumstances might seem like a stretch to our modern sensibilities but Sophia was a proud sort of woman and when she considered the question of her husband she reflected that she had resolved to love him no matter what, so she was relieved and not a little delighted to find that he was, at least, *amiable*.

Simply put, Sophia had made a conscious decision to love the man she was to marry regardless of whether he was loveable and often, he was anything but. Fortunately, she convinced herself that he *was* or at least that he might grow on her, which must have made her resolution easier to keep. Her union was certainly to prove more successful than some royal marriages were, including that of her brother and later, the disastrous match she made for her eldest son.

The *amiable* man who she was determined to adore sent his new wife to Hanover at the head of a magnificent and stately procession. During the journey she had spent an interlude as a guest of her marital uncle, George II, Landgrave of Hesse-Darmstadt, where the woman raised at first at the Winter Queen's chaotic court in exile, then in the fiery household of the Elector Palatine, caught a tantalising glimpse of just how protocol-ridden a court *could* be. Despite or perhaps because of her eventful youth, Sophia longed for order. It wasn't the stifling routine of her childhood with its multiple curtsies and mind-numbing adherence to precedence that she craved, but a sense of things being done correctly and according to rank and title. Here in Darmstadt, she saw that being taken to its extremes.

In her memoirs, Sophia notes the rigid etiquette she witnessed when she was a guest of the landgrave and his wife, Sophia Eleanor. From the ceremony of their first meeting outside of the town, when the married ladies could not ride with the princesses and the princesses could not ride with the countesses, to the carefully appointed rooms from which each rank was permitted to watch a firework display, she observed the full weight and discipline of protocol. Sophia's companions, used to being her constant shadow, were not at all happy to be kept so distant from her and when they saw the landgravine's ladies-in-waiting forming a guard of honour beside the halberdiers outside their mistresses' room, Sophia's attendants were flabbergasted. They *certainly* weren't about to snap to attention.

As a newly married lady of rank Sophia loved being treated as an equal by the landgravine, who joined her children to perform a ballet in honour of her guests. Now she knew what it was to be more than a sister or daughter and though she would miss her brother dreadfully, Sophia was more than ready for this next chapter.

Home at Last

When Sophia neared Hanover, her husband and his three brothers travelled to meet her at the head of a flamboyant cavalcade. Also in the procession was her mother-in-law, Anne Eleonore of Hesse-Darmstadt, at whose etiquette-observing brother's court Sophia had enjoyed a break during her journey. After a speech of welcome was given by Christian Louis, the dukes all crammed into Sophia's carriage to enter the city. It proved quite a challenge thanks to the bulk of the *very* portly John Frederick. Then the rather squeezed party proceeded to the Leineschloss where stunning apartments had been prepared for the new arrival. Sophia first saw her new rooms in the company of the court, not the husband whom she had longed to be reunited with, but they would be alone soon enough. No doubt she paid particular attention to the flight of stairs which she only need to descend to reach Ernest Augustus' own rooms, as they were situated directly beneath her own. This was the *establishment* she had craved and she was determined to make it work for everybody.

Once again, there was ceremony and show and once again, Sophia and Ernest Augustus were the centre of attention. The following day the couple were guests of honour at a celebration of their wedding but all the time, they longed to be alone together, rather than surrounded by adoring courtiers and family. Sophia was determined to fall in love, after all.

That moment finally came on the third day. Years later when her husband was long dead and her days of wine and roses were behind her, Sophia wrote that she took 'pleasure in remembering how rejoiced we were to be left to ourselves when all the guests were gone, and how great was the Duke's devotion to me.' She had not expected anything but the need to create both heir and spare, for this marriage was a business arrangement and with the benefit of hindsight, Sophia claimed that she would have been perfectly content with that arrangement too. Perhaps Sophia was surprised to find that Ernest Augustus, who had seemed keen to marry her only because it made business sense, was as adoring of her as she was of him.

> 'Marrying from interest only he had expected beforehand to feel nothing but indifference for me; but now his feelings were such that I had the fond conviction that he would love me forever, while I in return so idolised him that without him I felt as if I were lost.'

For all Sophia's claims that she would have been happy with nothing but a companionate marriage of convenience, I simply don't believe it.

Written in her dotage, Sophia's fond memories of the early days of her marriage positively shine from the page. Pragmatism and the years that had passed could do nothing to dim the memory, nor lessen the sense of a woman reliving her happiest hours.

Sophia wanted to spend her every waking moment beside her husband and her friends saw less and less of her with each day that passed. When the ever-loyal Miss Carey sought permission to leave Hanover and return to The Hague to marry Baron Franz Ludwig von Bonstetten, Sophia readily granted it, so enamoured was she of the company of Ernest Augustus. As far as she was concerned, she had no need of her female companions now, for she had the constant presence of the man she had resolved to adore.

Was this really wise, though?

There is much to be said for the company of friends, for wonderful though it is to have a devoted spouse, Sophia was soon to find that her husband's attention to her wasn't quite as idyllic as hers was to him. There were, to paraphrase another princess, three people in the marriage.

The third person in the union wasn't another woman, nor was it a lover, but a sibling. In fact it was George William, that brother who had not wanted to marry Sophia when her hand had been his to take. He was a constant presence in the Leineschloss and where Ernest Augustus and Sophia went, George William wasn't far away. He and Ernest Augustus were extraordinarily close, but George William seemed to be hinting that he would like to be extraordinarily close to Sophia too, which was a step too far for the husband and wife. Over the months that followed he became Sophia's shadow, as we will see, but should we be suspicious of the picture she paints in her memoirs, where he is always around every corner, popping up like an unwelcome smell? There is always the possibility that she exaggerated his interest to make herself feel better for his having rejected her but to me that's just not her style. Sophia never expected her memoirs to be made public and most importantly of all, she cared for her reputation far too much to risk it on fancies that weren't true. George William simply wanted what he couldn't have; he was a boy who couldn't reach the biscuit tin.

George William, that fast-loving, hard-living Duke of Brunswick-Lüneburg, was laid up by illness one day when his brother and sister-in-law paid him a visit. Ernest Augustus was relaxing with a book whilst his wife sat at George William's bedside and chatted about this and that, as she was quite happy to do with her husband's favourite brother and closest friend. By way of small talk, Sophia commented that George William must be sorry to be stuck here in bed rather than partying in Italy, his favourite place in the world. Never one to let an opportunity go by, George William declared that so long as Sophia was at his side, he didn't care *where* he was. She laughed off the comment and archly quoted the words of a song that the trio loved, telling him:

> 'Quand on n'a pas ce que l'on aime,
> Il faut aimer ce'que l'on a.'

Or to put it another way:

> 'When you cannot have what you love,
> Love what you have.'

Unfortunately, it was at precisely this moment that Ernest Augustus chose to look up from his book, just in time to hear his wife's throwaway comment. Having missed the first half of the conversation and any reference to not being able to travel to Italy, Ernest Augustus believed what he had heard was his wife dropping a fairly large hint that she had married him because she couldn't have his brother. To say that Ernest Augustus was furious doesn't quite capture exactly how distressed the misunderstanding left him and for what was left of the visit, he was mute. His silence continued until the couple was alone and Sophia begged him to tell her what had happened, but still she was faced with her husband's agonising silence.

Sophia was utterly bereft at the thought that she had upset the husband she was so keen to idolise and he, in true spoiled brat mode, had decided that the best response was to send her to Coventry. Faced with his silent anger, Sophia wished that she was dead, unable to imagine a life without her dashing duke. If this seems like a rather melodramatic reaction to a tiff, spare a moment to remember exactly how Sophia's life had been lived to date. She had never known a normal marriage between loving spouses and had seen no useful example of how a relatively normal couple would behave. Instead she had witnessed violent explosions in Heidelberg, seeing outbursts of physical violence and such extremes of emotion from both Charlotte *and* Charles Louis that it's little wonder that, at 28, she still burst into tears more suited to a child.

Eventually, with Sophia was in floods of tears, Ernest Augustus broke his silence. Upon hearing that he had mistaken her little Italian joke for a secret message of love to his brother, Sophia 'clearly proved to him his mistake. Thus peace was made very quickly between us.'

I suspect that *peace was made* may be the polite way of putting it.

Ironically, it was the siren song of Italy that tempted Ernest Augustus away from his dutiful, devoted wife when he and George William took a trip there to escape the Hanover winter. Though Sophia had hoped to join them, the journey proved too much for her and she was forced to turn back after just one day on the road, leaving the men to travel on without her company.

Bereft all over again, Sophia was caught in a cycle of being distressed by her own distress. She withdrew from public appearances so that nobody would see how unhappy Ernest Augustus' absence had left her, and delighted only when she received his letters. There was also a sniffy missive from a piqued George William and this was the cause of anything *but* delight. The duke, who wanted Sophia only when he could no longer have her, was behaving like a spoiled child with a favourite toy, trying to snatch back what he had already rejected. The cause of his annoyance this time was his belief that his sister-in-law had deliberately pulled her hand away from him when she exited the carriage to leave the brothers to their journey. He had been about to kiss Sophia's hand, he complained, and she had coldly robbed him of the opportunity.

Now, Sophia might weep bitter tears when Ernest Augustus slighted her, but she wasn't about to spare any of them for George William. His letter of complaint went unanswered and Sophia's fair hand stayed resolutely and happily unkissed.

There was to be one more rejection for George William. When the brothers returned, protocol demanded that Sophia greet *him* before her spouse. Instead she dashed straight past her brother-in-law and into her husband's arms.

Quite by accident, of course.

Even now George William wouldn't be cowed and less than a year after the wedding, he was *still* making loaded comments to his sister-in-law until, one day, he told her that he regretted letting her go. Sophia pretended not to have heard because what could she possibly say to *that*? Perhaps, she speculated, there was another aspect of Italian life that he hoped to emulate, this one rather eye-opening. Sophia had heard that in Italy, when one brother married, all declared, 'siamo maritati', meaning that *all* had married the bride of the favourite.

If that was what George William hoped for himself, he was to be sorely disappointed. Sophia was married to one man and one alone, but just as she had seen the destructive powers of jealousy in Heidelberg, now she was to experience it firsthand. No matter how much she adored Ernest Augustus, her jealous husband believed that his wife's affectionate demonstrations were nothing but elaborate ruses designed to throw him off the scent of the *true* object of her lustful thoughts - George William. In a world in where men took mistresses as a matter of routine, Sophia found herself accused without proof of a heinous betrayal, for Ernest Augustus judged all women by those he and his brother had cavorted with in Italy and beyond. As far as he was concerned, the mere matter of being female made one free with one's affections and it seemed as though the courtesans who had illuminated his travels had somehow followed him into marriage. In his loving and devoted bride, he saw the echoes of their spirits.

Sophia didn't dislike George William at first, but she wasn't particularly attracted to him and one begins to get the sense that his constant presence was not only wearying, but the source of some distress to her too. He was an omnipresent phantom in the couple's marriage and Sophia tried to take his closeness to his brother in good spirits, not wishing to give Ernest Augustus a reason to get any more annoyed. Rather than demand the company of her husband as Charlotte did in Heidelberg, Sophia instead attempted to fit herself into the symbiotic relationship of the brothers, smart enough to recognise that her husband would never agree to forego his sibling's company in her favour. No matter what she did, no matter how much unwanted flirtation she let George William get away with, it wasn't enough to calm Ernest Augustus' distrust. Like so many women before and after her, Sophia told herself that his extreme jealousy was merely more proof of his adoration for her, because what else *could* it be but that? She was sure that she could change his mind simply by loving him and continuing to behave as she always had, which was beyond reproach.

She was wrong.

Ernest Augustus was convinced that his wife and his brother shared a fatal attraction. He became so obsessed by his groundless jealousy that he took the most extraordinary lengths to keep the pair in check.

Each afternoon Ernest Augustus took a nap and when he did, he made his wife sit in a chair in front of his and then rested his feet on the arms, so she couldn't leave his presence without waking him. One can't imagine what a life it must have been, living with this Tweedledum and Tweedledee pair of ducal brothers yet Sophia endured it, claiming that she was happy to do so. Pious to the end, she later congratulated herself on her patience, noting that anyone who didn't love their husband as much as she did would have been terribly bored by the long hours in which she was pinioned to her seat by her snoozing spouse. Happily, so adoring did Sophia claim to be that she was supposedly quite content to wait until her husband awoke and restored her freedom once more.

Perhaps fearing the dreadful explosions of emotion and temper that had plagued the elector's court, Sophia did her best to keep Ernest Augustus' terrible jealousy from George William, fearful of causing animosity between the adoring brothers. What she *did* do was try to dissuade George William simply by becoming colder towards him, but he was not to be deterred. Put simply, he was the spoiled child who wanted what his brother had, what he *could* have had, and as his daily visits to Sophia's chambers continued, she grew more and more uncomfortable in his presence.

George William always insisted on arriving in Sophia's rooms before she had an opportunity to dress for the day. Her husband hated the practice but still it continued until Sophia hit upon the idea of asking George William to leave so that she could get dressed in private. She had a feeling that he would step outside, wait a few seconds then walk right back in, no doubt hoping to find her in a less than decent state. As soon as he left the room Sophia locked the door and she was proved right, because no sooner had she done so than he was rattling the handle trying to get back in.

The furious George William accused Sophia of toying with him and asked if she intended to make a scene with Ernest Augustus. She promised that she had no such intention but that if he continued and Ernest Augustus found out about his regular visits and unwanted attentions, then it would be *she* who suffered, not him. If he couldn't contain himself, Sophia warned, she would have to see him even less than she already did.

But this was George William, and George William didn't do as he was told. Faced with his continued attentions and her husband's unrestrained jealousy, Sophia did all she could to avoid his brother. Yet there was a devious cunning in George William, who went to pains to try and be in Hanover when he knew his brother was away. Sophia had no choice but to receive him but she refused to meet his gaze, keeping her eyes on the ground and her tongue stilled. When finally she broke her silence, it was to ask him to leave. He obeyed her wish but was sure to tell Sophia that she owed him one - *he* had done *her* a favour by agreeing to leave. Both knew that Ernest Augustus would direct his jealous anger in one direction and one alone if he learned of George William's visits in his absence, and it wasn't towards his brother. Still Sophia kept true to her refusal to engage with George William and gradually, bit by bit, Ernest Augustus came to see that his wife had no attraction to his brother.

Or so he claimed.

The Heidelberg Monkey

Once upon a time, Sophia had been shuttled from Leiden to her mother's court at the Wassenaer Hof to Heidelberg and the care of her beloved elder brother. Now a married woman herself, it was her turn to take in a stray. The wanderer in question was of course her 7-year-old niece, Princess Elizabeth Charlotte, better known as *Liselotte*[1]. As the daughter of Charlotte and Charles Louis, she had seen enough drama to last her a lifetime and hoped to have something approaching a normal childhood in the care of her aunt Sophia.

Liselotte exchanged the jealousy-ridden court of her family to come to the jealousy-ridden court of Hanover instead. Sophia had already placed her lifelong friend, Anna Katharina von Offen, at her beck and call. Once Sophia's childhood companion, now she would be Liselotte's beloved governess and later, she would even go on to care for both George I *and* George II[2]. Little Liselotte's four years in Hanover were the happiest she ever knew, and when one considers the sort of scenes her mother subjected her to it's hardly a surprise that she was keen to seek new surroundings.

> '[Charlotte] placed herself. 'soberly dressed, though not in widow's weeds,' close to where the Elector and his new wife were to pass in to supper. We are told that she held

the little [Liselotte] by the hand, having bade her cry with all her strength when she saw her father approach, "Mercy! Mercy!"[3]

Seeing his daughter used in such a manner, Charles Louis decided that his little girl must be removed from the influence and company of her mother. He was equally keen to be rid of Madame von Offen, in whom he suspected Charlotte had found a confidante, and what could be worse than that same confidante also being responsible for the upbringing of his child? No doubt he envisioned her deliberately poisoning Liselotte's mind against him in favour of her mother but, safely away from Charlotte, that influence would be effectively neutered. For her part, Liselotte was delighted to escape the stern discipline of the father who was determined to wring her mother's influence out of her. On her arrival in Hanover she found that the strict rules that governed her childhood were nowhere to be found. Instead, her aunt Sophia was determined to give her the youth that she herself had not been able to enjoy, shunted from one home to another until she reached the melodramatic court of Heidelberg.[4]

Sophia delighted in Liselotte's company even as Charlotte mourned her little girl's absence, and Liselotte flourished in her new home. In Sophia's care all was light and opulence, laughter and cheer. The child saw no trace of the strange and disagreeable trinity that was the Ernest Augustus, George William and Sophia triangle; she saw only the childhood that Sophia was determined she would enjoy.

Liselotte must have been charming indeed for she even enchanted her grandmother, Elizabeth of Bohemia, when they met for the first time. The Winter Queen wrote to her son, 'she is a verie good childe and not troublesome; you may beleeue me, when I commend a childe, she being one of the few I like.'[5]

High praise indeed.

Liselotte delighted in jumping, an activity far from suited to a little girl of her station, but she had been told in her early years that vigorous jumping could change her into a boy, which she quite liked the sound of. So she pogoed all over Hanover and The Hague, even when she learned that she was destined to remain a girl. Just like Sophia and her dog poo prank, the little girl had a devilish sense of humour and a love of making mischief. Elizabeth's great-nephew, Prince William Henry, was also visiting and the two children were soon partners in crime and naughtiness, one a future king, the other destined to become the mother of a regent.

Young William Henry's life had known its share of tragedy despite his tender years. His grandfather, Charles I, died on the executioner's block and one year later, just a week before William Henry was born, his father, William II, Prince of Orange, fell victim to smallpox. If William II sounds familiar he *should*, for it was he who was charged with ruining Sophia's reputation back in The Hague. You may recall that he singularly failed.

When the time came for Liselotte to visit the House of Orange and get to know William's mother and Charles II's sister, Mary, Princess Royal and Princess of Orange, Sophia had the perfect excuse to get out of the unwanted excursion.

In an extraordinarily frank letter to her son Elizabeth wrote that Sophia was in high demand in The Hague. In fact, to put it in the Winter Queen's less than flowery language, 'she is so visited by all the ladies here that she had not had time to piss.'[6] Liselotte had no such escape and was dragged off to meet the Princess of Orange, whom she loudly and publicly referred to as 'the lady with the fiery nose'. It was a bad start and things were about to get worse.

When Liselotte left for the Orange residence in the Binnenhof Sophia told her to follow Elizabeth step by step and not to dawdle. Unfortunately the little Electoral Princess took her at her word and when the Princess Royal went to follow on behind Elizabeth as protocol dictated she should, the cheeky princess tugged at Mary's skirt and bade her move aside, in order that she could remain step by step with the Winter Queen. In later life, just two years before her death, one can still hear the laughter in Liselotte's words when she recalled the incident in a letter to her half-sister, Louisa.

> 'When my aunt, our dear Electress, was at the Hague, she did not go to see the Princess Royal, but the Queen of Bohemia went and took me with her. Before I departed, my aunt said to me: "Lisette, take care not to do as you usually do and wander off so that you cannot be found. Follow the Queen closely, so that she will not need to wait for you."
>
> I said, "Oh, aunt, you will see that I have behaved very nicely."

I arrived at the house of the Princess Royal, whom I did not know, and there I found her son with whom I had often played. After having looked at his mother for a long time without knowing who she was, I turned round to see if there was someone who could tell me who the lady was. Seeing only the Prince of Orange, I went to him and said, "Please tell me who the lady is who has such a fiery nose!" He began to laugh, and replied, "That is the Princess Royal, my mother." I was flabbergasted and stood stupefied. To help me recover myself, Mademoiselle Heyde took me with the Prince into the Princess's bedroom, where we played all sorts of games together. I had asked them to call me when the Queen should be ready to leave, and we were rolling together on a Turkish carpet when I was called. I took one leap, and rushed into the ante-chamber. I was not frightened, however, and pulling the Princess Royal's skirt, made her a pretty curtsey, placed myself before her and followed the Queen step by step to the carriage. Everyone was laughing and I did not know why. When we returned the Queen went to find my aunt, sat down on her bed and burst into peals of laughter, and said, "Lisette has had a fine outing," and told her all I had done. Then, my dear Electress laughed more than the Queen. She called me to her and said, Well done, Lisette, you have revenged us on that haughty princess.'[7]

Elizabeth took great delight in describing this scene to Sophia and the two women howled with laughter, for Sophia's trips to The Hague were always far more cheery than her childhood there had been. Unfortunately Liselotte was rather pleased with herself when she realised that being naughty didn't always warrant chastisement, and became as willful and filled with mischief as Sophia had been. Remembering how Lady Goring's words had stopped *her* in her tracks all those years ago Sophia silenced the puckish little girl's worst excesses by telling her, 'Your brother has a better face than you.' It was left to Elizabeth to assure Liselotte that this wasn't the case, for she had become the apple of her grandmother's choosy eye.

A little monkey indeed.

It wasn't only Liselotte whom Elizabeth had something to say about though. On 7 November 1659 she wrote to her son that Sophia was 'monstrous fonde of [Liselotte]', but more importantly, 'I beleeue some six months from hence she will make you an Oncle, but God for bid it shoulde be beleeued, for her ladieship doth not beleeue it.'[8] A month later she wrote again, sagely noting on 2 December 1659 that Sophia, 'doth beginne to be in ernest bigg a little but not to confess it, you may imagine.'[9]

It's likely that we can put Sophia's reluctance to discuss her pregnancy down to a superstition of tempting fate. She and Ernest Augustus were keen to have a child and as month after month passed without her conceiving she began to fear that she might never become a mother. Even in advanced pregnancy she was as no-nonsense as ever and nothing shows this with more clarity than her behaviour in the face of disaster.

During the heavily pregnant Sophia's journey home from The Hague fire broke out as the party rested for the night at a roadside lodging. Sophia didn't panic - when did she ever? Instead she put on her slippers and robe and calmly left the scene. This wasn't some inconsequential nothing either, but an inferno that managed to lay waste to more than a dozen buildings in the space of thirty minutes.

Liselotte wrote, with no effort to conceal her awe, 'I saw her [Sophia] once, at Klagenberg, issue coolly out of a conflagration, saving herself in a night-gown from the flames, which had nearly closed round her in her sleeping-chamber, and she then was far advanced in pregnancy; but she only laughed, not being the least frightened.'

Sophia was a past master at painting on a happy face and one senses that with Liselotte in her care, the last thing she would have wanted to do was show any distress to the little girl. Of course, she must have feared for her unborn child but she had no need on this occasion because both mother and baby were completely unharmed.

On 28 May 1660 a child was born to Sophia and Ernest August. He was George Louis, destined to one day rule as King George I of Great Britain, the man who founded an era.

The following day, there was a party in England too. This wasn't to celebrate a birth, but a restoration. Charles II had returned triumphant from exile. The Protectorate had fallen and for the printers of England, there was money to be made.

'*Advertisements of Books new Printed and Published,*

England's Gratulation for the King, and His Subjects happy union. Preach'd on the Tenth of May, being the day of Publick Thanksgiving in London. Also an Apology in the behalf of the Sequestered Clergy. Both presented to our dread Sovereign, King Charles the Second, on the 29 of May, 1660. By *Robert Mossom,* Minister of St Peter's Pauls Wharf, London.

Both sold by William Grantham at the Black Bear in St Pauls Churchyard, near the Little North-door.

A Poem to the King, upon His Majesties happy Return. By Edward Waller, Esquire. Sold by Richard Marriot in St Dunstans Churchyard, Fleet Street.'[10]

The Firstborn

George William, the possible spectre at the feast when it came to his new nephew, was in Holland when his sister-in-law gave birth to her first child. It was a traumatic labour that lasted for seventy-two hours, leaving Ernest Augustus fearing for the life of both his wife and newborn babe. To the end of her days Sophia remained nervous of doctors, but she did place her trust in one physician. He was Doctor Otto Tachen, who she remembered as *Dr Tac* and sometimes, when she was feeling mischievous, as *Dr Tictac*. With the doctor's care Sophia and her child not only survived but the robust new arrival was positively hearty as his took his first breaths. Ever the dutiful wife, she wouldn't even credit herself for fighting to deliver her baby against the odds and her own exhaustion, preferring instead to thank Ernest Augustus. It was his terror at the thought of her death that gave her new determination to survive, Sophia later claimed. And George Louis didn't just survive, he flourished. From a healthy child he would grow into a robust young man and an irascible monarch, but there was a long way to go before that.

Though Sophia's memoirs don't mention it, young Liselotte, as mischievous and full of devilry as the young Sophia had been, also witnessed the first minutes in the life of George I. As her aunt laboured on, the little girl was merrily playing in the gardens where her attendants had hidden a doll in a rosemary bush, telling her that this was her newborn cousin. As Liselotte recalled, 'I heard loud cries, because the Duchess was in travail. That didn't agree with the story of the baby in the rosemary bush, so I pretended to believe them; but I slipped into my aunt's room […] and hid behind a large screen which had been placed before the door near the fireplace. They brought the baby over to the fireplace to bathe it and I came out of my hiding-place. I should have been whipped, but in honour of the happy event I was only well scolded.'[11]

'He is beautiful as an angel,' the proud and adoring new mother told her brother of the newborn. Yet there was no question that Liselotte continued to be as loved and spoiled as ever she was. There might be a long-awaited new baby in the house but Liselotte's uncle, George William, gave her something that entertained her even more: a puppy of her own. Not long afterwards she would add to her menagerie when Ernest Augustus indulged her with a little cart drawn by two hounds, in which she raced about the palace in between jumping breaks. When the time came to rest, the intrepid Liselotte once did so after downing a vast quality of wine and falling down drunk in the garden.

For a time all seemed happy at Hanover until, like a bad penny, George William showed up again. In a case of the gentleman protesting too much, he brought with him word of a new love who went by the unlikely name of *Mademoiselle Wattinsvain*. Liselotte, with the wisdom of a child, later reflected that in the case of George William and Sophia, there was unfinished business. As she wrote, 'old love does not rust.'

But the love was one-sided and for all his breast beating over the mysterious and marvellously named Mademoiselle Wattinsvain, George William was still bound by the document he had signed. He might love any number of mademoiselles, but marry them he could not. Ernest Augustus, however, found all of this a touch suspicious. Who was the enigmatic Wattinsvain? *Where* was she and what was his brother up to? Eventually he chose the path of least resistance and decided that she was nothing but another technique to distract him from his wife and brother's flirtations. Bang went the peaceful family home, exploded in a smoking temper tantrum that left Sophia terrified to speak to her brother-in-law. With Ernest Augustus in full flight soon she wasn't the only one and as he grew more annoyed, George William became more miserable until both brothers were prescribed a spa trip to heal their spirits. Wisely, the married couple stayed in one house, their shadow in another.

The trip was a success. So friendly were the siblings when they left the spa at Bad Pyrmont that they took another of their regular trips to Italy. Sophia and little George Louis, meanwhile, went to Heidelberg.

And it was all change.

Charlotte was now virtually invisible, her place taken by Marie Luise von Degenfeld who may or may not have been the wife of Charles Louis, depending on who you asked. She was by now mother to three of her thirteen children by the elector and Charles Louis placed his sister in the awkward position of having to somehow be on good terms with both Luise *and* the embittered, reclusive Charlotte. A born diplomat, Sophia did just enough to keep both women happy, fussing over Luise's children enough to flatter her but not enough to upset the hot-tempered electress. She was careful not to make their first encounter a formal one but instead met Luise and her youngsters casually, whilst engaging in some local festivities. She found Luise easy company and with the children there to break the ice that might have formed since the two women last saw one another, everyone was soon getting along famously.

Sophia had other things to think about besides her brother's messy love life though, for in 1660 the Stuart dynasty had been restored to the throne. Over the years, the Winter Queen finally began to thaw. She had mourned her husband and four of her children already, as well as losing her brother to the executioner's axe, and she was ready to leave those unhappy memories behind.

After decades spent in exile in The Hague, Elizabeth Stuart was ready to go home to England. A tearful and pregnant Sophia waved her off from Rotterdam and as the ship disappeared onto the horizon, one wonders if she knew whether she would ever see her mother again. Upon her arrival in her homeland Queen Elizabeth of Bohemia lived as a guest of her old friend and rumoured lover, Lord Craven, at his Craven House residence, but her health was already beginning to fail. Shortly after a move to Leicester House Elizabeth contracted bronchitis. She grew weaker with every passing day and on 13 February 1662, nine months after her arrival in England, the Winter Queen died. In one last act of revenge on Charles Louis, the son who had refused to dig her out of her debt, she left everything of value to his brother, Rupert. Elizabeth Stuart was laid to rest in Westminster Abbey, finally reunited with the brother she had adored.

It was the end of an era.

The Bishop and Doctor Faustus

At the time she bid farewell to her mother on the harbour of Rotterdam, Sophia was already pregnant with her second son. Despite her devotion and her pregnancy, which the jealous Ernest Augustus doesn't seem to have suspected was down to anyone but him, he continued to be mistrustful of her relationship with his wayward brother. George William, meanwhile, finally acknowledged that Sophia was purposefully avoiding him. Because this was George William he didn't take a moment to practise a bit of self-reflection and wonder why a woman who had once been content to be his friend had become aloof, but instead, he looked around for a rival. He saw it in the shape of a courtier named Villiers, who he was sure was Sophia's secret *amour*.

The furious George William took his suspicions to his brother, yet Ernest Augustus did nothing but laugh. Later he told Sophia that, 'I should never think of being jealous of any one but my brother,' and it is tempting to speculate on whether he *did* wonder at the paternity of that unborn child. That said, Ernest Augustus was anything but able to hold his temper so perhaps it wasn't really the threat of being cuckolded that aroused his jealousy, but the freewheeling lifestyle of George William, who managed to have both the company of Sophia - at least until she withdrew from him - and the bachelor freedoms of a man with no responsibilities and the money to indulge himself. His current *indulgence* was one of Sophia's ladies-in-waiting, which gave the pregnant woman some breathing space in which to escape both his unwanted flirtation and her husband's unwarranted jealousy.

Perhaps mindful of the difficult labour Sophia had experienced with George Louis, Ernest Augustus strove to make her pregnancy as free of incident as it could be. He even had her leave her chambers and move into his, where he remained her constant companion. Or perhaps he was motivated not by love but by that ever-present need to watch his wife, just in case she strayed. Whatever the reason behind his wish, it proved to be an ill-judged decision. Sophia caught a heavy cold whilst in his chambers that left her so weakened she would later blame it for the miscarriages she suffered in the years that followed.

On 3 October 1661, Sophia gave birth to the spare to go with her heir. He was named Frederick Augustus and he was as delicate as George Louis had been robust. In the looks of the former she saw the blood of the Palatine, in the latter, the blood of Brunswick, but both boys were loved. In the centuries since their birth, speculation has increased that Sophia favoured her second son over the first precisely *because* Frederick Augustus was so clearly a Palatine but there is no real evidence to support this. Far from it, in fact, for she was devoted to George Louis in his infancy, so it cannot be at Sophia's door that we can lay the blame for his aloof, curmudgeonly nature in adulthood.

Mother and father were delighted with their new arrival and since that troublesome uncle was off adventuring, all was peaceful in Hanover. Though one cannot hope but speculate that perhaps it was *too* peaceful, as Sophia wrote to her mother, 'one does not know how to fill a letter in a place such as this.'[12] Yet the value of a lack of drama cannot be underestimated. Sophia recovered from the birth at a sedate pace and her husband was once again in watchful attendance, doting on mother and son. It was during these peaceful court days that the next chapter in the life of the girl from the Palatinate began.

Sophia, Liselotte and the court were watching a performance of Doctor Faustus in early December when a messenger arrived with important news. The Bishop of Osnabrück[13] was dead. Let there be no mistake, it wasn't pure coincidence that made Sophia juxtapose the fate of the bishop and that of Faustus when she wrote of the troupe that came from Hamburg, 'I well remember their acting Doctor Faust, who was carried off by the devil. News reached the Duke that the Bishop of Osnabrück had also passed into another world.' This was Sophia's sense of humour at its most playful and arch. She didn't mean her memoirs for public eyes but instead as a way to occupy herself during her husband's absences. Had they been intended for publication, one might assume that she would have been somewhat more careful in her choice of content, and we would have been all the poorer for it.

She was about to become a bishop's wife, after all.

To put it bluntly, Sophia was delighted at the news, for this would mean an escape from Hanover at precisely the moment George William returned. This posed a problem for Ernest Augustus, as he didn't think that his investiture ceremony was an appropriate place for a wife, nor did he trust Sophia enough to leave her alone in Hanover with his brother. His solution to this problem of his own making was to send Sophia off to Celle to visit Sophia Dorothea of Schleswig-Holstein-Sonderburg-Glücksburg, the eminently respectable and childless wife of his brother,

Christian Louis. This she did but to her annoyance, George William wasn't far behind. He sent a note to Sophia asking if he might pay her a visit and she replied in no uncertain terms: the answer was an unequivocal *no*.

The Bishop's Wife

Ernest Augustus' appointment as a secular archbishop should not be dismissed without some comment. The diocese of Osnabrück was founded in 772 by Charlemagne and still exists today. It began as a means to impose Christianity upon the conquered lands of Saxony and grew to be a powerful force, with the bishop wielding considerable influence within the Holy Roman Empire. In 1633, Swedish forces overwhelmed Osnabrück during the Thirty Years' War and began to enforce a secular rule. Eventually, under the terms of that hard-fought Treaty of Westphalia, it was decided that the bishopric would be held alternately by a Roman Catholic then a Protestant representative, thus going some way to satisfying both parties. With the sitting incumbent a Catholic, the next appointed office holder would be Ernest Augustus.

This led to two anomalies that are worthy of further note. Because the terms of the Treaty of Westphalia guaranteed that a Protestant would hold office on a rotating basis, Roman Catholic canons in Osnabrück were bound by the treaty to cast their vote in favour of a Protestant when the time came. This was strictly against Papal law, for the thought of any good Catholic canon voting for a Protestant, that is to say, a heretic, was unimaginable and punishable by excommunication. Yet they had no choice so a quietly unofficial arrangement was put in place by which the canons would vote for the Protestant, in this case Ernest Augustus, and would be swiftly excommunicated as a result. They would then file a petition to set aside the excommunication. This petition would be granted and the canons would resume business as usual. This, the Vatican decided, ticked all the boxes whilst ensuring that fundamental Catholic tenets were still adhered to.

What of those Catholics who had established themselves in Osnabrück and suddenly found themselves ruled by a secular Protestant from Hanover? For these troubled souls help was at hand. It was agreed that their spiritual wellbeing would be entrusted to the Archbishop of

Cologne. Ernest Augustus, then, had no responsibility for the earthly souls of his subjects, but only for their mortal selves. It was a role that he felt amply prepared to assume and one that he no doubt envisioned buying him some plaudits from the Holy Roman Emperor, which might one day result in an electoral cap to call his own.

Ernest Augustus and Sophia moved with their family and Liselotte into the bishop's residence at Iburg Castle and Sophia received a gift of 7,000 thalers from Osnabrück. Here at last she found herself settled in a way that she had scarcely been before. Ernest Augustus was the first secular appointment to the Bishopric of Osnabrück and when he arrived in Iburg, he found that the official residence was not *quite* luxury incarnate. Though fully-furnished, it was too old and small to accommodate the courtiers who would also be joining the family. Indeed, the corridors were so narrow that they could only be traversed by one person at a time, because there was no room to pass!

The castle might have been the seat of the Prince-Bishopric since the twelfth century, but the time had come for change and Ernest Augustus conceived of a grand new palace, befitting what he saw as his station in the world. Construction began on the new residence in 1667 and continued for six years. Though Ernest Augustus didn't share his wife's love of philosophy and theology, they had in common a passion for theatre and design, so the chance to stamp their mark on the palace and its newly-laid grounds was one that they both relished. When completed, the palace became the new residence of the bishops of Osnabrück. Decades later it would also be the place where King George I would take his last earthly breath.

Sophia approved of the castle's furnishings and distance from George William, even if she was slightly less than enthusiastic about its small dimensions. Crucially, of course, she believed that it might afford her some space from her troublesome brother-in-law and for this she was inordinately grateful. It mattered less for now *where* she was, but more that George William wasn't there to annoy and harass her.

Whilst attending the wedding of one of her ladies-in-waiting[14], who also happened to be one of George William's former flames, Sophia was afforded the opportunity to have a good look at the ladies of Osnabrück. She was *not* impressed.

One wonders, why did she care? In fact, surely it would be in Sophia's better interests if Osnabrück was overflowing with gorgeous and eligible young women because George William was bound to appear at one time or another and what better way to distract him from his unwilling sweetheart than with a fresh conquest?

George William and Sophia, that *unwilling paramour*, however, were only two corners in the triangle. The third was Ernest Augustus, that jealous husband who would sleep with his feet on his wife's chair so that she couldn't escape. Let's not forget that this was the same Ernest Augustus who accompanied his high-rolling brother to Italy at every opportunity. How ironic that Ernest Augustus should see sexual intrigue everywhere he looked.

Might Sophia's interest in the ladies of Osnabrück have a deeper motivation than she was willing to let on, and just what was her husband up to when he took those extended trips to Italy with his sibling?

There's every chance that the person who was intriguing in the marriage wasn't Sophia at all, but her husband, and there's every chance that Sophia knew all about it too. It would hardly be unusual for a noble husband of the era to have mistresses and one of Ernest Augustus' will later play a major part in our story. One can only speculate but it's entirely possible that she hoped a lack of beauties in the bishopric's court might keep her husband faithful. Later in the couple's marriage, she knew of her husband's infidelities and permitted them but now, still relatively new to marriage and celebrating the birth of her second son, perhaps Sophia hoped that her husband might be as true to her as she was to him. Of course, it wasn't to be.

The year of 1663 was one of partings for Sophia. In March, she received news of the death of her brother, Edward, Count Palatine of Simmern. He had lived in Paris since 1645, when he had married Princess Anna Gonzaga, the daughter of Charles, Duke of Mantua. If you recall, the couple's relationship was hardly love at first sight but both Anna and Edward needed to marry, he for financial reasons, she to banish the memory of her cousin and lover, Henry II, Duke of Guise, whom she claimed to have married in 1639. Henry then denied her claim and wed another, leaving Anna's reputation in tatters.

The marriage solved the problems of both husband and wife but Edward followed his new wife into the Catholic church and earned his mother's fury in the process. The couple had three children and, had they been both Protestant, it's entirely likely that they would have jumped in front of Sophia's claim to the English throne, thus changing the course of history forever. Edward never lived to see that day though, as he died in 1663, without quite reaching his fortieth birthday[15].

The second parting in 1663 was one that Sophia felt keenly. Liselotte, that lively little girl who had been both a sister and daughter as well as a niece to Sophia, left to return to Heidelberg to get ready for her place on the marriage market. At just 11-years-old, she had made a friend for life and she and Sophia remained close for the rest of the older woman's days. Liselotte always maintained that she had never been happier than those years spent beside her aunt in Hanover. When Liselotte departed, her governess, the erstwhile Anna Katharina von Offen, did not go with her, for she had married Christian Friedrich von Harling, Hanoverian Privy Councillor, equerry and eventually Master of the Horse, the previous year. Anna Katherina was not forgotten though and she and her former charge remained in touch over the decades that followed, when Anna Katharina was employed as governess to the children of the House of Hanover and later the son and daughter of George I too[16].

When Ernest Augustus went off to Venice again in the winter of 1663, Sophia was too unwell to accompany him. She had still not fully recovered from the cold she had contracted in her husband's chambers and blamed the malady for what she saw as an inability to conceive. When her next pregnancies ended in tragedy, she was sure that the illness was the cause.

To Italy

> 'The bonds of holy matrimony had not changed the Duke's gay nature. He wearied of always possessing the same thing, and found a retired life irksome.'

With those words, Sophia identified a problem that would touch all of the kings of Georgian Britain, with the exception of George III. They pursued what they desired and when they won it, found its lustre quickly tarnished. So it was with Ernest Augustus and the woman he so jealously adored.

It was unusual for Ernest Augustus to ask his wife to accompany him and his brother on their trips but when he issued the invitation in 1663, she was keen to go along. An agreement was reached by which she would convalesce at Heidelberg and follow him to Venice once the weather grew more clement. We already know that Sophia wasn't stupid, nor was she easily duped and she knew full well that Ernest Augustus wanted her at his side so that all of Italy would be dazzled by his wife and her attendants. He charged her with a mission too, asking if she would call into Kassel whilst she was on the road and vet some *new* ladies in waiting, who were currently employed at the court of Emilie, Princess of Tarente. The princess also happened to be the sister of Charles Louis' fiery wife, Charlotte, she of the proud bosom and thick black brows. Sophia must have known that she was intended to provide a veneer of respectability to the endeavour but if she had her doubts about his motives she didn't question them. Instead, she simply did as her husband asked.

One of the ladies in the Princess of Tarente's service, Éléonore Desmier d'Olbreuse, was to be invited to Venice at the request of George William, who was rather taken with her. She was the companion of Marie Tour d'Auvergne, Duchess of Thouars, and when she and George William met whilst both were visiting Kassel, 'being of an amorous, though not of a marrying disposition, he fell in love at first sight'.[17] Éléonore chose not to accept the duke's request for her company and preferred to travel on to The Hague with the duchess. George William, no doubt much to Sophia's delight, chose to follow her.

The next stop on Sophia's journey was Heidelberg, where things had settled somewhat. The electress had departed for her family home leaving Charles Louis and Luise to play happy families. It was during this trip that Sophia miscarried twins and subsequently delayed her departure for Venice until her constitution was stronger. When she left to travel onwards her little sons, whom she affectionately called Görgen and Gustchen, remained in the care of Frau von Harling in Heidelberg. Sophia missed the boys keenly, having become a 'stupidly fond' mother. She absolutely adored them, showing a maternal instinct that her own mother had lacked. She blamed herself for her miscarriage and would torture herself when she lost more unborn children in the future, believing that she had not rested properly, but there is no evidence to support this. In fact, she seemed given to moments of worry despite her efforts to remain cheerful and perhaps this might have contributed to the difficulties she was experiencing. It certainly did nothing to heal her wounded spirits.

One senses that Sophia's heart was not in the journey she now had to undertake and she was forced to travel as part of an immense and opulent procession, with the bishop's wife the centre of attention at every stop they made. She had seen through the dukes' plan to add some new ladies from the court of the Princess of Tarente to the party under cover of the respectability her presence lent to the endeavour and now was ready to see exactly what kind of temptations kept drawing the brothers back to Italy.

And she wasn't impressed.

> 'I was prepossessed with the idea that only angels of beauty were to be seen in a country that had so often attracted the Dukes, from whom I had learned so much about the ladies of Italy. Great, therefore, was my surprise to see frightful faces, which even magnificence of attire failed to make tolerable. No sooner, however, did they speak than I was fascinated by their wit and charm of manner.'

One suspects that Sophia felt little relief at discovering that the women of Italy were not all *angels of beauty*, for hadn't she been asked to procure extra ladies for the journey? The official motivation behind the wishes of the dukes to have these women in their entourage might have been to show off a beautiful wife surrounded by beautiful retainers, but Sophia most likely had her suspicions that the true reasoning behind it was of a far more lurid nature.

Tired of winter and the sadness of the last twelve months, Sophia allowed herself to be beguiled by Italy. The women might not appeal but the landscape certainly did and she revelled in her surroundings. Here the woman who had been raised to know the importance of birthright and blood saw how her Italian hostesses whiled away the hours in a marketplace where, 'exposed to sun and dust, the ladies spend their afternoons, more delighted with the society of gentlemen than distressed by the ruin of their complexions.'

It's tempting to think that she envied them their freedom but is this too romantic? Possibly not. Given that she had just suffered a miscarriage and spent an ailing winter in Hanover and the Palatinate, it's not unreasonable to think that spring in Italy might have been enchanting to Sophia.

At first.

It didn't last.

Her next stop was Vicenza where the red carpet was rolled out for the visiting dignitaries. Meeting the ladies of the city, Sophia was surprised to find that even the chief magistrate's wife, the flighty Madam Legge, concealed her face beneath a mask. She believed that it would be inappropriate for her to meet Sophia with her face uncovered due to the marked difference in their social ranks. Any sense of satisfaction that Sophia felt about this was soon banished when she saw that rank seemed to be thrust aside when it came to these same women paying court to her husband. Those who had been respectful, welcoming and deferential thought nothing of 'flaunting [their] charms and giving my husband the pleasure of acting as [their] admirer in the Italian style.'

It was a warning sign for what was to come and from that moment on, one senses a definite decline in the spirits of Sophia. Not without compliments herself, when a dance partner compared her to the stars that same evening, she reserved comment on the matter. She did, however, note that the masked woman who had made eyes at Ernest Augustus in the garden that day was also at the dance. Not only that, but she was wearing the *same* gown.

Sophia - 1, Madam Legge - Nil.

The trip to Vicenza concluded with a visit to the Campo Marzio, where Sophia witnessed a ceremony in which carriages containing ladies were lined up along the meadow in single file, their windows lowered. The gentlemen then toured the carriages and entertained the occupants with improvised sonnets, performed through the open windows. It was a different way of life to Hanover or Osnabrück and Sophia began to see now that, regardless of whether she thought the witty and charming ladies of Italy *attractive*, there were things other than physical beauty that might make them appealing to gentlemen. She shrewdly identified how this more relaxed - though still strictly regimented - approach to socialising might show a woman off in the very best light to a fellow with stars in his eyes.

Even a bishop.

By the time the verdant gardens and sun-drenched marketplaces of Verona and Vicenza were replaced by the canals of Venice, Sophia's enthusiasm for her tour had begun to wane. She missed her children, learning from Frau von Harling of their progress and alarmingly, that both had suffered and recovered from smallpox. There was nothing in Italy that appealed to her as much as the thought of seeing those boys again, and she never took another long trip like this one again during their childhood.

Sophia's homesickness wasn't helped by her realisation of exactly what it was that drew her spouse back to Italy time and again, usually in the company of the brother who even now was pursuing his latest paramour across Europe. Unfortunately for her, she made the mistake of letting Ernest Augustus know how much she was missing her sons and this gave him not one but three people to be jealous of. Now, alongside his sibling, he could add his children to the roster of rivals who commanded his wife's attention. It may seem churlish but we already know that Ernest Augustus was not above a little pettiness when the mood took him. And the mood took him often.

From Vicenza the party moved on to what Ernest Augustus believed would be the highlight of the trip - his beloved, adored and much-visited Venice. For Sophia, it was hate at first sight.

> 'The Duke asked me if I did not think the town beautiful, and I did not dare to say "No", though in reality it appeared to me extremely melancholy. Nothing was to be seen but water, nothing heard but "Premi," and "Stali," the cry of the gondoliers as they guide their coal-black gondolas, which resemble floating coffins.'

The dances in dusty marketplaces and sonnets in lush meadows were replaced now by visits to nuns who had no interest in gawking nobles, and when Sophia was taken to view the city's churches, she was quick to note that they were employed by many locals not for worship, but as places where lovers might make a clandestine rendezvous. She loved the wide aspects and fresh air of the Grand Canal yet one senses a loneliness in her experiences, isolated in her gondola from those who glided past in those 'floating coffins.'

The noble ladies of Venice were not permitted to visit Sophia and her party thanks to a senate decree aimed at keeping influential Venetians from making potentially awkward connections. Of course, their husbands were free to make what visits they wished but Sophia found endless games of cards with her husband and his Italian friends trying and her isolation deepened. It's true that she had her attendants to keep her company but there was little respite from these same faces day after day. As her attention wandered and her mood grew darker, all she wanted was to return home to her boys.

Sophia's response to what she decided was a melancholic city was not to retreat behind her beloved protocol, but instead to break free and return to that little girl she once was, full of fun and life. She was emboldened by the realisation that the Venetians were willing to excuse her behaviour as, 'è la moda Francese'[18], and decided that, if she had such an exotic reputation, then she would give it free rein and full indulgence. Tired of churches and travelling the Grand Canal in splendid isolation from the Venetian ladies who passed her on the water, Sophia thrilled to 'dance out of doors in the evenings with the Duke and my ladies, and this French liberty was loudly applauded by some Venetian nobles who looked on. To complete our folly we went all dressed out like actresses in gold and silver brocade and quantities of feathers to tilt at the ring on the Lido before a crowd of over 100,000 persons. Each lady was attended by a cavalier, and the carriages were adorned with gilded copper laid on in festoons of raised work instead of carving, so that it might be light.'

Ernest Augustus was having a marvellous time in his favourite city and he even provided Sophia with a cavalier of her own for the evening but when the party ended and the shutters were closed, all cavaliers were banished and the couple was left alone to enjoy each other's company.

Since Ernest Augustus was so keen to play his part in the entertainments, Sophia could keep an eye on him and with George William in a different country, her husband's jealousy was curtailed for once. Though John Frederick, that plump younger brother who could be so hotheaded, was in attendance, Ernest Augustus sensed in him no threat and he certainly showed nothing beyond friendly civility towards his sister-in-law. Besides, John Frederick was having plenty of fun of his own getting to know the ladies of Venice and even maintained a palazzo on the edge of the city, *Casa Fascari*, for his private *assignations*. Perhaps on other trips there had been another palazzo on a different edge of the city that served the same purpose for Ernest Augustus. Sophia doesn't tell us if she considered this a possibility, but it's not impossible to think that she might have.

As though the dip in Sophia's spirits were determined to make its presence felt physically, her next trial was one that travellers had endured since the dawn of time and still do today. To put it bluntly, Sophia contracted diarrhoea. In fact, she had such a severe dose of traveller's tum that she was confined to bed with a fever and became so weak that she began to suffer regular fainting fits. Though all Sophia wanted to do was shut herself away and sleep under the care of Doctor Tac, who was travelling with the party, her sense of duty wouldn't allow her the luxury of rest. Instead she sallied forth from her chamber and attended the Doge's traditional *Marriage of the Sea*. The ceremony, which had been celebrated since the year 1000, symbolised Venice's power over the water and took the form of a grand and opulent celebration in which the Doge, the city's head honcho, processed through the city to the ocean accompanied by pilgrims and saintly effigies. He then headed out to sea on his boat, the luxurious *Bucentauro*, and there performed a blessing before taking a gold ring from his finger and casting it into the waves, pledging himself to the water. As the Doge returned to dry land every bell in Venice chimed out and Sophia found herself impressed by the sheer spectacle of the occasion, not to mention the eye-watering amount that it must have cost.

There were plenty of entertainments to choose from and the next outing that drew her from her sickbed was a concert that John Frederick had arranged in honour of the ladies in the party. It was a rare chance to socialise with Venetian noblewomen too, who might on this occasion circumvent the senate decree by meeting Sophia not in her own quarters or theirs, but at the concert. Despite her sickness and the fact that she was by now rail-thin and challenging even Doctor Tac's considerable abilities, she simply couldn't resist the temptation to indulge in her favourite pastime of checking out the local women, who always seemed to be wanting.

As a result of this outing Sophia found herself with an opportunity to play one of those pranks she had once been so fond of. A Madam Dolfine, one of the Venetian wives present at the concert, confessed that she had taken a fancy to Piero de Bonzi, a French diplomat, and she was desperate to get some time alone with him. Her plan was simple. Sophia was due to attend a masked wedding and the lady urged her to ask de Bonzi if he would make a request on behalf of the king of France for the ladies of Venice to be allowed to visit Sophia privately. One imagines that the lady would then conspire to visit Sophia at the same time as de Bonzi, thus stealing some time alone with her paramour. Sophia readily agreed and, masked and in her finery, met the similarly masked de Bonzi at the wedding. Keen to extend his own influence by making connections in Hanover, de Bonzi informed Sophia that Madam Dolfine had suggested that he might be of aid to her and asked what he and the king of France could do on her behalf.

Sophia thanked the hapless gentleman for attending and told him in no uncertain terms that she had a message for him. That message was simply to say that, if ever she *did* need the king of France to leap to her aid, it wouldn't be for something so mundane as to seek permission to be visited by Italian noblewomen. Still, she decided afterwards, the politically disappointed de Bonzi would at least have been able to guess that Madam Dolfine's interest in him went a little beyond diplomacy.

Coming at a time when she would rather have been at home, Sophia found it all very tiresome. She wasn't exactly a stuffed shirt but the constant focus on matters of the heart, when her own husband was happily occupied elsewhere, understandably began to chafe with her already rather stretched efforts to be merry. To put the cherry on top of the icing, one of Ernest Augustus' former Venetian flames became Sophia's eternal shadow for the duration of her stay. She dogged Sophia's every footstep and when challenged, claimed that she merely wanted to show Sophia half of the attention that Ernest Augustus had shown *her* when she was young and beautiful. Unsurprisingly, all the beleaguered Sophia wanted to do was to escape.

That escape came in the unwelcome form of her husband's decision to return to Vicenza, for she knew that what drew him back was not the Campo Marzio nor the lush gardens, but the society of Madam Legge, who helped him to pass the evenings by holding musical entertainments for the party. As if things weren't bad enough, Sophia's ladies-in-waiting suffered a dreadful accident when the carriage they were travelling in overturned on a steep hill road. The women were thrown from the vehicle and trampled beneath the hooves of the horses. It was only due to the quick thinking of one of their companions that they were saved, as Chevalier von Sandis - later to marry one of the women he rescued - dragged them from danger. This drama was followed by more as the ladies were hit by smallpox and another went into labour, meaning that the party was a little depleted when it finally left Vicenza for Rome.

As the procession of almost 200 courtiers and attendants - supposedly travelling incognito - trooped onwards towards the capital city, the husband who Sophia once declared she would have 'followed to the Antipodes', was all that was keeping her from returning home. She traipsed from place to place, trailing around churches and remaining resolutely unimpressed by both the supposed birthplace of the Virgin Mary and news of miracles performed by, 'a truly awful Madonna statue with a broken nose'. In our modern age of carefully choreographed media opportunities and well-oiled royal PR machines, it's a delight to learn that Sophia was having none of it. The more her guides entreated her to open herself to the power of the miracles the statue could perform the more cynical she became and she made no effort to hide her feelings. If the miraculous statue couldn't fix its own broken nose, then what hope was there for anyone else? There was no chance of a Roman Catholic conversion for Sophia.

On and on went the party on the road to Rome, visiting Parma and the family that Sophia once briefly considered being married into, before it paused in Modena. Even with a card table installed in her carriage, Sophia found the journey difficult. Travelling as part of a large procession of attendants and courtiers the carriages were often in danger of being overturned on difficult roads and even had to have their axels modified in order to pass through some particularly narrow passages. Eventually when the ladies became tired of being buffeted and terrified in their vehicles, they made a change and took to horses or simply their own two feet whilst Sophia retired to a sedan chair, completing the journey in comfort.

Finally they reached Rome and once again, Sophia found herself barred from receiving callers at her quarters. Ernest Augustus swiftly left her alone in the opulent lodgings provided by the Grand Duke of Tuscany and went off to pay his respects to Marie Mancini, the Connétable di Colonna, who was recovering after giving birth. Marie Mancini[19] had been the first love - though crucially, not *lover* - of Louis XIV and was now married to Prince Lorenze Onofrio Colonna. She was celebrated throughout France and Italy, so Sophia was very keen to see her.

Sophia far outranked Marie so should have waited for the Connétable to pay court to her but curiosity got the better of her during the long days and nights in which her husband played cards with his new best friend. It was decided that Sophia would visit her imagined rival without any announcement, thus catching the bedridden Marie unawares. Upon her arrival Sophia was delighted to find that Marie was not only wearing a mismatched gown and cap 'which, I thought, had a very bad effect,' but also addressed her as *Highness*. She quickly decided that she had nothing to fear and settled to join a game of cards, observing as the evening wore on that Marie seemed to come alive when surrounded by men in a way that she did not in the company of women.

Marie and Sophia became regular companions once the former was recovered but Sophia never let her rival forget her place. Even when the pair were incognito Sophia made sure than she asserted her precedence, going through doors and up and down stairs first as was her right. Marie was untroubled for she had little interest in trying to trump Sophia when protocol forbade it, but Ernest Augustus was agitated by his wife's subtle power plays. He was, after all, one of Marie's fondest champions.

To put these matters of protocol and rank in perspective, Sophia herself missed out on an audience with Queen Christina of Sweden in Rome. An arranged meeting was postponed when Sophia was forced to retire to bed with a fever. Though she was well enough to receive visitors, the queen's superior rank made it impossible for her to pay a call on Sophia. As a result they didn't meet for several years. Sophia likewise didn't meet Pope Alexander during her time in Rome as he would only see her if she was incognito. Her brother-in-law, the Catholic John Frederick, was absolute desperate to be invited to a papal audience but the pope declined and, in solidarity with her husband's sibling, Sophia made no effort to arrange a meeting of her own. John Frederick, meanwhile, was so outraged at the pope's dismissive attitude that he set off for Hanover at once in an almighty huff. It was a fateful decision.

Having exhausted the churches and monuments of Rome, Sophia received Ernest Augustus' decision to go home with delight. He explained that he would quite like to spend some time with Marie - who was probably his mistress - before he departed and Sophia, of course, made no complaint. Marie and Ernest Augustus accompanied Sophia to the gates of Rome and from there, she travelled for home without him. One again there were grand receptions - though she attempted to travel incognito - entertainments and treacherous carriage rides, culminating in a reunion with Ernest Augustus in Venice, just in time for Carnival. When they were settled in Hanover it was a tradition that Sophia and her husband would bring with them, holding enormous festivities that surely echoed Ernest Augustus' many trips to Venice.

Masked and in costume, Sophia relished the freedom of the city. She was just another person at Carnival with her face and rank concealed. In her memoirs she detailed the behaviour of some *other* women during a visit to a local convent where, at the sight of the men in the party, the nuns put on a desperate display, reaching through the grilles on the convent doors to hold their hands. So taken by the display was one of the chevaliers in the group that he generously passed the night with the holy sisters, no doubt in sacred prayer and silent worship.

Or something like that.

It was during this stage of the journey that Sophia realised that she was pregnant again. Disguised in men's clothes and a wig, she travelled with her husband for Milan in a post-chaise. Though on one hand this made sense as it was by now winter and the thought of completing the difficult journey to Germany was one that she could hardly entertain, there was an ulterior motive. Ernest Augustus had made plans to meet with Marie in Milan that he was determined to keep but, no doubt to his annoyance, she did not appear as planned.

Upon her arrival in Milan an exhausted Sophia was taken straight to bed. She spent much of the visit resting, remembering all too well the twins that she had miscarried the previous year, but eventually the lure of her two living children proved too great. The perilous journey resumed, sometimes in carriages, sometimes on foot and sometimes, when the mountains grew treacherous, on sledges, but eventually the party arrived in Heidelberg. Here they were told that Christian Louis, Ernest Augustus' oldest brother, was dead. He had passed away on 15 March 1665. The Dukes of Brunswick-Lüneburg were now three.

Lady Harburg

Much had happened since Sophia had last seen her children. John Frederick, having arrived home long before his travelling brothers thanks to the pope's refusal to grant him an audience, had swiftly seized control of Celle, the richer and larger of the two duchies[20] that had once belonged to his now dead brother. John Frederick had written to George William multiple times begging him to come home for one last visit before Christian Louis died but he had ignored the pleas, too occupied with his paramour. His official excuse, which is frankly absurd, was that he didn't want to see Christian Louis in case the dying man forced some of his less able household staff into George William's service. It was a preposterous excuse and Sophia was disgusted at him. Politically his delayed return was problematic too. If he had paid heed to the letters and headed back to Hanover, it's likely that John Frederick would have been prevented from making his grab for power.

As it was, there was now the potential for a fairly major upset between the remaining three brothers. Christian Louis had summoned only George William, signalling his intent that he was the choice of heir and George, their late father, had named George William as such before his death. To go against their father's wishes was usually unthinkable for all of the brothers but this time, John Frederick had shoved ahead in line.

Ernest Augustus pledged his support for George William's cause and began to gather an army to enforce the point. Luckily for everyone, John Frederick had a hot temper but not an unreasonable one and he knew as well as his brothers did that there would have to be concessions before there was literally a civil war. Accordingly, he handed the duchy over to George William just as their late father had wished. In return George William distributed the remaining lands between all three brothers, fulfilling the wishes of their parents. It was an admirable bit of diplomacy on the part of the siblings and relatively quick too given how long some negotiations like that could drag on, with an agreement reached within the space of six months!

John Frederick now considered that his prospects were far better than they had been and he swiftly found himself a willing wife. The 43-year-old duke took as his bride 16-year-old Benedicta Henrietta of the Palatinate. As the daughter of Anna Gonzaga and Sophia's late brother Edward, she was also Sophia's niece, which ensured that all the interests of the brothers were kept in the family, as it were. Contrary to what one might expect, the marriage was to be a happy one and produced four daughters, three of whom lived to adulthood.

George William, that brother who had once given his word that he would never marry, was still besotted with his beloved Éléonore Desmier d'Olbreuse. Éléonore was a Huguenot of noble birth and had been to all intents and purposes perfectly respectable before she caught the eye of the duke. Yet she exerted quite an influence over the men she encountered and during her sojourn in Kassel had so enchanted the

1. Electress Sophia, by
Petrus Schenck.

2. Sophia of the Palatinate,
by Jans Frans van Douven,
1706.

3. Friedrich V, Elector Palatine (Frederick I, King of Bohemia, The Winter King), by Michiel Jansz van Mierevelt, in or after 1621.

4. Elizabeth, Queen of Bohemia, by Robert Peake the Elder, 1606.

5. Portrait of Sophia Dorothea of Hanover, by Jacob Houbraken, after Antoine Pesne.

6. Charles I.

CAROLVS PRIMOGENITVS SERENISS. CAROLI
LVDOVICI. COM. PALAT. RHENI. &c.. PRINCIPIS
ELECTORIS. FILIVS.

7. Charles Louis, Elector Palatine.

FREDERIC ROY DE BOHEME
ELECTEUR PALATIN.

8. Portrait of Frederick V, by
Jan Lamsvelt.

FORTVNÆ DOMITRIX, AVGVSTI MAXIMA REGIS
FILIA, PALLADII GRANDIS ALVMNA CHORI,
NATVRÆ LABOR, HOC VVLTV SPECTATVR ELIZA.
ET EACIEM FATI VIM SVPERANTIS HABET.
EXVLAT ET TERRAS. QVAS NVNC SIBI VENDICAT ISTER,
IVRE, PATROCINIO. SPE PVTAT ESSE SVAS.
SI PATRIIS CÆSAR TITVLIS SVCCENSVIT, ILLVD
FRANGERE DEBEBAT CÆSARIS ARMA CAPVT.
Crispiaen Qeebooren Sculp: Caspar Barlæus.

9. Portrait of Elisabeth van Bohemen, by Crispijn van den Queborn.

10. Ernest Augustus, Elector of Hanover.

GEORG WILHELM.
Hertzog zu Braunschweig und Lunenburg.

Left: 11. Portrait of
Georg Willem, Duke of
Brunswick-Lüneburg, by
Hendrik Causé.

Below: 12. Prince Maurice
Accompanied by his
Two Brothers, Frederick
V, Elector Palatine, and
Counts of Nassau on
Horseback, follower of
Adriaen Pietersz van de
Venne, c.1625.

Sophie Electrice d'Hanover, Duchesse de Brunsuic
Et Lunebourg, Née Princesse Electoral Palatine.

13. Sophia Electress of Hanover,
mother of King George I,
RB Peake, 1690.

14. Prince Rupert of the Rhine, by
the Studio of Sir Peter Lely.

15. 'Madame'
Elizabeth Charlotte,
Dowager-Duchess of
Orleans [Liselotte].

16. Charles II.

17. Louise Hollandine, by
Gerard van Honthorst, 1643.

18. The Elector Ernest
Augustus of Hanover.

Georgius D.G. Mag. Britanniæ Francia et Hiberniæ Rex Fidei Defensor
Born at Lunen Dux: S.R.J. Arch. Thesau et Princeps Elector &c. Inauguratus xx die October 1714

19. Georgius D.G. Mag. Britanniae Franciae et Hiberniae Rex. John Benson Lossing.

20. Portrait of Marie Mancini, by Jacob Ferdinand Voet.

21. Gottfried Wilhelm
von Leibniz.

SERENISS™ PRINCEPS
SOPHIA CHARLOTTA
D.G. MARCHIO ET ELECTRIX BRANDENB.
NATA DUCISSA BRUNSV.

22. Sophia Charlotte of
Hanover [Figuelotte].

23. Éléonore Desmier d'Olbreuse, Duchess of Celle.

24. Portrait of Georg Willem, Duke of Brunswijk-Lüneburg, by Pieter de Jode, after Anselm van Hulle.

25. Jean-Frédéric de Brunswick-
Lunebourg, by Robert Nanteuil,
after Jean Michelin.

26. Portrait of Willem II, Prince of
Orange, and his Wife, Mary Stuart,
by Gerard van Honthorst, 1647.

27. Sophia Dorothea of Celle.

28. Count Philip Christoph von Königsmarck.

29. Clara Elizabeth von Platen.

30. The Electress Sophia, from the gardens of Herrenhausen.

31. Queen Anne. 1730, John Closterman, after John Faber.

32. Sophia, Electress of Hanover.

landgrave that he left his wife to pursue her. Éléonore, however, wanted no part of any of it and though she appreciated the implicit compliment to her in his actions, she rejected his advances.

Now, having spent a heady few seasons getting to know the intoxicating Éléonore in Holland, George William was desperate to install her in Hanover, if only to cut down on the travelling. But how was he to achieve this ambition?

The ever-cunning George William began to drop hints around the court that Éléonore was keen to meet Sophia, having been left disappointed that she couldn't join the party that had travelled to Italy. Some of Sophia's attendants on that trip had previously known Éléonore and George William claimed that his beloved was eager to make their acquaintance again too. When Ernest Augustus heard this he happily agreed for Éléonore to pay a visit, no doubt thinking that, if his brother's mistress was on hand in Hanover, then Sophia would soon cease to be of any interest to George William. Sophia was likewise delighted to welcome Éléonore to her household for precisely that reason and the lady was duly summoned. Sophia received the new arrival with her usual politeness and together the two women got to know one another over salt biscuits and coffee. At first Sophia seemed delighted to appoint Éléonore as a lady-in-waiting but as the months sped past, that pleasure was subsumed by something else entirely.

Born in 1639, Éléonore was fifteen years younger than George William and when she arrived in Iburg, Sophia didn't exactly take an instant liking to her. Aware of the rumours that had attached themselves to Éléonore in Kassel, Sophia was surprised at just how composed and serious she was, for she had expected someone very bubbly. She noticed also that Éléonore was leading George William a merry dance and keeping him on a tight leash with regard to her favours. Sophia correctly guessed that there was more to this than met the eye, surmising that what Éléonore wanted more than anything was to be his bride.

Remembering his agreement with the brother who had come to his aid when John Frederick had audaciously claimed the territory that was rightfully his, George William balked at the prospect. Instead he decided to offer Éléonore the position of his mistress on the understanding that she would be taken care of financially both before and after his death. It was agreed that Éléonore would receive 2,000 crowns per year as long as George William lived and 6,000 crowns per year after his death.

To avoid any misunderstanding, both parties signed an agreement and had it witnessed by Ernest Augustus and Sophia. It seemed like the best solution all round. There had still been no legal marriage, George William was still thought to be impotent, meaning that there was no threat of a child, and best of all, this unofficial marriage seemed to take him completely off the market.

The deed was done and the couple retired to bed but when the dawn came, so too did the tears. When Éléonore emerged from her room she was weeping, something that sounded alarm bells in Sophia's mind straight away. The reason for the tears, Éléonore sobbed, was her own realisation that she was married in her heart but not in the eyes of the world or God. She wanted everyone to know that she and George William were pledged to each other and now asked what her official title would be, advancing the suggestion of *Lady Celle*. To this, Ernest Augustus and Sophia were resolutely opposed, for the Dowager Duchess of Celle still lived and George William had no wish to upset her by lending her title to a woman of low rank and no legal standing. It was agreed instead that Éléonore would be known as Lady Harburg, and she agreed readily.

What Éléonore perhaps hadn't anticipated was how rigidly Sophia would insist on adhering to protocol, so she didn't only not have the title she wanted, she also had to behave in a manner befitting a lady's attendant. At mealtimes she didn't sit with the dukes and duchess, but at a table with other ladies-in-waiting. Whilst the ducal party dined like, well, *dukes*, Éléonore took her share of the far from grand meal served to their household. She did, however, enjoy the use of a carriage and the love of her husband, but this wasn't what Éléonore wanted. Éléonore wanted what Sophia had.

Oh, and George William's inability to conceive after that nasty bout of venereal disease?

Turns out it was somewhat overstated.

On 15 September 1666 Éléonore gave birth to a little girl, who was named Sophia Dorothea. As his wife recovered from her trying labour, George William was at her side, doting on her in a way that Ernest Augustus never did for Sophia anymore. Sophia Dorothea was to be the only child born to the couple and the bishop and his wife were extremely relived that the child wasn't a boy, as this might have led to all sorts of problems down the line. Of course, now George William had proven himself perfectly able to conceive, the threat of more children was worrying present all over again.

In fact, Sophia Dorothea would lead to plenty of problems of her own.

Three months later Sophia gave birth to twin boys and to her horror, the first was stillborn. Sophia named her surviving boy Maximilian William but suffered so greatly from the loss of her child that there were fears for her life. In an effort to cheer her up a little, Ernest Augustus moved his court to Lüneburg to enjoy the lavish hospitality of his brother, and Sophia was treated to a winter of entertainment and laughter. Here Sophia learned that Éléonore had led her lover to believe that she was from a high ranking family and far from being a lady-in-waiting at the French court, she had actually been a valued friend of the royal family. One rather gets the impression that she was content to let George William go on believing what he wanted, for as long as George William loved Éléonore, he would not trouble her.

Hysterics, Poison and Plot

George William might not be troubling Sophia but someone in her entourage certainly was. The new thorn in her side was Susanne de La Chevalerie-Manselière and this friend of Éléonore's was soon to become a firm *friend* of Ernest Augustus too. During a trip to the Danish court as guests of the king and queen of Denmark[21], Ernest Augustus made his move on the delectable Susanne. Unbeknownst to her would-be paramour, Susanne wasn't the romantic sort but was instead possessed of the sort of guilty conscience that one rarely comes across in the annals of court history. Every time her admirer came to pay his court, she was overcome by such extreme guilt that she would collapse in hysterical fits. So punishing was her conscience that she insisted on only meeting Ernest Augustus in public, hoping that this might assuage her guilt. It didn't. Instead her reaction grew more violent with every new encounter and Éléonore, seeing the opportunity to make some mischief not only for Susanne but perhaps for Sophia too, delighted in spreading rumours about what was going on between the duke and the lady's attendant.

Susanne became so distressed by the gossip at court that she asked for an audience with Sophia. Still recovering from the birth of her most recent child, Sophia Charlotte, who was born on 30 October 1668, Sophia reluctantly agreed. After three sons she was utterly ecstatic to have a daughter and the little girl was known by the pet name, *Figuelotte*, which stuck. Unsurprisingly, Sophia would rather have passed the time with her new arrival than the woman who had fallen for her own husband, but she invited her rival to come to her chambers and there the two women finally discussed the unfortunate situation. Sophia received Susanne with no small amount of sympathy, for she knew that Susanne loved Ernest Augustus with an almost absurd fervour, but she knew also that her piety and conscience would never allow her to act on it.

Only when Susanne had given her word that she valued her reputation more than her attraction to Ernest Augustus did Sophia admit that she wished the couple had shown more discretion. In fact, she told Susanne that their public shows of devotion were almost as damaging for a girl's name as a private assignation could be. Perhaps expecting only kind words and compliments on her piety, Susanne was shocked. As the tears began to flow Sophia tried to calm her, but her kindness only made things worse and Susanne flung herself upon the ground, screaming. Eventually Sophia had no choice but to have Susanne removed, if only to give herself a little peace.

The following morning, Susanne fled. Sophia was happy to see her go, for she suspected she might have proven to be a genuine rival if only she had been more willing to indulge her would-be suitor's whims. She knew that Ernest Augustus had his lovers - what married man of rank didn't - but those women were no threat to his heart. Innocent, virtuous, *hard to get* Susanne had never even played the game, and that made her the most dangerous opponent of all. Let's not forget the scenes that Sophia had witnessed in Heidelberg where a young woman of little note and precious little rank had stolen the heart of her brother, the elector, and left his highborn and fine-bosomed electress high and dry!

For her part, Susanne hoped that a swift departure would count as proof of her innocence but instead the rumours grew louder. Why would she flee so quickly, asked the courtiers, unless she had a pressing reason to make a hasty departure? And what reason could be more pressing than a not so happy event? Far from saving her reputation by leaving Hanover, Susanne was suddenly suspected of carrying Ernest Augustus' baby.

At this moment, when it would have been very easy for Sophia to turn her back on the woman who had almost been a rival, to abandon her to the rumour and the gossips, she did no such thing. Instead she sent Susanne gifts and letters, showing those who were spreading cruel stories that she had no quarrel with her presumed rival, thus dispelling the rumours. Soon the two women were in regular correspondence yet Ernest Augustus couldn't get the thought of Susanne out of his head. Before long, he and the woman he had fallen for were secretly exchanging letters.

Or rather, they *thought* they were secretly exchanging letters.

The canny Sophia actually knew *exactly* what was going on and as she always did, she let it slide. What she *wouldn't* let slide was her husband's request several years later that she allow Susanne back into the household, this time to become an attendant to Figuelotte. This was a step too far and Sophia said *no way*. As far as she was concerned, the ladies who surrounded her daughter must be entirely above reproach[22].

Motherhood, Marriages and Mistresses

In 1669 Sophia gave birth to a son, Charles Philip. That same year she was also instrumental in brokering the marriage of her nephew and future Elector Palatine, Charles, to Princess Wilhelmine Ernestine of Denmark. She was shy and the daughter of Ernest Augustus' sister, he was timid and the son of Sophia's brother, the elector, and his loathed wife, Charlotte. Though Charles Louis had nothing but love for the children he had of his second marriage, those he fathered by Charlotte were subjected to stern discipline and constant criticism and when Charles finally came to power, he did little to reward those half-siblings who had so occupied his father's love when he had been starved of it.

Charles was initially starry-eyed at the thought of marrying the daughter of a king but by the time the wedding rolled around in 1671, he had already cooled on his bride. There was no mutual attraction at all and the marriage was to remain childless despite Charles asking Ernest Augustus to give him a few pointers on what was expected of a husband when he took his wife to bed. When Charles died in 1685, the House of Palatinate-Simmern, which had existed since 1385 and the birth of Stephen, Count Palatine of Simmern-Zweibrücken, died with him.

The year 1671 was a time of new starts for Sophia and her family. In addition to the marriage of Charles and Wilhelmine Ernestine, it was also the year in which Sophia's beloved Liselotte, whom she had spent four such happy years with, was wed. Despite her closeness to the girl, Sophia knew nothing of the plans for the marriage until they were considerably advanced, though she and all of Europe *certainly* knew of the groom.

He was Philippe I, Duke of Orléans, brother of King Louis XIV and he was also a fellow with a chequered past, not to mention a Roman Catholic faith. The marriage was brokered by our old friend Anna Gonzaga, who had known the duke for years. She managed to negotiate not only suitable terms for a betrothal but even the conversion of the bride to Catholicism, something that would have had Queen Elizabeth of Bohemia spinning in her tomb at Westminster Abbey.

Philippe was a singular sort. Having been dressed as a girl in childhood by his mother, Queen Anne of France, it was a habit that he grew flamboyantly fond of. He appeared in public dressed in the guise of a shepherdess and he loved the company of young men, many of whom were just as effeminate as he was. He even had his own *mistress* in the shape of Philippe, the chevalier de Lorraine, who was his constant but not always faithful bisexual companion for three decades.

Philippe would happily have remained unmarried but he had a job to do and that job was to produce some heirs, so it was vital that he wed and get on with the task in hand. The first lady to wear the ring of *Monsieur,* as he was known, was Henrietta Anne of England, Sophia's cousin and a girl better known by her nickname, *Minette*. Despite Philippe's well-known preference for the company of men, two of the couple's children lived to adulthood - their only son died at the age of just two - though not always without a little whisper of scandal when it came to questions of paternity.

Things had not gone well for *Monsieur* and *Madame* once Minette and Philippe began to share a lover in the considerable form of Armand de Gramont, Count of Guiche. As both had vied for the handsome noble's attention, the initially happy marriage had slid into misery. Minette was just 26 she died, having suffered with extreme abdominal pain for several months. Though rumours of poison consumed the French court, the official verdict was gastroenteritis. It's believed now that the tragic death was a result of natural causes[23].

Philippe didn't really miss Minette much but he was all too aware that he had yet to produce the heir, let alone the spare. After some considerable searching for a wife the role went to Liselotte, who would henceforth be known as *Madame*. Though the couple was not exactly wild about each other sexually, Liselotte managed to find comedy in the situation. She recalled years later that her husband always prayed to his chapelet, a rosary decorated with religious medals, before he retired for the night. One evening as they were settling down, she heard the sound of the chapelet rattling beneath the bedclothes but when she asked Monsieur what he was up to, he told her to go to sleep. Instead she seized up the nightlight and pulled back the bedclothes to find her husband passing his medals and rosary over his body as though he needed holy courage to perform his marital duty! Liselotte laughed and asked if he thought the Virgin Mary would be pleased to have been used in such a way and Monsieur couldn't help but laugh too, even as he asked her to keep his habit a secret.

Madame and Monsieur got on well enough in most things but Liselotte found the constant presence of her husband's lovers, particularly the self-serving Guiche, occasionally difficult to take. Regardless, the mismatched couple eventually became parents to three children, two of whom lived to adulthood. One of those who survived was the all-important heir, Philippe II, Duke of Orléans and Regent of France[24].

It suddenly seemed as though marriage was on everybody's mind and in Celle as well as in Osnabrück, there was suddenly a flurry of activity from people who were very definitely on the make. The first of these opportunists was a man named Johann Helwig Sinold, Baron Schütz, Chancellor of Celle, who was the sort of fellow who could turn any situation to his advantage. Seeking to win influence over George William for his own ends, he knew that the first thing he needed to do was to weaken his employer's relationship with Ernest Augustus, his most trusted friend.

When Schütz looked at little Sophia Dorothea, who was only 5-years-old, he saw not a child, but an opportunity for a man of ambition. A girl was never too young for marriage plans to be made on her behalf, he decided, and she was no exception. In Wolfenbüttel Duke Anthony Ulrich was also seeking to match-make and when he looked to Celle he saw not only a girl who had yet to be betrothed, but also the rich coffers of the duchy, just waiting to be shared. What a perfect bride Sophia Dorothea would make for his son, Augustus Frederick, he decided, and he would be the one to broker the deal. There was only one problem and that was Sophia Dorothea's status. She was technically illegitimate and there was no way that his son, a prince, could marry her.

What to do?

Schütz took George William into a secluded corner and suggested that perhaps a legally binding marriage might be the way forward. He knew that Éléonore's ambition was as strong as his own and hoped that a combination of love and the cajoling of his left-handed wife[25] might be enough to prompt George William to set aside the promise he had once made to his brother and make an honest woman of Madame Harburg.

Such a manoeuvre could have catastrophic consequences for Ernest Augustus and Sophia and she wasn't about to let it happen. She had always suspected Éléonore of being a woman of ambition and this proved it, for if the couple was to legitimately marry and have a son[26], all that would one day be inherited by the heirs of Ernest Augustus would be split once more, as it had been split between the four dukes of Brunswick-Lüneburg. For a woman so aware of birthright and protocol the very idea of it was too much and she spat in a letter to Liselotte, 'We shall soon have to say "Madame la Duchesse" to this little clot of dirt [Éléonore], for is there another name for that mean *intrigante* who comes from nowhere?'[27]. Yet what could she do? Duke Anthony Ulrich liked the sound of Sophia's dowry of 100,000 thalers and Éléonore loved the idea of being mother to a princess. She wasn't going to back down.

George William was a little more loyal than his chancellor and wife and he wouldn't agree to break the promise he had made years ago. What he *would* agree to do, however, was bend it a little. He decided to ask Leopold I, Holy Roman Emperor, to legitimise the marriage and by extension, Sophia Dorothea's birth, but only if Ernest Augustus would agree to it. Schütz huffed and puffed and decided that it would do, though he told his employer that it would cost 16,000 crowns to secure the emperor's approval. Sophia, always able to spot a chancer, believed that it cost no more than half of that amount. Where did the other half go? If her suspicions were correct, the answer is straight into Shütz's pocket.

The brothers agreed that nothing so extreme as a broken promise was required. Instead they asked the emperor to legitimise Sophia in such a manner that she could adopt the arms of whatever house she might marry into without being forced to use the *bend sinister*. This heraldic symbol would instantly identify its holder as illegitimate and it was important to George William that if his daughter stood a chance of marrying into the House of Brunswick-Wolfenbüttel, then she wouldn't be marked as such. In return for George William's promise to lend his considerable armies to the emperor's campaigns, it was agreed that this would be done. Just to complete the picture, George William began assembling a considerable portfolio of territory as well, so that he knew his wife and child would be properly cared for after his death. For now at least, Lady Harburg was satisfied. It wouldn't last.

When Sophia heard that the Holy Roman Emperor had privately referred to Éléonore as *duchess*, she was disgusted. Worse still was the public persona Éléonore cultivated of a dutiful, respectful wife when Sophia believed she was nothing of the sort. With no ammunition presenting itself, Sophia dredged up some old gossip and wrote to Liselotte:

> 'Never would any respectable girl have entered the house of the Princess de Tarente[28], for, though she is my aunt - to my intense disgust - she is not a person with whom any one can live and remain clean. [...] However, d'Olbreuse being a nobody, it does not matter much.'[29]

Éléonore wasn't living like a nobody and she had an implicit understanding of the value of good PR. She and her daughter took regular rides out to meet the people of Celle, who adored the smiling and approachable pair. She encouraged George William to expand his territories and swell his coffers, to improve his estates and to do all he could to establish himself not as one of three dukes, but as *the* duke. Sophia dismissed this rapidly growing court as the folly of a mistress and when Éléonore employed a genealogist to establish that she was descended from the ancient kings of France, she couldn't contain her hilarity. She shared Éléonore's latest escapade with Liselotte, who promptly drew up a family tree of her own, proving once and for all that her cook was a descendant of Philip the Bold! Always arch, the wounded Sophia had toppled into spite.

Sophia, highborn whether in exile or not and granddaughter of the king of England, was no longer tolerating Éléonore. Instead, she had actively begun to dislike her. The women went to Altona to an audience with the Danish queen and Sophia was received with a kiss and an invitation to dinner. For low ranking Huguenot Éléonore there was a place at the table, but *definitely* no kiss. No longer was Éléonore the respectful, quiet lady who had become Madame Harburg. Now, safe in her position, her status legitimised by the emperor, she was showing her true colours. She was rich, respected and her daughter was set to be married to a Crown

Prince, so she wasn't about to let the matter of the queen's kiss, or lack of it, pass unremarked. Instead Éléonore complained loudly and at length about the food on offer, driving Sophia to distraction. One suspects an element of good old-fashioned rank pulling in her reaction though, for how dare someone like Éléonore criticise the quality of the food on a queen's table?

She had come a long way since salt biscuits and coffee.

Never one to miss a chance to better her rival, it was left to Sophia to exact a silent but deadly revenge on Éléonore for her rudeness. When she heard that Éléonore was in the early stages of plotting a marriage for her daughter and Prince George[30], heir to the Danish throne, Sophia *may* have had a little word in the ear of his mother, Sophie Amalie, because the negotiations ended before they properly began. Watching from a safe distance, Sophia crowed with bitter delight, 'Fancy a king's son for that bit of a bastard!'.

Not her finest hour.

But fancy a clot of dirt's daughter for an electoral prince.

That attraction that Sophia once wielded over George William was gone, replaced by his new *amour*. Is it too much to suspect that perhaps she missed the attention she had once commanded? Ernest Augustus was still regularly admiring the *sights* of Osnabrück just as he had regularly admired those of Italy and Sophia had lost the only man who had been content to lavish her with affection when her husband didn't. Though Sophia's court was relatively small and her finances always on a tight rein, Éléonore's life in Celle was a constant round of luxuries and parties, all of which might have been Sophia's but for that broken engagement years earlier. She had gone from being the centre of attention, a possible bride for the king of England, for the duke of Palma and a clutch of others, to being the wife of a man who had plenty of other things - including women - to occupy him, and mother to an ever growing brood of children. She was bored.

With another pregnancy announced, Éléonore twisted the knife in Sophia's side and told her that, should she have a boy, George William would certainly marry her. As travelling companions on the road to Heidelberg for the wedding of the electoral prince, Sophia and Éléonore were forced together more intimately and for longer than ever before. Eventually Sophia escaped her nemesis by travelling with Frau von Harling in a fast-moving sedan chair, which must only have annoyed

Éléonore all the more. This wasn't a subterfuge to get away from Éléonore. The heavily pregnant woman was suffering badly throughout the uncomfortable journey.

Upon her arrival, Sophia went straight to bed and was there delivered of her next child, Christian Henry. Whilst she was resting, Charles, the sheltered bridegroom, sought advice from Ernest Augustus about the duties he was expected to perform on his wedding night and beyond. One imagines that Ernest Augustus had plenty of helpful tips to impart and perhaps it gave him some ideas of his own because he immediately bade Sophia and the children farewell and headed off for the delights of Venice once more. Left alone in Heidelberg Sophia was lonely. She rose from her convalescent bed to travel with Liselotte as far as Strasbourg.

Here the young lady consented to be married to the flamboyantly bisexual Duke of Orléans, though she later reflected, 'It is true I came to France simply out of obedience to my father, my uncle and my aunt, the Electress of Hanover. My inclinations didn't lead me there at all.'[31]

There the women parted ways, one to become a wife, the other to meet a mistress.

Clara

In 1671, as Sophia was recovering from the birth of her son, Christian Henry, the influence of a woman who would become notorious first began to be felt at court. She was Clara Elisabeth von Meysenburg, and she was a lady on the make. Sophia had not enjoyed her extended sojourn to Italy with her husband so when he planned future trips, he didn't invite her along. Instead he took with him the woman who was to become his most enduring and most troublesome mistress. By the time she died her name was synonymous with cunning, plot and bloody murder.

But was that strictly fair?

Clara and her sister, Catherine Marie, were the daughters of Count Georg Philipp von Meysenburg, an adventurer of no particular fortune. His girls had been raised with an eye on making an impact, for both were striking in appearance and possessed naturally witty manners and keen intelligence. Indeed, some might say *cunning*. Schooled in the ways of courtly etiquette they dressed, behaved and spoke with utmost care, and their father had initially aimed for his daughters to make their fortunes at the opulent and decadent French court. When they had arrived, they had found that the followers of Louis XIV were more generous in number than they were in spirit and the sisters had been run out of town before they had had a chance to make much of an impression, let alone a royal conquest. It was time to adjust their sights and their next quarry, which seemed far more winnable, was Ernest Augustus and the Osnabrück court.

Count von Meysenburg introduced his daughters to Osnabrück, apparently with no greater ambition than finding a place for them at court. Once he had achieved this it was up to the sisters to make their own way and they did it in fine style. At a fete in 1673, the young ladies dressed themselves as storybook shepherdesses and recited a dramatic scene they had composed in honour of the bishop. Singing and dancing in the moonlight, their faces painted and their voices harmonious, they won the heart not of Ernest Augustus, but of two of his most influential advisors.

The sisters were soon married to George Louis' governors, Franz Ernst von Platen[32] and Johann von dem Busche[33], but Clara had higher aims than von Platen. Her husband proved a valuable stepping stone for he exerted some influence over the bishop and through this, Clara was soon safely in position as a lady-in-waiting to Sophia. It was only a matter of time before Ernest Augustus noticed her amongst his wife's circle, which was just what Clara was counting on.

Clara was eighteen years younger than Sophia. She was glamorous, accomplished and sensual, and Ernest Augustus fell for her just as she knew he would. With Clara enchanting the father just as her sister was enchanting the eldest son, the pair had soon sewn up the household of the Bishop of Osnabrück.

Sophia knew of the romance between Clara and George and she bore it with stoicism because this was just something that women of her rank had to put up with. The thought of complaining to her husband wouldn't have occurred to her, so she found her own ways to get back at Clara. She wasn't without her little moments of revenge and indulged her more mischievous instincts by taking long summer walks in the gardens of the palace, always accompanied by Clara. Draped in the heaviest of opulent fabrics and thick with makeup, the mistress sweated and laboured in the heat as Sophia glided serenely, smug in these little victories. Though Sophia had been raised to believe that women must be above reproach, in her world men were not held to such high standards. Instead they were free to consort with whomsoever they chose on the unwritten understanding that they would not do so ostentatiously or in a way that might cause any embarrassment to their wives.

And sometimes, this meant that there would be children.

In 1674, both women gave birth to sons by Ernest Augustus and both sons, perhaps unexpectedly, were named Ernest Augustus. This was a man who knew all about building a dynasty.

Sophia had witnessed first-hand in Heidelberg the catastrophic effect a wife might have by trying to separate her husband and his mistress and she had no wish to see a repeat of it here. Sophia was no Charlotte, likely to go after her rival with a knife, and Clara was no Luise, wide-eyed and fresh. Luise was innocent, young and inexperienced, whereas Clara had experience in spades and she wasn't looking for romance so much as influence and power. Clara posed no threat to the future inheritance of Ernest Augustus' children. That unpleasant position was held by the loathed Éléonore.

The Lady of Celle

Sophia would have no more children, but in Celle Éléonore was almost a decade her junior and still at an age where she might give birth to a boy. Despite the animosity between the two women she and Sophia remained civil - how could they not? - And Éléonore continued to delight in flaunting her wealth and taunting the bishop's wife. Gone was the young woman with a pretty face and serious aspect and in her place was glamour and ambition and a lady who knew her malleable partner was wrapped around her little finger.

Sophia could still stir it up when the mood took her though. Catching a moment alone with George William, she faithfully recounted to him a conversation in which she said that Éléonore had told her that, if she were to have a son, George William would certainly marry her. The furious duke was determined that he would have such loose talk out with his wife but Sophia, graceful and forgiving as ever, asked him not to. She only had his best interests at heart, after all.

If Sophia thought she had finally pushed a stick through the wheels of Éléonore's ambition, however, she was to be badly disappointed. Duke

Anthony Ulrich of Brunswick-Wolfenbüttel came calling again, with more news regarding the mooted union between Sophia Dorothea and his eldest son. The duke's brother, Rudolph Augustus, Duke of Brunswick-Wolfenbüttel, was far, far from happy at the proposal. He had shared power with his younger brother only on the implicit understanding that Anthony Ulrich's sons would marry his daughters[34] so to find his girls shoved aside in favour of a bastard from Brunswick did nothing for family relations. Anthony Ulrich knew exactly how his brother would react, but he also knew that Sophia Dorothea was sole heiress to a fortune and though she couldn't inherit the duchy itself, the cash she would one day gain went a long way to making up for that.

The only fly in the ointment remained the unmarried state of Éléonore and George William, so Anthony Ulrich approached Chancellor Schütz again and asked if he might drop a word in the right ear. He would happily consent to the marriage of Sophia Dorothea and his son if the bride's parents would agree to be married too, he said. The benefits to both sides were clear. Duke Anthony Ulrich offered the opportunity to marry into a royal family, whilst Sophia Dorothea offered him a fortune in dowry and future inheritance. All things considered, George William decided that there was nothing for it, he must abandon the promise he made his brother all those years ago and make an honest woman of Éléonore, thus fully legitimising their daughter.

Just as he had once negotiated the substitution of Ernest Augustus for George William in the marriage bed of Sophia, now the diplomatic powers of George Christopher von Hammerstein were called upon once again. This time he was charged with obtaining Ernest Augustus' permission for the marriage between Éléonore and George William. The future happiness of 8-year-old Sophia Dorothea, so her parents claimed, depended on it.

How horribly right they were.

George William knew his brother well enough to know that Sophia would play her part in Ernest Augustus agreeing to or refusing the request. Before Hammerstein reached Osnabrück he and his employer had already considered all of the questions that might be asked and they were sure that they had an answer for everything. The marriage would be morganatic, which meant that Éléonore and any children she and George William had would be unable to inherit the ranks and privileges of their father. Éléonore would give up any hopes of ever being titled a duchess in return for the respectable title of Countess of Wilhelmsburg and in the future, neither George William nor his descendants would seek any advantage over the descendants of Ernest Augustus. The bishop and his wife listened to all of this and when the promises and plans had been outlined to him, Ernest Augustus agreed to the marriage only on the condition that it would never come back to bite him. Realising that she had been outwitted by the party from Celle and that she couldn't disagree with her husband, Sophia had no choice but to bite her tongue hard and agree.

So grateful was George William that he sent Éléonore to Sophia with instructions to thank her in person. The meeting was awkward, with Éléonore ungracious and apparently ungrateful too. Only when she had her audience with Ernest Augustus did she turn on the waterworks, assuring him tearfully that she sought nothing for herself, only a good future for her beloved daughter. When Duke Anthony Ulrich asked Sophia for one last favour, however, it was the final straw. He wondered whether she might put word about that George William and Éléonore had been married prior to their daughter's birth, just to make it all purer than pure. The answer was an unequivocal *no way.*

The two brothers came to an accord by which the marriage and the little girl could both be legitimised, but only on the understanding that there would be no future ramifications for Ernest Augustus and his heirs should George William have a son. The two siblings both agreed to a legally binding document that detailed each point of potential future discord.

> '1. The Bishop [Ernest Augustus] promises not to oppose the said marriage, but will acknowledge and countenance the said Countess [Éléonore], and the children that may be born of this marriage; and also the daughter now living, Sophia Dorothea, agreeing to uphold her in the possession of her estates, and in her state and rank conferred upon her, and which may be conferred upon her, by the Emperor, and his Serene Highness Duke George William, in so far as such may not be to the prejudice of the heirs of the Bishop, as regards the sovereignty of this Duchy and its appurtenances.
>
> [...]

2. The Duke promises that this marriage shall not be to the disadvantage of the Bishop or his male heirs […]

3. Should one or more children be born in this marriage, they are to remain satisfied with the property the Duke, with the consent of the Bishop, may leave them at his decease and renounce any pretension to the Duchy and its appurtenances, as long as male heirs exist in the Bishop's family."[35]

Sophia must have been furious. She had been outmanoeuvred by her rival at every turn and had no choice but to remain gracious. Now she had to find other ways to needle Éléonore, who never knew when to turn the other cheek. The chance presented itself when George Louis went off to taste battle for the first time alongside his father at Conz, where the forces of the empire faced down and claimed victory over the French. George Louis distinguished himself alongside the Osnabrück troops but those soldiers who came from Celle deserted, resulting in injury to their commanders. Sophia quickly dashed off a letter to Éléonore to let her know of the poor show from her husband's men. Éléonore, of course, reached out and snatched the bait.

Steam must have shot out of Éléonore's ears, for she got it into her head that Sophia was claiming the entire victory was down to Ernest Augustus. She wanted to know why her rival hadn't so much as mentioned George William's prowess on the battlefield to which Sophia churlishly asked, *why should I?* After all, as far as she was concerned, that was Éléonore's job, not hers. Poor, innocent, wounded Sophia duly reported Éléonore's annoyance to George William, who ordered his wife to apologise and to seek Sophia's forgiveness. Naturally Sophia was the wounded party all over again and decided, all things considered, that she wouldn't write again since Éléonore was so ready to misunderstand her oh-so innocent comments.

Éléonore remained a thorn in the side of our heroine. Duke Anthony Ulrich, who had already achieved so much in pursuit of his son's marriage to Sophia Dorothea, now began to seek even more concessions, chief among them being the request that Éléonore be given the title of *princess*. Sophia once again sought to recover some of the influence she had once held over George William and she begged him to reconsider, reminding him that the marriage had been arranged only to legitimise Sophia Dorothea, so there was nothing to be gained by awarding Éléonore such a title. Did he not remember what John Frederick had done in the aftermath of the death of Christian Louis, when he had attempted to snatch power and territory from his brothers? Was he content to sow the seeds of future civil war should he have heirs of his own? The sons of a princess, she reminded him, naturally enjoyed a greater influence than those of a duke, and she would not be party to laying the foundations of future conflict for anything in the world. Though she loved him as a sister would a brother, she simply could not bring herself to agree to this most outrageous request.

Despite his assurances that he would never do anything to wound his brother nor his offspring, George William couldn't understand why Sophia was so distressed. The truth was, Sophia saw scheming in every ambition that Éléonore held and immediately reached the worst possible conclusion where her sister-in-law was concerned. It's perfectly possible that she was right of course and that Éléonore did indeed have long-term dynastic plans, but it's equally possible that she sought nothing more than her own advancement and that of her daughter. Sophia had been born to rank and title and Éléonore was hustling to elevate herself. Regardless of motive, to the highborn Sophia that made a very poor show indeed.

It must have been galling though to see Éléonore, who had really come from nowhere in noble terms, on the verge of outranking her. She was being prayed for in the churches of Brunswick-Wolfenbüttel where she was regularly referred to as a duchess and worse still, the envoy of the Holy Roman Empire had referred to her as *Highness*. Could it get any worse?

What do you think?

As soon as the couple was married in the spring of 1676, Éléonore was letting all and sundry know that she was pregnant once again and this time she had every intention of delivering her husband his first heir. In France, Liselotte did what she could to dispel the notions of future rank and title that Éléonore was putting about to anyone on the continent who would listen, but it was like trying to hold back the tide. She was an unstoppable force and though Sophia told herself that any sons of Éléonore and George William would only be counts, not dukes or, worse still, *princes*[36], it seemed as though she was losing her grip on her brother-in-law. If a son was born to him now, who knew what the future might bring?

In fact, Éléonore was delivered of a stillborn daughter. It was too late to silence the courts of Europe though and they were left reeling from the gossip of the two brothers, once so close, who were being driven apart by Lady Harburg.

It was ironic then that Crown Prince Augustus Frederick, the boy whose hand had prompted all this change and argument, didn't live long enough to marry Sophia Dorothea anyway. He died on 9 August 1676 from the horrendous injuries received from a cannonball that slammed into his head on the battlefield. Not to be deterred, Anthony Ulrich duly produced another son to take his place, but George William suddenly called a halt. He took the death of the groom as the worst of ill omens and asked if he might have a few years to think about it.

Until Sophia Dorothea reached the age of 16, in fact.

George William and Éléonore reluctantly agreed. It would prove to be a decision that echoed down the centuries.

France and Beyond

The battle with Éléonore left Sophia exhausted. Her children were growing, her husband had Clara to occupy him and she had walked the gardens of Osnabrück a thousand times. Though one senses that Sophia might have been a rather astute stateswoman had she been given the opportunity, Ernest Augustus never dreamed of giving his spouse such responsibility and instead she was left to be a professional wife, as so many of her peers were likewise. Let us not forget the Stuart blood that flowed in her veins though and if she had been raised to one thing by her mother, it was to remember where she came from.

It's hardly surprising for a woman who adored court protocol and rank that the Bourbon court proved irresistible. Years of conflict between France and the Holy Roman Empire had finally come to a head but that didn't mean that there wasn't still a world to get out and see. Despite the immense cost, when the opportunity came for Sophia to take a trip to France in 1679, she grabbed at it with both hands. She was keen to breathe some fresh air, far away from the power plays of family politics.

What she might *not* have expected was to find herself as a pet project of the flamboyant *Monsieur,* who became her personal shopper for the duration of the visit. He showed off his jewels and finery and picked out the latest trends for Sophia, teasing her hair and making up her face until she was the picture of French fashion. In spite of herself she grew fond of him despite Liselotte's grumbles, for it seems that she rather liked his unorthodox approach to life!

More than anything though, Sophia was delighted to be reunited with her sister, Louise Hollandine, who had by now been Abbess of Aubusson for fifteen years[37], and to renew her acquaintance with her beloved Liselotte. She devoured the world of the French court, determined not to miss anything of this once in a lifetime opportunity. One senses once again the keen eye of the little girl who had watched the comings and goings of her mother and brother's courts; the child who had grown into a woman without enough to occupy her mind. She witnessed too the devotion of Louis XIV to his current mistress and perhaps wondered at her husband, who had begun to suffer from the same bouts of melancholy that had plagued her late father, and his attachment to Clara, his social-climbing mistress. That absurd jealousy that had once occupied Ernest Augustus had long since dimmed and she held no grudge against him, believing that it was only natural for an older wife to become part of the household furniture. Besides, for all her professed devotion to her husband in their earlier marriage, that had long since passed too. Now they were like so many long-married couples, just sort of rubbing along.

The visit was intended to mark the betrothal of Liselotte's stepdaughter, Marie Louise d'Orléans, to Charles II of Spain[38]. *Monsieur*, Liselotte's husband, turned his charm up to eleven throughout the visit and Sophia saw no sign of the flamboyantly promiscuous husband with a parade of male lovers. In fact, she never guessed how dissatisfied Liselotte was with her dazzling life and for the rest of her days, remained one of Monsieur's loudest champions.

Marie Louise, however, was *very* open with regard to just how much she didn't want to marry the king of Spain. He was well known for his ugly looks and strange behaviour and she knew that her only purpose was to bear his children, which she singularly failed to do. Though the bride was distraught, all at court did their best to pretend that it was a marvellous opportunity for the young woman, when in reality it was the diplomatic outcome that interested the courtiers most of all.

Regardless of Marie Louise's distress, Sophia delighted in the attention that the French king paid to her and together the two discussed the current political state of the continent, in relation to their respective nations. Both shared a hope for peace but Louis had a few other observations to make, all of which left Sophia glowing with spousal pride as she decided that her welcome reflected well not on her, but on her husband, who had forged a fine reputation. Louis, however, seemed particularly interested in the beauty and fine nature of Sophia's daughter, Figuelotte, who was visiting France with her. He had a son of his own, he mentioned casually, and Ernest Augustus quite liked the idea of uniting Figuelotte with the dauphin[39]. Ultimately that wasn't to be her fate though.

Sophia had never seen anything quite like the Bourbon court. All was opulence and glittering wealth and she was treated to a taste of it herself while she was there. Liselotte's husband, who adored jewels and finery, delighted in showing off his clothes and those of his wife and daughter and he even had all Sophia's own gems reset in the French style. Her wardrobe was replenished with the latest fashions and Sophia, wife and mother, was for a brief time the toast of society all over again, but this time with added fashion maven credibility thanks to Monsieur's helping hand. Yet amongst all the glamour and glitz, just as there had been in childhood, there was that same sense of stifling protocol with multiple bows and curtsies, long ceremonies in boiling hot chapels and palaces and a dazzling array of new names and faces to remember. Sophia came a little unstuck when protocol slipped though and, alone with the queen and her ladies, she found herself so well-trained by life in Osnabrück that she simply *couldn't* relax.

As Maria Theresa - beautiful if not for her rotten dental work, Sophia tells us - lounged around and invited the others to join her, Sophia remained standing, ramrod straight, no part of her careful adherence to etiquette allowing her to just kick back in the presence of the Queen of France[40]. One thing she *wouldn't* do was kiss the hem of Maria Theresa's dress; Sophia had her breaking point, it seems.

One memory in particular that remained with Sophia when she left France was the utter horror of Marie Louise, the new Queen of Spain, whenever she thought of her husband. She and Figuelotte had become so close that the unhappy bride declared that she wished the other girl was a boy, so that they might be married and she would be saved from her miserable fate. Her unhappiness infected the whole court and Versailles echoed with tears of sadness as the courtiers waved goodbye to their sacrificial lamb.

There was disappointment of a different kind for Sophia who, having been dazzled by the sheer opulence of the Bourbon court, now found that her parting gift was a few imperfect gemstones. Monsieur, who knew a thing or two about giving presents, had them exchanged for something a little finer, but the damage had already been done. One senses a little satisfaction in Sophia at the initial gift, proof after all that the Bourbons and their jewels were as far from perfect as she had suspected!

The fate of Marie Louise was food for thought for Sophia, whose own daughter was now of an age to consider future husbands. She chewed it over during her happy reunion with Louise Hollandine, who seemed to her to be the happiest of the few surviving children of the Winter King and Queen, living out her peaceful days in the convent cushioned by faith and friendship. Sophia remained contemplative as she made her way home once more.

An Unhappy Reunion

Sophia's joy at returning home was soon stymied by the various bits of news that awaited her there. First among them was the announcement that Ernest Augustus, whose health had been frail of late, intended to take one of his trips to Italy, which his duties in Osnabrück had prevented him from doing for a while. Second was a report from the convent in Herford that its abbess, Sophia's sister, Elisabeth, was gravely ill and not expected to recover. Charles Louis, meanwhile, had become obsessed by melancholy and religious mania since the death of his beloved Luise in 1677. And just to complete the set, because bad news always comes in a heap, Ernest Augustus was seriously considering the prospect of marrying George Louis off to his cousin, Sophia Dorothea of Celle. After the young man singularly failed to impress the future Queen Anne during a visit to England, this would become *Plan A*.

Ernest Augustus made all the right noises of course, inviting Sophia to join him and John Frederick on their trip, all the time knowing full well that she would decline. And decline she did, leaving them to go off alone and in the case of John Frederick, for the very last time. Sophia had no wish to travel so far again anyway but even if she had, her fears for her ailing sister would have prevented it. Instead she hurried to Herford where she found Elisabeth lingering on the verge of a drawn out death. Her body was ravaged by dropsy and over the exhausting, agonising months that were left to her before she passed away in February 1680, the two sisters spent long hours together, though it pained Sophia to witness her sister's horrendous suffering.

More sad news was to follow when Sophia received word that John Frederick had died on the road to Italy. With Ernest Augustus still making his own way to the revels, Sophia recalled him to Osnabrück where he met the news with a shrug and said simply, 'I am glad it was not I who died.'

Ernest Augustus wasn't a monster though and he did mourn the brother whose death resulted in his receiving not only the duchy of Hanover, but the royal title of *Prince of Calenberg* too. All that had once been shared between four had come down to two. Looking back, Sophia ruminated on the differing fates of her sister and John Frederick. All things considered she concluded that she would rather go as he had, peacefully in his sleep after a few glasses of booze, rather than suffer the merciless physical collapse and debilitating pains that Elisabeth had been forced to endure.

Nostalgia began to prick at Ernest Augustus' conscience as he bade farewell to John Frederick and he remembered the way he and George William had once been the best of friends, sharing everything right down to their jealous attraction to Sophia. That had long since ebbed on both sides but now that brotherly love returned and Ernest Augustus decided to do what he had always sworn he never would. He would recognise Éléonore as a duchess at last. After years of pushing and infighting, Éléonore claimed the prize that she had fought for from the very start.

She had won.

At least Sophia could occupy herself with her forthcoming relocation to the Leineschloss where, in his new capacity as ruler of the Duchy of Hanover, Ernest Augustus would establish his court. She and her husband would be able to indulge their shared love of renovation and estate design, which was one of the few things they still actually did together.

She still hoped, though the hope was fading, that the mourning Charles Louis might yet remarry and have another son. His heir, the recently married Charles, was showing no signs of becoming a father and though Charles Louis had a whole brace of illegitimate children with Luise, none of them could inherit. If Charles and Wilhelmine Ernestine didn't have a son and there was no other boy waiting in the wings, then the Palatinate would pass into fresh hands. Rupert, the only other hope, had no interest in returning to the lands from which he had been banished and was happily settled in England in the arms of actress, Peg Hughes, the mother of his daughter, Ruperta. It was here that he was determined to remain, for he had no wish to marry and pursue power on the continent. In the end, Sophia's worst fears were realised. Years later, when Charles died without an heir in 1685, the Palatine was inherited by the Catholic Neuburgs.

For now all she could do was get on and with their building plans continuing apace, Sophia and Ernest Augustus travelled to Denmark as guests of the royal family. Here Sophia went on her first hunt and proved to be an unexpectedly crack shot, no doubt to her husband's delight. One gets the impression that she really enjoyed this short interlude, particularly seeing Ernest Augustus away from the cares of his court *and* the temptations of Italy. Sadly her brief happiness was shattered by news of another death, this one more painful than any other.

Charles Louis, Elector Palatine, the elder brother who had been as good as a father to Sophia, died on 28 August 1680. Never having fully recovered from the death of his beloved Luise, he had fallen victim to a stroke and lingered on through all manner of painful treatments before he died in his daughter's arms. Just as Sophia would decades later, he passed away in a verdant garden, the very same garden in which his initial stroke had occurred. This death more than any other to date cut Sophia to her core, for this was the man who had been her anchor through the unsettled early years after the death of their father and the disinterest of their late mother. He had taken her in, cared for her and been a devoted and loving friend. She nursed hopes of bringing his children to live with her but Ernest Augustus rejected the idea, citing their illegitimacy and the difficulties it might cause for court protocol. Sophia had to content herself with making financial gifts to them instead but she pined dreadfully for her deceased sibling and became convinced that her own life would soon be over too.

'My grief passes the power of words to express. He had always loved me as a daughter, and put such confidence in me that he wrote by every mail, and in a style of such fire and charm that this correspondence formed one of my chief pleasures. This loss has so increased my malady of the spleen[41] that it constantly reminds me that I am now fifty years old, and must soon follow my sister and brother.'

This belief that she too would soon be cold in the grave may well be what prompted Sophia to write her memoirs[42], for she was intent on looking back on what she doubtless considered her past glories, reliving those days that she would never see again. The manuscript ends on this melancholy note, but the low-spirited Sophia had many years yet to live.

A Marrying Man

With the death of her beloved brother, Sophia was catapulted into the position of elder stateswoman of her family and she took it upon herself to care for Charles Louis' children with Luise just as she had cared for Liselotte, though she must do so from afar. The newly-minted Duchess of Hanover now turned her attention to securing wives for her own eldest sons but even as she did, she knew that her husband was increasingly keen on uniting Celle and Hanover by means of a wedding between George Louis and Sophia Dorothea. If he could negotiate this union then who knew what might come next? Certainly it would replenish the suffering coffers of Hanover, for Celle was rich indeed. It would also put paid to any ambitious dynasties elsewhere who might fancy their chances at marrying into George William's family and mounting their own challenge for his territories. Crucially though, if Hanover's bank balance could be improved with money from Celle, then there was every chance that Ernest Augustus might be able to convince the Holy Roman Emperor to elevate Hanover from a mere duchy to the holiest of holies, a bona fide *electorate*.

Sophia, however, had thoughts not of an electoral cap, but a royal crown. When Charles II, with whom she was so briefly matched, was restored to the throne, she wrote him a warm letter of congratulations and began to watch events in England with a more personal interest.

Later she told Lord Dartmouth, 'she was once like to have been married to King Charles the Second, which would not have been worse for the nation, considering how many children she had brought.'[43] It's a fair point and how keenly she must have kept an eye on England, where Charles' marriage to Catherine of Braganza remained childless. Sophia traced her finger along the branches of the family tree all the way to Princess Anne, whom she knew might one day stand to inherit the throne.

Trying her hand at a little matchmaking, Sophia suggested to Ernest Augustus that it might be a good idea to send their eldest son off to England to charm his way into Anne's marital bed. Her husband was somewhat less keen. The fate of Charles I was all too fresh in his memory and he didn't regard England as a place that was politically *that* settled just now. Ernest Augustus had his backup plan of Sophia Dorothea ready and with this fallback in mind, he agreed to Sophia's plans. George Louis was duly dispatched across the sea. The young man didn't impress his effervescent and beautiful cousin one bit and soon he was headed home to Hanover, where Ernest Augustus was busy trying to sell Sophia on the idea of the possible marriage of Sophia Dorothea and George Louis.

Sophia, who rarely if ever said *no* to her husband, didn't like this latest scheme at all but Ernest Augustus wanted to stuff his purse before he made his bid to turn Hanover into an electorate. The plan to pursue an electorate was not what gave her pause, but the idea of the marriage that would be needed to set the wheels in motion. She loathed Éléonore but she recognised, despite herself, that the benefits of such a match would be myriad. There was another woman in Hanover who also had a stake in the marriage, one who had once been a mistress but was now much more. Clara, Countess of Platen and Hallermund, was scheming with a breathtaking skill.

Being mistress to a duke was quite a win, but being mistress to an elector - and a rich one at that - would be better still. With her sister sharing George Louis' bed, Clara knew everything that was going on in her adopted home and she was determined to make sure that Ernest Augustus made the right decision, which was to make a grab for the marriage and the money. With that in mind, Clara crooked one charming finger in the direction of a gentleman named Bernstorff, the prime minister of Celle, who was more than a match for her in terms of ambition. She presented him with a diamond-studded golden snuffbox - did somebody say *bribe* - and asked if he might have a little word with George William about the many merits of George Louis, promising to indulge in a little pillow talk with Ernest Augustus about Sophia Dorothea in return. For her plan to work, however, she needed Sophia to have the same ambition for her son and luckily for Clara, after some soul searching and close examination of the Hanover exchequer, Sophia reached the same conclusion.

Sophia Dorothea and her cousin, George Louis, must be married.

There were two flies in the ointment. They were Éléonore and Anthony Ulrich, in whose son Éléonore still had great faith. As far as this pair was concerned, when Sophia Dorothea reached 16 there would be much to discuss for the hopeful Duke of Brunswick-Wolfenbüttel, who still considered that his son had first refusal on her fair hand, and Éléonore was of the same opinion. If she was to learn of the scheming that was going on at Hanover she would doubtless be able to convince George William to refuse the plan when it was set before him, so it was vital that those plotting in Hanover gave no indication of their wishes.

There is no evidence that Clara and Sophia were in any way co-conspirators when it came to the marriage of George Louis, but they certainly both decided that it would be the best course of action. Ultimately Clara could operate only in the background, influencing her lover and his followers, but it was left to Sophia to make the official approach. For a woman so hung up on etiquette, it was an audacious moment.

As night fell on the evening before Sophia Dorothea was due to turn 16, Sophia climbed into her carriage and travelled through a violent storm towards Celle and her brother-in-law's home. For the first time, she abandoned her all-important protocol and rejected any sort of ceremony, intent only on reaching George William before Anthony Ulrich could do so. She strode through the castle like a woman possessed and headed straight for the private chambers of Éléonore and George William. Here she caught George William out in precisely the way he had, years earlier, attempted to catch her with her metaphorical pants down. He was in the middle of dressing and his wife, unaware of the ensuring drama, was still sleeping.

When a bleary-eyed Éléonore appeared, Sophia explained away her unexpected appearance by claiming she was there simply to wish her niece a happy birthday, which Éléonore was touched to hear. As soon as the duchess took herself off to dress though, Sophia revealed the true reason for her visit. Cunningly, she made her case for the marriage in Dutch, a language that she knew Éléonore couldn't understand. Sophia couldn't risk any interruptions before an agreement was reached. All too aware that Anthony Ulrich might even now be hastening towards Celle, Sophia told her brother-in-law that Ernest Augustus sought only reconciliation with the sibling to whom he had once been so close. It was a masterpiece of diplomatic skill and politicking. George William's weakest spot had always been the collapse in relations between himself and his brother as a result the years of squabbling over titles and the like.

Only when she had George William on side did Sophia even mention marriage and electorates. In doing so, she explained that George William too could expect rich dividends if one of the duchies was raised to be an electorate. She was smart enough not to say *which* duchy she was thinking of and he, quite naturally, assumed she meant Celle. George William's eyes must have widened at her descriptions of territories that might be theirs for the picking with the backing of the mighty Holy Roman Empire and when he asked how all of this might be achieved, Sophia told him that the means were simple. All it would take was a marriage. Only then did she produce the birthday gift she had brought for Sophia Dorothea: a miniature of her sullen son, George Louis.

It was Éléonore's first real failure and she simply didn't see it coming. All her years of courting Anthony Ulrich and extolling the virtues of Brunswick-Wolfenbüttel had come to nothing and in the space of one dramatic morning, her sister-in-law had recaptured the imagination of the man who had once dogged her every footstep. Without consulting Éléonore, George William said *yes*. He sent his disbelieving wife off to tell Sophia Dorothea of the news and settled down to breakfast with Sophia, who was finally able to taste the sweet victory that had too often belonged to her rival.

The young lady's reaction was violently emotional and she famously howled, 'I will not marry the pig snout!' and smashed the miniature that had been her betrothal gift. Sophia Dorothea had been raised by her mother to think of Hanover as a miserable place where mind-numbing protocol ruled all. Thanks to Éléonore's descriptions she thought little of Sophia too, and now she was not only to be shunted to that unhappy court, but she was to marry the son of the woman who had, as far as Sophia Dorothea was concerned, made a pariah of her own mother. Think too of what George Louis had been told of Sophia Dorothea, *that bit of a bastard*, the daughter of that *clot of dirt*, the woman whose mother Sophia saw as the lowest of the low, a liar and schemer, *a nobody*.

When Anthony Ulrich arrived later that day to discuss a possible marriage to his son, he found himself in a strange sort of parallel world. Instead of Éléonore he was greeted by Sophia, who was seated beside George William to form the official welcome party. Barely able to contain her triumph she invited her unwitting rival to stay for tea not only to celebrate the birthday of her niece, but also to congratulate her on her betrothal.

You couldn't see the furious Anthony Ulrich for dust as he made his getaway.

Let there be no doubt that Sophia had any hopes of romance between the cousins, for she wrote to Liselotte of the marriage and Sophia Dorothea's dowry in plain-speaking terms:

> 'One hundred thousand thalers a year is a goodly sum to pocket, without speaking of a pretty wife, who will find a match in my son George Louis, the most pigheaded, stubborn boy who ever lived, and who has round his brains such a thick crust that I defy any man or woman ever to discover what is in them. He does not care much for the match itself, but one hundred thousand thalers a year have tempted him as they would have tempted anyone else.'[44]

The betrothal was announced without delay, perhaps partly to ensure that Éléonore didn't get to George William and work her wiles. In fact it's likely she would have been unsuccessful even if she had got a chance to try and talk him out of it. George William loved the thought of being close to his favourite and only remaining brother and he too knew that this marriage secured the union of the duchies ruled by the two siblings. What he *didn't* know was that the electoral family's ambitions didn't centre on his territories in Celle, but on Ernest Augustus' domain in Hanover.

The couple was married at Celle on 22 November 1682 amid great celebration, though Éléonore and Sophia Dorothea didn't share in the joy. Mother and daughter parted tearfully and the newlyweds returned to Hanover and a joyous welcome. Sophia had let it be known that Catherine Marie von dem Busche, the sister of Clara and mistress of George Louis, should be gone before they arrived but when Sophia

Dorothea climbed from her carriage, who should be glowering down at her but the bitter frau? Determined to let nothing get in the way of her son's nuptials, Sophia commanded her not only to leave the window but the duchy itself, with immediate effect.

Sophia's spirits, which should certainly have been high, were dampened somewhat when she received word of the death of her brother, Rupert, who had passed away a week after the wedding in his adopted home of England. Ernest Augustus didn't want to spoil the party so there was no mourning for him in Hanover, but of course Sophia felt his loss, though she kept smiling through her tears. Of all the children of the Winter monarchy only two now remained, Sophia and her ecclesiastically-inclined sister, Louise Hollandine. Time was slipping away.

At first, Sophia Dorothea made a concerted effort to fit into her new home, though the lifestyle in Hanover was unlike anything that she had experienced before. In Celle she'd had the run of the household but here at the Leineschloss all was etiquette and whatever she did, she didn't *quite* make the grade. The more Sophia tried to correct her, the more she rebelled and in Sophia Dorothea's willful nature Sophia must have seen the echoes of Éléonore. To make matters worse, Ernest Augustus was fond of the new arrival even though Clara took an instant dislike to her, perhaps fearing a rival for her lover's influence.

For now though Sophia's work was done, but another project already awaited.

She had a Figuelotte to marry off!

Figuelotte Gets Married

Sophia had achieved her aims with the marriage of George Louis, even if she singularly failed to capture Lady Anne of York and push her family one step closer to the English throne. Not only that, but in 1683 Sophia Dorothea had done her duty and produced an heir who would one day rule as King George II. It's not surprising therefore that now Figuelotte was of marrying age, her mother intended to make the very best match for her that she could. Perhaps mindful of the damage religion had wrought to her father's kingdoms, Sophia had been determined not to impose any faith on her daughter but instead had left her as a blank canvas. Besides any metaphysical considerations, this of course meant that she would make an appropriate bride for a well-born gentleman of *any* persuasion.

Maria Theresa, the French queen whose hem Sophia had declined to kiss during her trip to France, died in 1683 and Sophia's first thought was that this might be a chance not just to get her daughter married, but to get her married into some serious power. Yet the Sun King was perfectly happy in the company of his adored Françoise d'Aubigné, better known to history as *Madame de Maintenon*, and wasn't in the market for anyone else[45]. Sophia's net widened and when she pulled it in who should be caught but Frederick, heir to the electoral cap of Prussia.

Though Frederick was only a decade older than Figuelotte, he was already a widower and had not yet fathered an heir, so a young bride with plenty of childbearing years ahead of her was a must. The couple had met before and if not firm friends were certainly on good terms, so it was decided that the match was an eminently suitable one. Sophia took her daughter to Berlin for the wedding and was delighted for the young woman as she started on what was to be, perhaps unexpectedly, a successful union. Figuelotte's husband adored her and although his official mistress, Catharina von Wartenberg, remained close at hand, she was nothing more than a friend to the electoral prince, so besotted was he with his bride. It was a rare success for Sophia's matchmaking and within a decade her daughter was sitting at the head of her own court, reigning in a manner that her mother could never have dreamt of in Hanover.

A few years later Sophia took it upon herself to care for Figuelotte and Frederick's tearaway son, Frederick William, who was proving to be what might be politely termed as *a handful*. The little boy was educated alongside her other grandchild, George Augustus (later George II), and proved himself to be rather more of a nightmare than she might have anticipated. He raged through Herrenhausen like a thing possessed and he and George Augustus were often to be found engaged in brutal combat. So out of control did Frederick William become that it seemed as if the end must be nigh for him when he swallowed a silver shoe buckle, sending his poor grandmother into a meltdown. The pragmatic lady wasn't to be low for long and as she watched the willful child devouring plateful after plateful of food, she declared him fully recovered. Soon after this incident Frederick William was packed off home, leaving his cousin George Augustus to rule the roost once more.

It was a rare happy ending for the House of Hanover.

Dividing the Spoils

What Sophia didn't know as she made her way home from Berlin was that her husband had once again decided to go rogue, just as he did with his initial plans for George Louis and Sophia Dorothea. With no son yet born to his brother, George William, and the possibility of that happening now swiftly slipping away, Ernest Augustus looked to his own sons, the same young men who would one day split the lands of the family just as he once had with his own siblings. He remembered his own battles with his brothers, the grabs for land and the long-winded legal documents, and decided to nip it in the bud before it had a chance to happen again.

Ernest Augustus had first considered the adoption of primogeniture in 1682. If he went through with his plan it would mean that George Louis alone would inherit and unite the divided duchies held by the dukes of Brunswick-Lüneburg. It will come as no surprise that George Louis thought it was a great idea, whilst his five brothers were less keen! As far as anyone knew, the plans had gone no further but in fact Ernest Augustus had been quietly plotting and scheming, waiting for the moment to make his move. Imagine Sophia's surprise when she realised that her husband had advanced things along without her knowledge and had now decided that primogeniture was the only way forward for his duchies. It was a reminder that, though she might be the boys' mother, she had little power to decide their fates.

With Ernest Augustus living it up in Italy with Clara, Sophia Dorothea and George Louis, it was left to Sophia to try and keep the home ship steady. With her sons under one roof and now agitated beyond belief by their father's plans that was easier said than done. Of most trouble to her was Frederick Augustus who, as second son, rightly felt that he would lose the most by the adoption of primogeniture. Although the remaining boys would all receive generous incomes and be given what Ernest Augustus firmly believed was every opportunity to forge hugely successful futures, Frederick Augustus didn't want to hear about any of that, all he cared for was his inheritance. He became so recalcitrant that Ernest Augustus eventually had him 'thrust out, and his father will give him no more keep. I laugh in the day and cry all night about it, for I am a fool with my children.'[46] In fact Sophia was heartbroken and fretted for her son dreadfully, desperate to keep her children close as her own mother never had.

Off went Frederick Augustus to forge a career in the military, leaving his mother to wring her hands at home. He never resolved his differences with his father. The pattern of fathers becoming estranged from sons, started by Frederick Augustus and Ernest Augustus, would become a mark of the House of Hanover down through the generations.

With Frederick Augustus' departure things seemed to settle at home and the remaining brothers reached an uneasy peace on the matter of primogeniture, thus granting Ernest Augustus his wish subject to the formal nod from the Holy Roman Emperor. Sophia occupied herself with matters philosophical, entering into a long and enduring friendship with the philosopher Gottfried Wilhelm von Leibniz, who had served as John Frederick's librarian and, some claimed, resident alchemist! Now commissioned to write a monumental history of Brunswick, he and Sophia were kindred spirits indeed. It was a welcome distraction for the duchess who had always had an abiding interest in philosophy and precious few people around her who shared her passion, for her husband saw himself as a man of business and action, and had no interest in matters of the mind. In the years to come Leibniz would endear himself to Sophia's daughter, Figuelotte, and Caroline of Ansbach too, long before she became George II's queen. Together, he and Sophia even discussed uniting the divided faiths in Europe though it was a plan on paper only. Who knows what might have happened had she been born later or lived longer or even spent a spell on the throne of Britain.

Sophia was glad for the mass exodus from Hanover to Italy though, for Clara was always more politically-minded than she and when Ernest Augustus was busy railing about his ungrateful son, far better that it be his mistress who absorbed his rants and temper tantrums. Clara and Sophia Dorothea had taken against one another in a big way too so getting them both out from under her feet guaranteed Sophia a modicum of peace, even if it always seemed to be swiftly shattered by feuding sons.

In 1685 Sophia's nephew, Charles II, Elector Palatine, died without an heir. He had squandered the money that Charles Louis had so carefully saved and had proved to be a highly ineffective ruler. At his death, he was just 34 years of age. He had promised to take care of his half-siblings but had done no such thing and when he passed away, the Simmern line died with him. The Electoral Palatinate now slipped into the hands of the Catholic Philip William of Neuburg, but Louis XIV wasn't about to let that happen without a literal fight. He pressed his sister-in-law Liselotte's claim to the electorate, leading to the outbreak of the Nine Years' War.

Charles Louis wasn't the only loss that Sophia suffered in 1685. In fact there was another death that year that later had important ramifications for the family. This one, however, was a little further from home.

> 'On Monday last in the Morning our late Gracious Soveraign [sic] King *Charles* the Second was seized with a violent Fit, by which his Speech and Senses were for some time taken from him, but upon the immediate application of fitting Remedies He returned to such a condition as gave some hopes of His Recovery till Wednesday night, at which time the Disease returning upon him with greater violence, He expired this day about Noon.'[47]

The late King Charles II was succeeded by James II, a Roman Catholic monarch in a land that was keeping an increasingly suspicious eye on that particular faith. Sophia looked on with interest and awaited the next developments in the tale, but little did anyone know just how much trouble lay on the horizon.

Considerably less volatile for now were relations between Sophia Dorothea and her pig snouted husband, George Louis. They were able to enjoy the fruits of their Italian sojourn in 1687 with the birth of their second and last child, who was christened Sophia Dorothea[48] after her mother. Sophia was passing from the role of mother into that of grandmother, just as she had passed from girl into wife and around her, the world was changing. Yet one never gets a sense that Sophia thought that it was leaving her behind. Instead she adapted, as was her way, and enjoyed visits to her beloved Figuelotte, ministering to her daughter through her pregnancies[49] and celebrating when she and her husband were elevated to the rank of Elector and Electress of Brandenburg.

But in England, could the family from Hanover be destined for even greater heights?

Act Three

Electress

'I care not when I die, if on my tomb it to be recorded that I was Queen of Great Britain.'[1]

England and the Electorate

The year 1688 began with another passing when Frederick William, Elector of Brandenburg, died. He was succeeded by Figuelotte and her husband, Frederick, who became the new electress and elector. His death also removed an obstacle from the path of Ernest Augustus, as the late elector had always rather looked down on the ambition of his lesser neighbour and was likely to have stood in the way of any ambitions Ernest Augustus had for his duchy. Now those plans could set off at full steam ahead.

Far away from Hanover in 1688, the Glorious Revolution swept through England and changed the face of the nation and the path of the future. The catalyst came with the birth of James, Prince of Wales, that same year. His father, King James II, had him baptised into the Catholic faith. Faced with at least another generation under Roman Catholic rule the so-called Immortal Seven[2], a group of seven Protestant nobles, took action. They issued an invitation to William III, Prince of Orange, who was married to James II's daughter, Mary, and invited him to come to England and claim the throne. The seven offered him the full support of their forces and enforced their point with claims that the Prince of Wales was not really the son of the king at all, but had been passed off as such to ensure Catholic succession.

As a result, William sailed for England with an army. Louis XIV offered his military support to James but the English king rejected it, believing himself more than able to combat the Orange threat. Instead, he could only look on as William landed in November 1688 and was immediately joined by a number of defecting Protestant soldiers and even James' daughter, Princess Anne, who was 23 at the time of the Glorious Revolution. James lost his taste for the fight and attempted to flee but was swiftly captured and for a time held in custody. However, William had no wish to drive England into another Civil War or to deal with a displaced king, so James was generously allowed to escape. He fled to St Germain, where he was welcomed into exile by the French court. William and Mary ascended the throne of England, ending the short-lived reign of Catholicism and sending shockwaves through the country's Catholic community.

Sophia was torn. On the one hand, she perfectly understood the fears of Protestants under James but on the other, she felt no ill-will towards the dethroned king. Her conflicted feelings can be clearly seen from a letter she wrote to William that congratulated him warmly before going on to address the question of James' fate with admirable honesty. This wasn't a shameful sentiment that the electress felt she should hide, it was simply something that she needed to speak of in plain terms.

'AFTER the profession which I have always made of being an humble servant to Your Majesty, I believe you cannot doubt of the part which I take in every thing that contributes to your elevation and your glory: yet I lament King James, who honoured me with his friendship. I should be afraid that Your Majesty would have a bad opinion of my sincerity if I concealed from you this sentiment. I am even persuaded that my candour will give you a better opinion of me, and that Your Majesty will the more easily believe the protestation which I make you of my prayers for your prosperity, and of the opinion I have, that you deserve the crown which you wear, in a thousand respects which I am unable to name, from the fear of shocking your modesty. However as it has pleased God to make Your Majesty the protector of our religion, I hope you will put it also in a state to have its arms free, to assist us poor mortals, who by the desolation of our neighbours, are near to that roaring beast which endeavours to devour us, in order that all those who are not papists may successively maintain the religion we profess to all eternity, in England and elsewhere.'[3]

The following year the Bill of Rights established the constitution under which the joint monarchs would rule, limiting sovereign powers, setting out the role of Parliament, the rights to free speech, and stating that no Roman Catholic could ever reign in England again as 'it hath been found by experience that it is inconsistent with the safety and welfare of this Protestant kingdom to be governed by a papist prince.' Although Sophia now stood in line to the throne, the bill didn't name her or her descendants as heirs despite the House of Lords giving the nod to an amendment that would do exactly that. The House of Commons rejected that amendment and the bill continued on its way with no mention of the family from Hanover.

Regardless of what the bill explicitly said, William and Mary had no children who would succeed them and Anne, the next in line, had no living children at that precise moment. However, Sophia was still not guaranteed to succeed at any point either, as the future of the crown was dependent on how long those in line ahead of her lived. With Anne still only in her twenties and married to Prince George of Denmark, it wasn't impossible that she might still fall pregnant for a seventh time, though her previous children had all died in very early infancy or were miscarried. Either way, Sophia thought it very unlikely that she would ever actually become queen given her age compared to those who were in the line of succession before her. Despite this realistic outlook, she was far too adept in matters of court and rank not to see that her own sons stood a strong chance of one day ruling in England, for a good many Catholic heirs had been unceremoniously shunted aside thanks to the Bill of Rights.

> 'This morning about Four o'clock, her Royal Highness the Princess *Anne of Denmark* was lately delivered of a Son: The Queen was present the whole time of her Labour, which lasted about 3 hours, and the King, with most of the persons of Quality about the Court, came into her Royal Highness's Bedchamber before she was delivered. Her Royal Highness and the young Prince are very well to the great satisfaction of Their Majesties, and the Joy of the whole Court; as it will doubtless be of the whole Kingdom.'[4]

It looked as though the Hanoverians would be staying in Hanover after all when Anne and George's seventh child was born in July 1689.

He was Prince William, Duke of Gloucester, and he seemed a *little* stronger than his six short-lived predecessors. Not robust by any means, but alive at least.

For now.

Ernest Augustus had more prescient things on his mind than overseas kingdoms though, for he had big plans for his duchy. In fact, he was sure that it would make a fine ninth electorate for the Holy Roman Empire - an electorate that George Louis alone stood to inherit thanks to primogeniture. Of course, it wasn't unthinkable that Frederick Augustus would start rattling his sabre all over again now the prospects of England *and* an electoral cap were being thrown into the heady mix of power. How Sophia's heart must have sank, for what would those other brothers do if Frederick Augustus started complaining again? In fact, it was a situation that the family never had to face, because Frederick Augustus was killed in battle at St Georgen in 1690.

This was the second death that Sophia received news of that year. She had lost her favourite son, her beloved Charles Philip, in battle at the beginning of that same year and descended into a depression and illness so severe that some wondered if she would ever recover at all. The Leineschloss was too full of memories of her lost child and for the first time in her life she fled, taking refuge with her husband in Carlsbad before withdrawing to Herrenhausen.

In her refuge Sophia passed her days in quiet contemplation and the company of her friends. Now more than ever she could indulge her love of philosophy and Leibniz's company, both in correspondence and in person, was a constant comfort to her. Yet there was an understandable sense of melancholy in her and she wrote to Leibniz in a contemplative mood of, 'listening to the nightingales in my garden of Herenhausen [sic], to divert my mind from thoughts which might distract me.'[5]

It was just the balm that Sophia's grieving soul needed. Peace and space to mourn became her comfort and slowly, little by little, she began to rally. She had scarcely begun to emerge into the world once more when news of Frederick Augustus' death hit Hanover like a bomb, shattering Sophia to her core. He had never reconciled with his father and she wondered now at the chasm that had never been bridged, at the tragedy of a father and son forever parted first by anger and then by death. Ernest Augustus somehow managed to look on the bright side even in the face of such tragedy. With the death of Frederick Augustus, the loudest opponent to his plans for primogeniture was permanently silenced and he saw nothing in the path of his ambitions. Blinded by the dazzling lights of the empire, he had reckoned without Maximilian William, the third son and the hardy twin who had survived the difficult birth that killed his brother.

Initially quite happy with his father's schemes for primogeniture, now *he* was the second son, Maximilian William changed his mind. At first he went down the diplomatic route, requesting that Ernest Augustus abandon his plans for primogeniture but when that approach failed, he assembled a conspiracy of associates and began plotting on how best to overthrow his father and take control of Hanover. Figuelotte learned of the plan and warned their father of the danger. He had the conspirators arrested immediately. Maximilian William was punished with temporary exile, but he was lucky to escape execution, a fate some of his co-conspirators faced[6].

This was also the first time that Sophia herself came under suspicion from her husband as Ernest Augustus demanded to know just exactly how much she had known about the plot. Hauled before the duke and his council, Sophia was not found guilty of any wrong doing. Perhaps she had fronted her sons some money and offered a shoulder to cry on when they were at odds with their father, perhaps not. The answer is that we simply don't know how deeply Sophia's involvement went, but I suspect it was very likely that she knew nothing more than the obvious fact that Maximilian William was as furious as his late brother had been at being denied what he believed to be his birthright. She was simply too loyal, too well-drilled to have been part of a conspiracy against the husband to whom she was steadfastly devoted. If she seemed to be taking Maximilian William's corner against Ernest Augustus, which must be what aroused his suspicions against her in the first place, then isn't this more likely to be out of a sense of guilt at having somehow let the late Frederick Augustus down than a wish to be part of a coup in Hanover?

Simply put, she wasn't the type.

She *was* the type to keep up her formal duties of course, so it's no surprise that a note from Sophia was recorded in the state papers of William and Mary that read, 'Though my heart is full of grief at the loss of my second son [Frederick Augustus] I nevertheless express my joy on hearing of your safe arrival in Holland. I hope that you may soon accomplish everything to your satisfaction, and I have charged the

Chevalier de Klenck to assure you of my sentiments and to tell you how grieved I am that I cannot come myself to see you.'[7]

And though her heart, so full of grief, would have to face even more heartache in the years to come, for now at least it was time for a celebration.

It had taken a long time, a great fortune and the lives of innumerable troops from Hanover who had died in the service of the Holy Roman Empire, but Ernest Augustus finally stood on the threshold of his dreams – the electoral cap.

The pinnacle of his achievements was finally with his reach, so close that he might reach out and touch it. All that stood in his way was the final agreement of the Holy Roman Emperor and in the shape of the Nine Years' War, fate threw Ernest Augustus exactly what he had been waiting for.

Emperor Leopold knew without a doubt that he could always count on Hanover to be at his side and when the moment of crisis came as the empire faced down French forces on the field of conflict, Ernest Augustus made his move. He would once again throw the weight of Hanover behind Leopold's outgunned troops but this time, it would come at a price. In return for his assistance, he wanted a guarantee that Hanover would finally become the ninth electorate of the empire.

Leopold, as they say, had been played.

The answer came back in the affirmative and Ernest Augustus could finally breathe a sigh of victorious relief, for he had achieved all that he had ever wanted[8]. The ceremony held to mark the elevation of the duchy into an electorate took place in December 1692 and was a spectacle of splendid pomp and ceremony. In every sense of the word, the electoral cap had cost an unimaginable price and it had taken the lives of two of Ernest Augustus' sons[9]. The price had been high but as one dashing count was about to discover, the price for passion in the cold court of Hanover could be higher still.

A Deadly Attraction

When she was a young girl, Sophia had initially been enthralled by the constant comings and goings at her mother's court, but she was now tired of the revolving door of exiles and intrigues at her own court. She might have sent the shameless Madame van dem Busche into unofficial exile but there was no point in trying to bat away every ambitious mistress, for as soon as one departed there were plenty more were lining up to take her place. Instead the years had taught Sophia to tolerate and to even ignore Clara, having convinced herself that it would be folly to expect a husband to be loyal to his wife, let alone once she was in her fifties and their initial attraction had long since cooled. She placed dignity above everything else and in turning a blind eye to Clara and the other scandals that swirled around Hanover, she kept herself above it all, or so she hoped.

Sophia Dorothea, of course, lacked her mother-in-law's experience in the hothouse world of the court. She had been raised by parents who adored and indulged her and she'd had no experience of mistresses and the like, since George William and Éléonore had eyes only for each other. Éléonore had her man *very* well trained in most things… if only she had been able to speak Dutch, how different life might have been for her only child.

But things *weren't* different. Sophia Dorothea had been left to her fate and that fate included, inevitably, a mistress.

In George Louis's case, that mistress came from within his mother's inner circle. She was Sophia's Maid of Honour as well as Clara's best friend and her name was Melusine von der Schulenberg. It was thanks to Clara that she had got her position in the electoral household at all, but we can only speculate whether Clara conspired to arrange the romance. Later nicknamed *the Maypole* on account of her lanky frame, Melusine didn't have Clara's scheming nature and love of drama but that didn't matter to Sophia Dorothea, who had never faced a humiliation like it. Her husband openly consorted with his *Maypole* and visited her opulent chambers every evening, caring nothing for the finer feelings of his wife. As far as mistresses go, this one was actually fairly inoffensive and relatively unambitious, but that did nothing to quell the unhappy Sophia Dorothea, who expected to command the attention of her husband just as she had the devotion of her parents.

Into this hotbed of gossip and intrigue waltzed a man whose fate would ring through the annals of the House of Hanover. Carefree, handsome and dashing to a tee, Count Philip Christoph von Königsmarck had known Sophia Dorothea in childhood when he had trained in Celle and now, having proved himself on the battlefield, he was a boy no longer.

The romance of Count von Königsmarck and Sophia Dorothea began innocently enough when the Swede arrived in Hanover in 1688 to attend a masked ball. He danced with Sophia Dorothea and perhaps she saw in him a glimmer of the love that she had never really received from her husband, because she was soon smitten. Yet George Louis had a temper, as Sophia Dorothea discovered when she remonstrated with him for spending so much time with his mistress. He responded by physically attacking her, throwing her to the ground. She had no wish to arouse his ire again so Königsmarck became a *what might have been*, a handsome daydream on which to ponder.

When this inexcusable assault took place, Sophia *did* intervene. Putting up with mistresses was one thing but making a show of oneself and one's spouse was quite another. It simply wouldn't do. Sophia Dorothea took to her bed in distress but the suddenly plucky Sophia wouldn't let her languish. Instead she took the young woman and her children to Herrenhausen and told George Louis that what he had done couldn't go unchecked. In fact, Sophia showed kindness to Sophia Dorothea at first and did her best to make the unhappy bride welcome, no doubt having some understanding of how it felt to be relegated in her husband's affections. It wouldn't last, but it would be wrong to tar Sophia with the brush of an uncaring mother-in-law because at the beginning at least, she did her best to keep things on a civil footing. Her eldest son was due a pep talk or two.

When Sophia Dorothea returned home she was surprised to find her husband a *little* more attentive. Rather than completely ignoring her, he forced himself to spend the odd few minutes in her company, but it was *far* from a loved up, moonlight and roses sort of marriage. Sophia was not a cold and unfeeling woman but she viewed noble marriage as a business arrangement as much as a meeting of hearts. In keeping with her upbringing, she believed that a man had certain rights that were not afforded to his wife but if that same wife was to dutifully tolerate her husband's mistresses without complaint, then he ought to show the outside world that he still held his spouse in some regard. Ernest Augustus had neglected Sophia, of course, but she had been quite content with the attention he had showed her when he saw fit to do so. This is all very bizarre to modern eyes, but in Sophia's time and class, it was all a matter of business. Sophia, above all things, believed in putting on the public face that her rank dictated.

She didn't like drama.

Clara, of course, had no such scruples and soon Königsmarck was a notch on her own well-whittled bedpost. She was pleased at her younger conquest, but when the count was given the choice of remaining in Hanover where he would serve as Clara's lover when Ernest Augustus had better things to do or going off to risk his life on the battlefield, he chose the latter.

Quite a review.

In fact, Königsmarck was fighting alongside Sophia's son Charles Philipp when he died and the dashing count was also thought dead for a time. This seems to have been the catalyst for the romance that later unfolded as Sophia Dorothea realised, apparently when it was too late, what she had lost. Happily Königsmarck was not killed on the field at all and returned to Hanover a little battered but resolutely alive. From that moment on he and Sophia Dorothea were lovers. They wrote to one another in the most florid terms, sometimes signing letters in blood and loudly proclaiming that death would be better than being parted, for their love was of the most hot-blooded kind. Communicating in a series of elaborate codes, they gossiped about court life and scandal, with the electress referred to by the pair as *La Romaine*. Sophia Dorothea hid her lover's letters in curtains and quilts and anywhere else she could find a nook or cranny, employing her faithful attendant and friend, Éléonore von dem Knesebeck, to help her maintain the subterfuge.

It is a mark of Sophia Dorothea's curious naïvety that she genuinely thought that her romance might remain undetected. This was a court in which Clara ruled the gossiping classes just as Sophia reigned over protocol and etiquette so between them, there was little that stayed secret for long - except primogeniture, of course. Clara soon discovered that Königsmarck had jettisoned her for the proverbial younger model and soon after that, *somehow*, Sophia learned of her daughter-in-law's heated affair.

Her reaction was very curious indeed. Rather than warn Sophia Dorothea off, she began praising Königsmarck as though she too were joining his fan club alongside Sophia Dorothea and Clara. There are two ways of looking at this. The first and most generous is to assume that Sophia was attempting, in her unusually clumsy way, to chum up to Sophia Dorothea, perhaps to give her a friendly nudge and say, *all the ladies have a thing for Königsmarck*. She didn't have a thing for him, of course, but identifying him as a charmer might have possibly stopped Sophia Dorothea from letting flirtation turn into something more. As we know, it was already far too late for that.

Perhaps Sophia even remembered the willingness with which Königsmarck had gone into battle alongside her son but this sentimentality simply doesn't fit with the character of the woman we've met in these pages. Nor was she a *nudge nudge, wink wink* sort of woman either, but she *was* a shrewd one. Rather, I think, she was hoping to win Sophia Dorothea's trust and draw her into either confessing or denying her affair, thus giving a definite answer to the gossip that was swirling around the court. It spread out to Celle too, where Éléonore beseeched her daughter to stop her affair before things went too far.

It was too late for that.

George Louis, busy being loved up with Melusine, was blissfully ignorant of all of this at first, but Clara soon put *that* right. In a plot worthy of romantic fiction, she sparkled at a masked court ball and used all her charms to tempt Königsmarck out into the garden for a little tryst. Beforehand she had made sure to tell her husband to bring George Louis for a stroll in the grounds at that same moment, deliberately ensuring that she and Königsmarck were discovered. Masked and anonymous, Clara fled the scene leaving behind not a glass slipper, but a discarded glove. This wasn't just any old glove though, it was one of a pair that George Louis had given Sophia Dorothea as a gift. Clara had pilfered it, planting the evidence so the bad-tempered George Louis would think his own wife had been romping with the dashing Königsmarck.

To Clara's surprise and annoyance, when George Louis found the glove dropped at the scene of the tryst, he took no action. Instead he bided his time and with each day that passed, Sophia Dorothea and her lover became bolder, little knowing that they were being watched. Now Sophia Dorothea knew the joy of a real romance and she didn't want to turn her back on it. She had never had any ambition to come to Hanover to start with and now, more than anything, she wanted to be as far away from the place as she possibly could.

The final straw came in 1692 when Melusine gave birth to the first of three children she would have with George Louis. Devastated at this latest humiliation, Sophia Dorothea appealed to her mother-in-law, perhaps hoping that she might intervene somehow. Sophia's answer was unsympathetic. She told Sophia Dorothea, essentially, to suck it up - it was a man's right to take mistresses but a wife had no such privilege. After all what if she fell pregnant and her lover's bastard was presented as a child of the marriage? Such a changeling might even be introduced into the line of succession! No, it would never do. Putting up with a mistress was all part of the job and just as Sophia had endured Clara and those never-ending trips to Italy, she expected the same of her daughter-in-law. Sophia Dorothea had other ideas and when she asked for a copy of her marriage contract and began going through it with a fine tooth comb, the writing was on the wall.

For Sophia, this was the worst thing that could have happened. She was willing to turn a blind eye to so many things but now she knew that her son would likely one day inherit the English throne and the humiliation that his wife's possible desertion might bring was too much to bear. Realising that her considerable inheritance had been entirely settled on her husband, Sophia Dorothea began to pursue her father in the hope of receiving some money of her own. Why she wanted it she wouldn't say, but it wouldn't take a genius to know that her plan was one of escape. To leave Hanover behind the couple needed cash, yet she had none and nor did Königsmarck, who was heavily in debt himself.

That changed when a man who owed the count some serious money was suddenly in a position to pay his debts. Frederick Augustus I had been made Elector of Saxony and with that honour came cash, so Königsmarck took off for Dresden to claim what was owed to him. Unfortunately drink rather got the better of him and he entertained the court with some eye-opening tales of life in Hanover, reserving his more caustic comments for the character of Clara. Unbeknownst to the Swede his audience contained a close friend of that particular lady and when word reached her of what had been said, she was apoplectic. Sophia bears no involvement or blame for what happened next, but it would be remiss of me not to finish the story that has been started and unveil the final act in the life of Count Philip von Königsmarck.

The endgame began with Clara's fury, which she was quick to share with Ernest Augustus. Furious at being made Saxony's latest laughing stock, she told the elector that it was worse for him than anyone. It wasn't *her* son that was the punchline to every joke in the empire, after all, but *his*. What a thing it was for the Elector of Hanover to have a dupe for a son. Didn't it make a fool of the father too? George Louis, meanwhile, finally gave vent to the fury that he must have been keeping in check ever since he found that glove and he turned both barrels on his wife. She responded with a rage of her own and the couple hurled accusations and insults at each other until George Louis, unable to contain himself any longer, fell upon Sophia Dorothea. He seized her by the throat and choked her with so much force that it took all of Éléonore von dem Knesebeck's strength to prevent tragedy.

Sophia Dorothea fled for Celle but she found little sympathy there. Her mother was kind but her father was resolute: he couldn't afford to upset the Elector of Hanover, for power had very definitely flowed into Ernest Augustus' hands. Sophia Dorothea wouldn't return to her marital home and lingered in Celle for as long as she dare until finally she had run out of excuses. Only then did she return to the Leineschloss where Sophia and Ernest Augustus waited to welcome her ceremonially back to the castle. In a deliberate two fingers to the couple, Sophia Dorothea had her carriage drive straight past her waiting in-laws. She shut herself into her private apartments, where she gave word that she would see no visitors, no matter who they might be.

But there was an exception to that command.

Not far behind her came Count von Königsmarck, with plans to steal away his lover and fly to the protection of Duke Anthony Ulrich in Wolfenbüttel. The duke still remembered the way Sophia had outsmarted him over Sophia Dorothea's marriage and this was a small but very significant instrument of vengeance, served *exceedingly* cold indeed.

On 1 July 1694, Count von Königsmarck opened a note that he believed had been sent by Sophia Dorothea, summoning him to her apartments. He hurried to the Leineschloss only to find that she had not been the author of the missive at all. Despite this proof that someone was intriguing against them the couple tarried, getting up to whatever love-struck, hot-blooded couples with a penchant for overheated notes get up to when alone. Finally, in the darkest hours of the night, the count left his lover's rooms. He was never seen again.

Nobody knows what happened that evening and those who once did are long since dead, but the most likely narrative seems to be one in which Clara Elisabeth von Meysenburg, Countess of Platen and Hallermund, looms large.

Let's try and piece together a likely scenario.

Having convinced her lover that Königsmarck and Sophia Dorothea's affair was making Hanover the laughing stock of the Holy Roman Empire,

Ernest Augustus agreed that the time had come to have Königsmarck arrested before the couple had time to flee and embarrass the electorate still further. Believing his mistress to be loyal and not in the least bit murderous, he agreed to let her oversee the operation. At no point were Sophia or George Louis ever involved in the plans. Ernest Augustus wanted the matter dealt with quietly and efficiently, something he hoped Clara would be able to achieve.

He was wrong.

Clara assembled four of her favourite and most biddable courtiers, all of whom had had enough of the Swedish Casanova in their midst and together they lay in wait for their prey. As he made his way from Sophia Dorothea's rooms in the Leineschloss they attacked him, leaving him badly wounded but still alive.

The outnumbered Königsmarck was powerless against his armed assailants but somehow found the strength to beg not for his own life, but for that of Sophia Dorothea. As he lost consciousness he was dragged through the castle into a room where Clara waited, ready to dispense the last judgment on the man who had once had the nerve to reject her. She was standing over Königsmarck when he regained his senses and at the sight of her, he muttered an oath that dripped with loathing. Clara's response was to kick him as hard as she could in the mouth. It was the last thing Count von Königsmarck would ever know, for he succumbed there and then to his wounds.

What became of his body is just as much a mystery as how he ultimately died but it's highly likely that the courtiers, now their bloodlust was sated, panicked. They had no permission or order to commit murder and had been told by Ernest Augustus only to bring the count into custody. Instead they had slaughtered him. George Louis' biographer, Ragnhild Hatton, posits that the body was thrown into the Leine River and despite later fanciful tales of skeletons under floorboards and bodies flung onto bonfires this seems like the most sensible explanation. As to who committed the murder, there have been some tantalising clues over the years.

Professor Georg Schnath concluded at the close of his investigation into the mysterious disappearance of Königsmarck that Duke Anthony Ulrich of Brunswick-Wolfenbüttel had received intelligence that named one of the killers as Don Nicolò Montalbano. As estate manager at Osnabrück on a modest salary of 2,000 thalers, Montalbano mysteriously received a payment of 150,000 thalers from Ernest Augustus not long after the count was last seen alive. This does indeed seem to be proof that Montalbano was involved in *something* and why not the murder, the cleanup or both? Despite this tantalising clue, the true facts of the case will likely never be fully known now, more's the pity.

Sophia, unsurprisingly, remained aloof from all of this drama. No doubt she remembered that Königsmarck had been there when her favourite son met his death, but if she felt that he deserved some justice, she did nothing to seek it. If we look from a darker perspective, perhaps she resented his survival when her son had died but to me that seems a bit *too* Gothic. Sophia was well-drilled in European politics and king making, she knew that death was an occasional byproduct of battle and though she missed her son dreadfully, the thought that she might have nursed some festering resentment for Königsmarck's survival is a bit of a push!

The daughter of Sophia's loathed 'little clot of dirt' was locked in her rooms. She was watched day and night by Clara's scheming husband, Prime Minister von Platen, who had played such a pivotal role in the subterfuge of the glove. Sophia Dorothea wasn't allowed to see her children nor her furious spouse and the wheels began to turn towards an inevitable divorce. Ignoring Sophia's pleas to confess the truth of her involvement with the late, not very lamented Königsmarck, she longed only to be allowed to go home to Celle. With the love letters between the couple now in Ernest Augustus' hands Sophia Dorothea knew that she had lost her greatest ally in Hanover and there was no way she was going to be returned to the care of her parents, where that vast dowry might never be seen again.

In December 1694, the marriage of the electoral prince and princess was dissolved on the grounds of her desertion and bad character. Even Sophia Dorothea's own adoring father turned against her, ashamed at her behaviour and disgusted at how carelessly she had thrown the family honour away.

All this from a man who contracted a nasty dose of VD, swapped his fiancée with his brother then proceeded to pursue that same fiancée for years, just hoping for a kiss!

Sophia, however, was disgusted at her daughter-in-law's behaviour. Not only had it been bad, it had been public. The worst thing in the world was that her family might be shown up and now, all across the empire, they were a hot topic.

Sophia Dorothea's dreams of going back to Celle were dashed when her Hanoverian prosecutors decided upon her fate. She was to be held under house arrest in Ahlden House and never allowed to see her children again, a sentence that was artful in its cruelty. For more than thirty years the Lady of Ahlden languished in her opulent prison, counting the unthinkable cost of desire

Death Comes to Hanover

'A Panegyrick on our late Sovereign Lady *Mary*, Queen of *England, Scotland, France* and *Ireland*, of glorious and immortal memory; who died at *Kensington* on the 28th of December 1694.'[10]

When Queen Mary died without heirs in the winter of 1694, there were some who saw it as divine judgment against a daughter who had dethroned her father. Others regarded it as a tragedy and mourned a woman gone too soon, but Sophia saw it in more pragmatic terms, though she didn't expect to live long enough for this to make any difference. Besides, nothing official had yet been laid out regarding Hanover's part in the future of the English monarchy. Of more immediate concern to Sophia was the fact that Ernest Augustus had fallen ill, weakened by years of gout and high living. With Sophia Dorothea's unhappy fate now decided, the electress devoted herself entirely to her elector. As he grew frailer Clara's influence began to grow weaker and the ailing man had no desire for intrigues either in the bedroom or the debating chamber.

Sophia's only relief from nursing the dying elector was an interlude with Figuelotte to enjoy an audience with Peter the Great during his tour of the continent. Rarely did Sophia have the chance to play gracious hostess and she was determined to make a great show of it for this most important fellow. It was to be quite a challenge. Things looked hopeless at first as Peter refused to see anybody face to face and wouldn't accept the offers of hospitality, preferring instead to set up a bivouac with his men next to the poised-for-action kitchens. Sophia and her daughter weren't about to be deterred and little by little they tempted the tsar out his shell until he was having a roaring time.

As the hours went by it became clear that the electress enjoyed Peter's company as much as he obviously did hers, with Sophia convinced that the meeting had been such a success thanks to the modest demeanour of the women from Hanover. She did note shrewdly that the tsar was more used to women whose natural complexion 'cannot be seen for white and red.' As she shadily added, given the Russians' love of heavily made up women, the flamboyantly painted Clara 'was immensely admired by the Muscovites.' The night passed in music and dancing and when Peter was finally ready to leave he seized up young Sophia Dorothea, Sophia's granddaughter, and kissed her cheek so heartily that it brought the sensitive little girl to tears.

Just as the Sun King's presents had disappointed when Sophia departed from France, so too did those of the tsar, who left her with some flea infested sables and a few tiny squares of unusable damask. Sophia, who rather liked to occupy herself with making chair covers, found that the damask was too small for even this though once the sables had been deloused, they were at least wearable. It was a welcome if brief diversion and once Sophia returned to her husband's bedside, where he was by now immobile and unable to speak, her already narrow horizons shrank even further.

Ernest Augustus died on 23 January 1698, with his devoted wife at his side. In the days following his brother's death George William arrived from Celle to mourn the man who had been his closest friend. It signalled the start of an uneasy truce between Sophia and Éléonore as they had become united in their grief, the latter perhaps more concerned by the suffering of her husband who had lost a beloved brother.

Ernest Augustus' body lay in state as his family and court paid their respects. On either side of the casket were the two symbols of his reign and achievements, the electoral cap at one shoulder, the ducal crown at the other. In his right hand was his sword, in his left the bishop's staff, signifying the curious combination of warrior-bishop that his reign had represented. Thanks to his own empire-building nous the bishopric did not pass to a Catholic as had been originally intended by the Treaty of Westphalia but to his youngest son, also named Ernest Augustus, whilst the electoral cap was inherited by George Louis, his eldest child.

Just as Ernest Augustus had wished when he made the decision to pursue primogeniture, the duchies were united under George Louis. Should there be any trouble from the other sons, the newly-capped elector had already taken the time to ensure that they had no leg to stand on. With the backing of the emperor, his brothers could do nothing to stop George Louis from fulfilling his father's wishes.

> 'The Elector of Hanover has obtained a Decree from the Emperor's Council, by which his two Brothers Maximilian and Christian, are obliged to contend themselves with their deceased Father's last Will and Testament.'[11]

It was the beginning of the long last act of Sophia's life too and as she donned her widow's veil, she prepared to recede into the background and, she speculated, 'join my dear Elector in the other world'. George Louis, of course, had no *official* electress at his side to take her place, though all knew that Melusine ably filled the role despite the lack of a marriage certificate. It was left for Sophia to take the title of Dowager Electress and her son no doubt hoped that she would continue her quiet life in the background. He wrongly believed that he had nothing to fear from her interference in political matters. She had enjoyed no influence during her husband's reign so he thought her unlikely to start seeking it now.

And he was right.

At first.

The newly-widowed Sophia quietly prepared to move to the palace of Herrenhausen, which Ernest Augustus had left her in his will. She felt no sadness at leaving the Leineschloss for her new home, where no doubt she looked forward to her walks and the peaceful gardens in which she could mourn for her late, much lamented spouse.

In the sanctuary of Herrenhausen, all was peaceful. Sophia's pride and joy were the grounds and particularly the orangery, which was richly decorated with classical frescoes. The pickings were extravagant and the estate, with its well-tended greenhouses, produced verdant crops of not only apples and oranges, but pineapples too, all nurtured by the heat provided by carefully monitored stoves which had been specially installed for the purpose. The gardens ranged from an artful wilderness to manicured lawns and lime trees, whilst secluded ponds were fed by waterfalls and streams, lending the dowager electress an ideal place in which to gather herself once more. She did renew her attempts to bring her late brother's illegitimate daughters into the household but like Ernest Augustus before him, George Louis wouldn't allow it, believing that introducing them into Hanover would only cause problems of rank and precedence with Melusine and other courtiers. As guests of the Catholic Elector Palatine, he pointed out, no harm would befall them, so it was better for all that they remain safely out of harm's way.

Eventually Sophia stepped out of her sanctuary and told herself firmly that 'one does not die of grief.' In 1700 she took a trip to the Netherlands in the company of her daughter. The ladies were actually intent on taking the waters at Aix-la-Chapelle but hearing of an important visitor on the continent, a detour was in order. During their journey they secured an audience with King William III of England, who was visiting Het Loo Palace. Here it was agreed that Figuelotte's husband would be recognised as the King of Prussia but William, supposedly, had another scheme in mind. He audaciously suggested that Sophia might try to nudge herself into the line of succession ahead of Anne, but she wisely chose not to entertain the plan. All in all the trip had been a successful one but to all intents and purposes, the dowager electress was now in retirement.

Filling her time with her gardens and trips to the theatre, Sophia couldn't help but take an interest in matters of state too. Now more than ever, Sophia was free to watch events in England. She did so safe in the knowledge that the *little clot of dirt* junior would never take her place as electress, since Sophia Dorothea had been gifted only the title of Duchess of Ahlden after her divorce. Nor would she sit beside George Louis should he ever assume the throne of England, which was becoming an ever more likely proposition. When the unhappy Sophia Dorothea wrote to her husband to beg at the very least a chance to see her children again, he ignored her letters. For those same children, even whispering the name of their mother was forbidden. Sophia heartily encouraged him in these draconian rules, wishing that the erring Sophia Dorothea might be entirely forgotten and scrubbed from history, where she could do no further harm to either the reputation of the House of Hanover or its chances of snatching that tantalising crown.

Sophia's quiet life was in marked contrast to the court she had departed, which William Makepeace Thackeray chronicled with a gleeful and mischievous twinkle in his eye.

'There were the princes of the house in the first class; in the second, the single field marshal of the army [...] Then follow, in due order, the authorities civil and military, the working privy councillors, the generals of cavalry and infantry, in the third class; the high chamberlain, high marshals of the court, high masters of the horse, the major-generals of cavalry and infantry, in the fourth class, down to the majors, the Hofjunkers or pages, the secretaries or assessors, of the tenth class, of whom all were noble.

[...]

There were two chamberlains, and one for the princess; five gentlemen of the chamber, and five gentlemen ushers; eleven pages and personages to educate these young noblemen - such as a governor, a preceptor, a fecht-meister, or fencing master, and a dancing ditto [...] There were three body and court physicians, [...] a court barber, [...] a court organist; two musikanten; four French fiddlers; twelve trumpeters and a bugler; so that there was plenty of music, profane and pious, in Hanover. There were ten chamber waiters, and twenty-four lackeys in livery; a maître-d'hôtel, and attendants of the kitchen; a French cook; a body cook; ten cooks; six cooks' assistants; two Braten masters, or masters of the roast - (one fancies enormous spits turning slowly, and the honest masters of the roast beladling the dripping); a pastry baker; a pie baker; and finally, three scullions [...] In the sugar chamber there were four pastry cooks (for the ladies, no doubt); seven officers in the wine and beer cellars; four bread bakers; and five men in the plate-room. There were 600 horses in the Serene stables - no less than twenty teams of princely carriage horses, eight to a team; sixteen coachmen; fourteen postilions; nineteen ostlers; thirteen helps, besides smiths, carriage masters, horse-doctors, and other attendants of the stable.

The female attendants were not so numerous; I grieve to find but a dozen or fourteen of them about the Electoral premises, and only two washerwomen for all the Court. These functionaries had not so much to do as in the present age.'[12]

Though Sophia's life had grown quiet, the Grim Reaper seemed to have a busy year in 1700. The first to be carried away was Clara, the lady whose manipulative schemes had caused such misery. Her final illness - claimed by some to be syphilis - left her blind, her reliance on cosmetics and the ravages of the years robbing her of her striking good looks. Legend has it that she died in torment and 'constantly saw Königsmarck's ghost by her wicked old bed.'[13] With the death of Ernest Augustus her influence had disappeared entirely, but now she was really gone for good. The old guard was being swept away.

> 'On Tuesday betimes in the Morning, we Received an Express from Windsor, with the disagreeable News of the Death of his Highness the Duke of Gloucester, who to the inexpressible Grief of their Royal Highness, the Princess, and the Prince of Denmark; as also of the whole Nation in General, Died between 12 and One a-Clock that Morning, after 5 days Sickness; upon this occasion the People of all Ranks in his City, shewed a very great concern for this irreparable loss, extremely Lamenting the Death of this hopeful Prince.'[14]

A death of considerably more importance than Clara's occurred on 30 July 1700 when Prince William, Duke of Gloucester, passed away at Windsor. Aged just 11, this was a decisive turning point in the future of the electoral house. After the death of his beloved Queen Mary, William III had continued to rule alone, no heir in the wings to follow him. Next in the line of succession was his sister-in-law, Princess Anne, followed by her children. The only problem was that the Duke of Gloucester would eventually prove to be the sole survivor of seventeen pregnancies and now he too was dead. The Protestant line of succession was dwindling at an alarming rate until only William and Anne stood between the Dowager Electress Sophia and the crown. William was 50-years-old but Anne, the heir apparent, was still only in her mid-thirties.

Though Anne's health was notoriously poor, Sophia remained resolutely certain that at 70-years-old, she was 'no longer of an age to think of any kingdom other than that of heaven'[15]. George Louis, however, currently fighting alongside his surviving brothers in the War of the Spanish Succession, could likely begin to look forward to becoming king so long as he came back from battle!

That wasn't all that was happening on the continent though. The supporters of James I, who had been forced into exile by the Glorious Revolution, had been gathering allies to their cause. Should there be any wobbles when it came to the succession, they wanted him poised to swing into action and lead the Catholic claim for his restoration.

The more supportive biographers of Sophia Dorothea poked around in Sophia's affairs for some scandal to hurl at the dowager electress and they found it in rumours that she had conspired with William to push ahead of Anne in the line of succession. When she modestly declined, they claimed, she instead put forward the suggestion that William should attempt a reconciliation with James and his son, James Francis Stuart, the Prince of Wales.[16] Of course, Wales would have had to convert to Protestantism to have a crack at the throne and on this point he was immovable. Wilkins, a champion of the wronged Sophia Dorothea, unequivocally states that Sophia 'would not stand in her own light, but short of that she was a Jacobite.'[17]

Quite a claim!

Yet as we already know Sophia *did* still feel some affection and respect for James II. He was now living in exile at St Germain as a guest of Louis XIV and she wished no ill upon him. In fact, it wasn't in her nature to celebrate her own advancement at the cost of her kinsman. When driven into exile, it's telling that she referred to the Pretender *in a letter* as 'le pauvre prince de Galles' or *the poor Prince of Wales*. In the same letter, sent in 1700 to George Stepney, an envoy in Vienna, she fretted as to whether George Louis was suitable to make the transition from absolutist elector to constitutional monarch. Famously her letter became known as *the Jacobite letter*, but to suggest that she was a committed Jacobite is a step too far. Her sense of duty weighed more heavily than any sense of family and the thought of her rejecting the crown of England is unlikely, but it's perfectly natural to feel that she still harboured a sense of sympathy for those of her own blood who had been forced into exile, just as her own parents had been all those years ago.

Though Sophia must have nursed secret and perhaps unconscious hopes, she had mostly reconciled herself to dying before she assumed the throne. As she confided in Stepney:

> 'If I were thirty years younger I should have sufficient good opinion of my blood and my religion, to believe that people might think of me in England. But, as there is little

likelihood that I should survive two persons (King William and the Princess Anne) both very much younger, though more sickly, than I am, it is to be feared that my sons will be regarded as strangers; and the eldest of them is much more accustomed to give himself the airs of a sovereign.'[18]

She feared how the aloof and famously cold George Louis might come across when he landed on English shores and as history would tell, she was right to do so. As Liselotte later recalled, 'it is not wonderful that one no longer finds the gaiety in Hanover that was once there, the Elector is so cold that he turns everything into ice. His father and uncle were not like him.'[19]

The Act of Settlement

Across the sea, the English Parliament swung into action to ensure that nothing untoward could occur to upset the future of the Protestant succession. The result was the Act of Settlement, which established that, though any as-yet unborn heirs to William III and the future Queen Anne would take precedence, should there be no children born, then the English crown would pass into Hanoverian hands. Since Sophia's elder sister and only living sibling, Louise Hollandine, was as a Catholic banned from inheriting the throne, this meant the crown would go to our very own dowager electress.

Even at this late stage, hope wasn't lost for the Pretender. As the Catholic half-brother of Anne, should he convert to Protestantism he could still inherit in her place. Yet convert was something he was utterly unwilling to do, so the wheels of constitutional change continued to grind, leaving him behind.

'That the most excellent Princess Sophia, Electress and Duchess Dowager of Hanover, daughter of the most excellent Princess Elizabeth, late Queen of Bohemia, daughter of our late sovereign lord King James the First, of happy memory, be and is hereby declared to be the next in succession, in the Protestant line, to the imperial Crown and dignity of the said Realms of England, France, and Ireland, with the dominions and territories thereunto belonging, after His Majesty, and the Princess Anne of Denmark, and in default of issue of the said Princess Anne, and of His Majesty respectively: and that from and after the deceases of His said Majesty, our now sovereign lord, and of Her Royal Highness the Princess Anne of Denmark, and for default of issue of the said Princess Anne, and of His Majesty respectively, the Crown and regal government of the said Kingdoms of England, France, and Ireland, and of the dominions thereunto belonging, with the royal state and dignity of the said Realms, and all honours, styles, titles, regalities, prerogatives, powers, jurisdictions and authorities, to the same belonging and appertaining, shall be, remain, and continue to the said most excellent Princess Sophia, and the heirs of her body, being Protestants: and thereunto the said Lords Spiritual and Temporal, and Commons, shall and will in the name of all the people of this Realm, most humbly and faithfully submit themselves, their heirs and posterities: and do faithfully promise, that after the deceases of His Majesty, and Her Royal Highness, and the failure of the heirs of their respective bodies, to stand to, maintain, and defend the said Princess Sophia, and the heirs of her body, being Protestants, according to the limitation and succession of the Crown in this act specified and contained, to the utmost of their powers, with their lives and estates, against all persons whatsoever that shall attempt anything to the contrary.'

The Act also laid down a series of vital constitutional points including specifying that all future monarchs must be loyal to Protestantism and that any future monarchs who were not a native of England (such as, let's say, someone from Hanover) could not compel England to engage in conflict for the defence of another realm. A further clause, which George I later had repealed in order to be allowed to visit Hanover as often as he liked, ruled that the monarch couldn't leave England, Scotland or Ireland without the agreement of Parliament. Again, one can't help but feel that these clauses were intended not only to protect English interests, but to contain Hanoverian ambitions too.

All of this seemed to be coming not a moment too soon. In France, the exiled James II died and the French proclaimed his son James III, king in exile. What this would mean for the future nobody could guess but for now at least, the English were getting their paperwork in order.

Any sense of celebration Sophia felt at Parliament's official recognition of her position must surely have been diluted in the early months of 1702 when her lifelong companion, Anna Katharina von Harling, died after a long and debilitating illness. It was left to Sophia to break the news to those other members of her family whom Frau von Harling had cared for, from the two Georges to Liselotte. As one of the old guard of the Hanoverian court, her loss was one that Sophia must have felt more keenly than most. Once again she retreated to her gardens and the company of nature, walking the avenues in which she had grieved so often.

An Official Visit

With the Act of Settlement explicitly naming Sophia and her heirs as successors to the throne, George Louis began to prepare in earnest for his forthcoming role. Things were moving on apace and that summer, William sent Charles Gerard, 2nd Earl of Macclesfield, to Hanover to officially hand over a copy of the Act of Settlement and award the Order of the Garter to George Louis. With him was the philosopher John Toland, who wrote an account of the ceremonial visit, mentioning the members of the electoral family who received him in Hanover.

And paid handsomely for the privilege.

> 'The Earl of Macclesfield's Reception at the Court of Hanover was extraordinary magnificent, and that a Person who came on his errand must needs be very welcome. You deserve an Account of it, and I take this to be a proper place.
> [...]
> There one of the largest Houses in the whole City was align'd for his Entertainment, and to lodg [sic] as many of the Gentlemen that accompany'd him as he wou'd please to have near him, the rest being dispos'd into other Houses of the Neighborhood at the Elector's Charge. During all the time of his stay, not only between thirty and forty Gentlemen who came along with him, but likewise all

Englishmen that pass'd that way, were treated on free cost. It was a continu'd Feasting, and I do not exceed when I say, that the two great Tables kept in this English Hotel were as plentifully and as sumtuously [sic] furnish'd the last Day as the first. All the Servants had half a Crown a Day given 'em in good Silver Pieces to provide for themselves; for they wou'd not disgrace 'em, it seems, with their Master's broken Meat, nor be at the trouble to dress for them in particular. The Citizens had Orders, which they observ'd, not to take any thing for Meat and Drink of any English Gentleman if his humor should lead him to desire it. The Elector's own Servants waited on them every Morning with Silver Coffee and Tea-pots to their Chambers. Burgundy, Champaigne [sic], Rhenish[20], and all manner of Wines were as common as Beer. A number of Coaches and Chairs were appointed to being 'em every Day to Court, to carry 'em back to their Lodgings, and to go whithersoever else they wou'd. They were entertain'd with Music, Balls, and Plays; and every Person made it his Business to oblige them. There was a very fine Ball, and a splendid appearance of Ladys, the Evening after my Lord deliver'd the Act of Succession to the Electress. His Lordship did often eat at the Electoral Table, and som [sic] of the Gentlemen were always there in their Turns. They were frequently entertain'd by the Ministers of State; and if any of 'em (as I know of none) did misbehave himself, it cou'd well be otherwise among so many young People; and I defy the like number, unless they shou'd be pick'd on purpose, to carry themselves more decently.'[21]

No expense had been spared to make a massive impression and from Hanover the party travelled to Celle. There they met George William and Éléonore whose grandson, let us not forget, was now also part of the line of succession. George William still refused to see his disgraced daughter, but he had regular contact with his grandchildren. In addition, Éléonore and Duke Anthony Ulrich, whose son had long ago hoped to marry Sophia Dorothea, were now reconciled with Sophia, three remaining members of the ever-dwindling old guard together. Of course, Sophia Dorothea was not included in these festivities. When Macclesfield returned to Hanover the celebrations continued and the electress handed over the expensive gifts that were part and parcel of such an event. It's fair to say that Sophia Dorothea's fortune and dowry probably came in rather handy in footing the eye-watering bill.

'[Macclesfield] was presented by her Royal Highness with her own Picture set in Diamonds, and the Electoral Crown of the same Materials over it, to the value of several thousand Pounds. The Elector's Present was a huge Bason and Ewer of Massy Gold to a very considerable value; and the Duke of Zell gave him a great many Gold Medals, to dispose of at his pleasure. Mr KING the Herald, who brought the Garter to his Electoral Highness, tho his Lordship perform'd the Ceremony, was nobly presented.

[…]

A Present was also given to Mr WILLIAMS his Lordship's Secretary; and what Marks of Favor their Highnesses were pleas'd to confer on my self, I pretend not to have deserved by any Services I could render their Family, not on any personal Account. The Present was partly in Gold Medals; but what I much esteem, and will always preserve, is the Queen of Prussia, the Electress, the Elector, and the young Prince's Pictures done in Oil colors, and very like.'[22]

Wonderfully, just as Sophia had documented her opinions of her sisters, Toland records his opinion of Sophia and what emerges is a portrait of a strong, sprightly woman, who had borne her tribulations well.

'The Electress is three and seventy Years of Age, which she bears so wonderfully well, that had I not many Vouchers, I shou'd scarce dare venture to relate it. She has ever enjoy'd extraordinary Health, which keeps her still very vigorous, of a cheerful Countenance, and a merry Disposition. She steps as firm and erect as any young Lady, has not one Wrinkle in her Face which is still very agreeable, nor one Tooth out of her Head, and reads without Spectacles, as I often saw her do Letters of a small Character in the dusk of the Evening. She's as great a Worker as our late Queen, and you cannot turn your self in the Palace without meeting som [sic] Monuments of her industry […] She has bin long admir'd by all the Learned World, as a Woman of incomparable Knowledge in Divinity, Philosophy, History, of which she has read a prodigious quantity. She speaks five Languages so well, that by her Accent it might be a Dispute which of 'em was her first. They are Low-Dutch, German, French, Italian, and English, which last she speaks as trull and easily as any Native; which to me is a matter of amazement […] the Electress is so intirely [sic] English in her Person, in her Behavior [sic], in her Humor, and all her Inclinations [and] was ever glad to see Englishmen, long before the Act of Succession.'[23]

So far, so good and no doubt this bit of flowery flannel gave Sophia a rosy glow, but what of her son? Toland knew better than to be anything other than totally complimentary, of course, and when he turned his pen on George Louis, it was equally adoring if a little less focused on looks!

'[George Louis is] a proper, middle-siz'd, well-proportion'd Man, of a gentile Address and good Appearance [and] tho he be well vers'd in the Art of War, and of invincible Courage […] he's naturally of peaceable Inclinations, which mixture of Qualitys [sic] is agreed by the Experience of all Ages to make the best and most glorious Princes. He's a perfect Man of Business, […] equitable, mild and prudent. He's the most belov'd by his Subjects of any Prince in the World. […] he understands English, and in a little time will speak it readily.'[24]

No mention, perhaps unsurprisingly, of the wife.

For a time, things were very bright indeed in Hanover. There was even some discussion of an annuity for Sophia from England but when William died in 1702, all of that changed.

'On Wednesday last Our late Most Gracious Sovereign King *William* the Third was seized with an Ague Fit and a Feaver [sic], which returning upon him the following days, reduced him to a very weak and languishing Condition; All proper Remedies were applied, but not having the wished-for Effect, His Majesty expired at *Kensington* at Eight a Clock this morning.'[25]

Now Queen Anne was on the throne and for Sophia, that possible annuity was nothing but a memory. Anne had no love of William, her predecessor, and even less for those who had been his allies, Sophia included. The new queen did make one concession and added Sophia's name to the Prayer for the Royal Family in the Book of Common Prayer. Though Anne hoped that she might still have another child, the inclusion of the dowager electress in those all-important prayers was a clear indication of just how the wind was blowing. With the press also reporting the change to the Book of Common Prayer, England was being prepared for the future, and the future came from Hanover.

> 'On Sunday last the Princess Sophia, Electress Dowager of Hanover, was publickly pray'd for in the Chapel-Royal at St. James's; and her Majesty hath published an Order to pray for her henceforward in all Churches and Chapels throughout the Kingdom.'[26]

Losing Figuelotte

In 1703 Sophia's second youngest son, Christian Henry, died. He was killed during an engagement with the French at Ulm, leaving his mother bereft. Now only four of her seven children still lived and that number would soon dwindle even further. With George Louis needing little help with the business of being Hanover's elector, Sophia travelled to stay with Figuelotte and made a new friend in the shape of a young orphan who had been taken in by Figuelotte to live at court. She was Caroline of Ansbach, later to become queen at the side of George II.

By now Figuelotte and Frederick were the King and Queen of Prussia and their court was one of philosophy and intellect pursuits, championed by Figuelotte. Young Caroline couldn't have asked for a better place in which to grow up, especially having suffered through a very unsettled start in life. Her father, John Frederick, Margrave of Brandenburg, had been killed by smallpox at the age of 31, leaving Caroline and her brother, William Frederick, to be cared for by their mother, Princess Eleonore Erdmuthe of Saxe-Eisenach. With an eye on the financial security of her children, she married again. The decision would prove to be a disastrous one.

Unfortunately Eleonore's second husband, John George IV, Elector of Saxony, proved to be as neglectful as he was rich. After a confrontation ended in violence and John George came for Eleonore with a knife, she fled for safely with her children. Like John Frederick before him John George also fell victim to smallpox, but life wasn't about to get any better for the little family without him and Eleonore died when Caroline was just 13. It was this unhappy turn of events that saw the orphaned young lady being raised by Figuelotte and Frederick, where she made the acquaintance of Sophia.

Alongside the electress and her daughter, Caroline had also found a great intellectual sparring partner in Leibniz, who was a key figure in her intellectual development. Of course, just like those two women before her, education wasn't her only focus and she too was being prepared for a good marriage. She was intelligent, witty and beautiful and so sought after that Sophia called her, 'the most agreeable Princess in Germany'[27], yet it seemed likely that Archduke Charles of Austria would be the one to win her hand. Destined to become the Holy Roman Emperor, Charles had one condition that must be satisfied if the two were to be wed, and that was for Caroline to convert to Catholicism.

Sophia didn't interfere in the negotiations, but she did look on with interest. She watched as Caroline sparred with Father Ferdinand Orban, a Jesuit priest who had been sent to try and convince the young lady of the wisdom of conversion. One senses that Sophia enjoyed watching the comings and goings and she commented, 'First the Princess of Ansbach says "Yes" and then "No". First she says we Protestants have no valid priests, then that Catholics are idolatrous and accursed, and then again that our religion is the better. What the result will be I do not know. The Princess is shortly leaving here, and so it must be either "Yes" or "No". When Urban [sic] comes to see the Princess the Bible lies between them on the table, and they argue at length. Of course, the Jesuit, who has studied more, argues her down, and then the Princess weeps.'[28]

On and on went the tearful negotiations until they collapsed but the talks were still in full swing when Sophia made her way home to

Hanover. When Caroline of Ansbach finally wrote to her suitor to tell him that she would not convert to Catholicism and become his bride, it was Leibniz who drafted the letter on her behalf.

Frederick, Caroline's guardian, was utterly fuming. He believed that his mother-in-law had exceeded her brief in introducing Leibniz to the young lady. It was he, Frederick believed, who was responsible for spiking the wedding plans with Archduke Charles and for this, he simply couldn't forgive Sophia. For a time he wouldn't even allow his wife to visit her mother but eventually he relented and once again, mother and daughter were making plans. Figuelotte set off for Hanover full of excitement for the longed for reunion, delighted that her husband's anger had begun to ebb. Tragically, it was a reunion that would not last. During Figuelotte's visit to Hanover, disaster struck.

On 1 February 1705, Figuelotte, Sophia's only daughter, her loving and loved friend, died.

It began as a sore throat on the road to Herrenhausen but the party travelled on regardless towards their destination. By the time they arrived in Figuelotte's homeland she was definitely ill but she nevertheless insisted on attending the festivities held in her honour. Soon what had initially seemed like nothing more serious than a severe cold began to look like something far more sinister, possibly even a tumour in Figuelotte's throat. After rejecting the attentions of a priest who was looking to save her immortal soul the philosophical Figuelotte took to her bed and told her ladies in waiting, 'I am at last going to satisfy my curiosity about the origin of things, […] to understand space, infinity, being and nothingness; and as for the King, my husband – well, I shall afford him the opportunity of giving me a magnificent funeral, and displaying all the pomp he loves so much.'[29]

Thinking Figuelotte's symptoms innocent enough and suffering from a cold of her own, Sophia took to her bed. She was still recovering when she received word that her daughter had died. Though Sophia had not been there, George Louis, realizing how critical Figuelotte's condition had become, was with his sister at the end. She was only 36 when she died, leaving behind her only surviving child, Frederick William. The exact cause of her death remained uncertain but she declined with such horrifying speed that some at court spread rumours that she had fallen victim to poisoning by 'Diamond Powder, for when she was opened her Stomach was so worn, that you could thrust your Fingers through at any Place.'[30]

With her daughter's death Sophia sank lower than perhaps she ever had before in all her many bereavements and setbacks. She was desolate and believed, 'I have lost what I loved most in the world'. In a castle hung with black drapes and filled with silence the body of Figuelotte waited for its return to Berlin, a constant spectre of the light that had been extinguished in Sophia's life. No longer a young woman, she tumbled into the mire of grief and became so unwell that for a time her life was believed to be in danger. She refused to eat or rest and wanted only to mourn the daughter who had been her closest friend during some very tumultuous times.

It was to be an emotional year.

That summer, George William, Sophia's brother-in-law and the man she had once almost married, died. Following so hot on the heels of Figuelotte's passing it must have seemed like just one more body blow heaped upon a woman whose spirits were already teetering. In France, Liselotte fretted over her beloved aunt, wishing that something might be done to prompt her to seek out some life and company. That something, a light in the darkness as it were, came in the shape of Caroline of Ansbach, who was in so many ways the natural heiress to Figuelotte's place in Sophia's aching heart.

Having resisted all of Father Orban's considerable efforts to convert her to Catholicism, Caroline had remained true to her faith. Now she was about to be wed to Sophia's grandson, George Augustus. For Sophia, it was the perfect tonic.

The courtship of Caroline of Ansbach and George Augustus had been like something out of romantic fiction and though Sophia knew nothing of it as she navigated her way through grief, when she heard the story she was delighted. George Louis, who knew a thing or two about forced marriage, decided that his son must be allowed to have a say of his own when it came to his bride. He had heard all about Caroline from his mother but he also knew that Sophia had been instrumental in fixing him up with Sophia Dorothea, so it was vital that George Augustus agree with the match before it was made. George Louis also thought that Caroline should get to know her would-be suitor as nothing more than a man, with no rank or title to his name. Only then, he decided, would she show George Augustus her true self as opposed to a version that had been created to snare a future king of England.

George Augustus travelled to Triesdorf to meet Caroline in the guise of Monsieur de Busch, a minor noble with nothing to single him out as remarkable. He and Caroline fell for one another and when she learned of his true identity, she was stunned and thrilled in equal measure. The couple was married at Herrenhausen on 2 September 1705 and few could have been happier than Sophia, who doubtless saw in Caroline much of the beloved daughter she had lost so recently. They lived with her at Herrenhausen for almost a decade and the presence of the young bride did much to restore Sophia's spirits. It was as though Figuelotte had returned and to the end of Sophia's days, she and Caroline were devoted to one another.

Just over a year later the dowager electress was able to witness the marriage of George Louis' second child, Sophia Dorothea, to Frederick William I. Of course, Sophia Dorothea, the imprisoned Lady of Ahlden, did not attend the wedding of either of her children, nor was she free to do so though no doubt she would have dearly loved to be present. She would have dearly loved to have been *anywhere*.

Ultimately Sophia, the woman who had lived in exile, passed between suitors and family members alike, had become grandmother to a king and a queen.

Not a bad showing really.

A Crisis in England

Don't be fooled into thinking that all was now well in Hanover though, for that was *far* from the case. The grandchildren were married, Sophia was wiling away the days in her garden and George Louis was on active military duty in the service of his country, navigating the electorate's path through the War of the Spanish Succession. He must have wondered what mischief could befall the court in his absence, perhaps comforting himself with the knowledge that there was really little of note that might go wrong.

How mistaken he was.

Things in England had not been at all settled in the years since William's death and they came to a head in 1704 with the Act of Security, when the Scottish Estates made it plain that they would not accept any Hanoverian as the legitimate heir to the throne of Scotland. Instead they would select their own sovereign from the legitimate descendants of earlier Scottish monarchs when the moment came and neither Sophia nor George should expect to find themselves on the shortlist.

Negotiations between Scotland and England intensified and ultimately ended in a lack of anything approaching agreement, which can hardly have come as a surprise to anyone. The response was the sledgehammer of the 1705 Alien Act, which offered the Scottish two choices. The first was the option to discuss uniting the two parliaments into a single body, allowing free trade between Scotland and England. If this wasn't attractive, the second option open to the Scottish was the right to reject any negotiation and the Hanoverian succession. In this case, there would be a ban on the import of all Scottish products into England and citizens of Scotland would be considered foreign nationals. This meant they would no longer enjoy certain fundamental rights outside Scotland, throwing into question the fate of property and land owned by Scottish people in England. Faced with a choice that was no choice at all the Scottish people were forced to accept the union *and* the Hanoverian heirs to the throne. In 1707, the twenty-five articles of the Acts of Union joined the countries once and for all. Today, that relationship is still far from harmonious!

> 'I. THAT the two Kingdoms of Scotland and England shall upon the first day of May next ensuing the date hereof, and for ever after, be united into One Kingdom by the Name of GREAT BRITAIN; And that the Ensigns Armorial of the said United Kingdom be such as Her Majesty shall appoint, and the Crosses of St Andrew and St George be conjoined, in such manner as Her Majesty shall think fit, and used in all Flags, Banners, Standards and Ensigns, both at Sea and Land.

> II. THAT the Succession of the Monarchy to the United Kingdom of Great Britain, and of the Dominions thereto belonging, after Her Most Sacred Majesty, and in Default of Issue of Her Majesty, be, remain, and continue to the Most Excellent Princess Sophia, Electoress and Dutchess Dowager of Hanover, and the Heirs of her Body being Protestants, upon whom the Crown of England is settled by an Act of Parliament made in England in the twelfth Year

of the Reign of his late Majesty King William the Third, Intituled, An Act for the further Limitation of the Crown, and better securing the Rights and Liberties of the Subject: And that all Papists, and Persons marrying Papists, shall be excluded from, and forever incapable to inherit, possess, or enjoy the Imperial Crown of Great Britain, and the Dominions thereunto belonging, or any Part thereof, and in every such Case the Crown and Government shall from time to time descend to, and be enjoyed by such Person being a Protestant, as should have inherited and enjoyed the same in case such Papist or Person marrying a Papist, was naturally Dead according to the Provision for the Descent of the Crown of England, made by another Act of Parliament in England in the first Year of the Reign of their late Majesties King William and Queen Mary entituled An Act declaring the Rights and Liberties of the Subject, and settling the Succession of the Crown.

III. THAT the United Kingdom of Great Britain be Represented by one and the same Parliament to be stiled The Parliament of Great Britain.'

Of course, then as now, Parliament didn't seem happy unless it was indulging in a little drama and no sooner had the union been settled than the newest wheels of conflict were turning. This time, however, Sophia was front and centre.

Whig supporters published a pamphlet entitled *The Memorial of the Church of England*, suggesting that Queen Anne was being badly advised by those around her, with an aim to undermine religious stability in the country. Anne responded with a speech in which she redoubled her assurances that she was dedicated to the faith of the nation. This wasn't enough for the Tories though, they wanted the Whigs punished to the fullest extent of the law for daring to even *suggest* that the sanctity of the church was not in safe hands under Queen Anne's stewardship.

As the ruling party in Queen Anne's Parliament, the Tories rather fancied making a little mischief. What better way to do so than under the cover of sending a welcoming invitation to the heiress presumptive? They also knew it was important to curry favour with the incoming family from the continent and to this end Lord Haversham, a Whig who had crossed the floor to join the Tories, gave a speech in the House of Lords in which he censured his political opponents and their supporters. Only at the end of the speech did things take an unexpected turn when he requested that Queen Anne formally invite Dowager Electress Sophia to move her entire court to England and reside there as a guest of the crown, thus ensuring that she and her family recognised the strength of public support for the succession. It was a masterstroke of political bad behaviour and Haversham knew it.

Sophia quite liked the idea but Anne was less keen. Should the electress accept the invitation and move lock, stock and barrel to England then Queen Anne could look forward to a life that would be anything *but* settled. She would have her own successor living on her doorstep, complete with a rival court, courtiers and advisers. The thought horrified her but her reaction was, I think, a rather melodramatic reading of the situation. Sophia had no wish to stage a coup nor to destabilise the monarchy, she certainly had no intention of suddenly unveiling hidden Jacobite leanings and making an attempt to enthrone the Pretender. Rather Sophia considered herself to some extent English and was sorry that she had never seen the land of her mother. Her motives were more sentimental than cunning.

Despite this, Haversham's invitation had stymied his Whig opponents good and proper. Whilst they quite naturally didn't want to support a Tory suggestion, they couldn't argue *against* the invitation without offending the heirs in Hanover and calling into question their enthusiasm for the Protestant succession. Nor could they support the suggestion without offending Queen Anne, who would've seen it as a deliberate move to rile *her* if they did.

Queen Anne, likewise, couldn't complain too loudly about the suggestion lest it be interpreted as a sign that she wasn't too fond of her successor and simply didn't want her around. She was sure that the suggestion had been made out of devilment though and had to be seen to be at the very least encouraging of Sophia's claims to the throne. That didn't mean she had to roll out the red carpet and welcome her with open arms, of course.

And what of Sophia?

What position did all of this leave *her* in?

When one recalls the enthusiasm with which the dowager electress plunged into her visit to France, not to mention her jaunt in Denmark and any number of regular trips to see her late daughter, it's hard to imagine Sophia being anything other than enthusiastic about the proposed adventure to England. Should the invitation be formally issued then protocol would make it very hard to say no without it being taken as an implicit rejection of England itself. Despite all this, one still suspects that she would have been very keen to find herself on English shores, if only for a break from the familiarity of Hanover.

The Whigs responded with a conciliatory act to establish a regency council that on the occasion of Queen Anne's death would rule until the new monarch arrived in England. This meant there was no reason for anyone from Hanover to be in the country just in case, for there would be a contingency plan firmly in place. At the same time though it signalled their clear support that the next monarch should be someone from Hanover. The Regency Act allowed Sophia to name her own Lords Justices[31], thus ensuring that the Regency Council should reflect the interests of the woman in whose name it would rule.

Mindful that Sophia might still decide to take offence at the lack of an invitation to England, Queen Anne suggested a compromise. She sent the Duke of Marlborough and Lord Halifax to Hanover to hand over the Regency Act in person. In addition, they were charged with conferring upon George Augustus the Order of the Garter and the title of Duke of Cambridge, which would signify the queen's respect and esteem for the family without actually going so far as summoning them to England.

Sophia welcomed the English party with all due ceremony but little enthusiasm. She was of the opinion that there was nothing particularly useful amongst the offerings in real terms, just titles and bits of paper. Besides which she had to stump up for presents in return, including 30,000 florins for a gold plate that was destined to go home with Lord Halifax. Like her brother, she had never been fond of extravagant spending.

In fact, Halifax was to take something else away from his visit to Hanover and this was a rather curious event that occurred during his audience with Sophia. With the whole court gathered amid great ceremony to witness the meeting in the Leineschloss, Halifax made his speech and waited for Sophia to reply. Instead of speaking she leapt to her feet and with a speed that belied her years, darted across the room into the shadows. Here she remained to observe what was left of the ceremony. What had prompted this bizarre occurrence was actually Sophia's realisation that she was sitting right opposite a portrait of the Pretender, the man who she had usurped. Faced with this unflinching sight throughout Halifax's exhortations of delight at the prospect of Sophia's inheriting the crown of Great Britain, when the moment came to escape his painted gaze she seized it.

Little wonder some thought her a Jacobite down to her bones.

Queen Anne, of course, was never without worries for long and soon the thought occurred to her that George Augustus might use his new title as a reason to come to England anyway, with the excuse that he wanted to take up his seat in the Lords. Marlborough counselled that she had no need to fear. George Augustus was far too well-occupied with affairs in Hanover to even *think* of a trip and, trusting in his decision, Anne agreed that the visit could go ahead.

Unfortunately, there was to be another spanner in the works that *nobody* could have foreseen.

Sophia's friend and champion, Leibniz, came up with the not-so marvellous idea of writing a pamphlet which denounced those who had attempted to meddle in the succession by stirring the pot of whether or not Sophia should be invited to England. In it, he accused them of being motivated by hidden Jacobite sympathies. Also included in the pamphlet was a letter Sophia had written to Thomas Tenison, Archbishop of Canterbury:

> 'I thank God, I am in good *Health*, and Live in *Quiet* and with *Content* here, therefore I have no reason to desire to change my way of Living, on the Account of any Personal Satisfaction, that I can propose to my self.
>
> However, I am ready and willing to comply with what ever can be desired of me, by my Friends, in case that the *Parliament* think, that it is for the *Good* of the Kingdom, to Invite me into *England*.
>
> But I suppose they will do this is such a manner, as will make my Coming agreeable to the *Queen*, whom I shall ever *Honour*, and Endeavour to deserve Her *Favour*; of which She hath done for me in *England* and *Scotland*, which you can judge of more particularly; And I most remember that She Order'd me to be Pray'd for in the *Churches*.'[32]

In all honesty, it hardly reads like a woman plotting a coup but to Queen Anne who by her own admission was wont to worry, Sophia's apparently respectful words carried with them a hint of trouble. Although Leibniz wrote the pamphlet, the name on it was that of Sir Rowland Gwynne, an English Whig who had lately been in residence at the court of Hanover.

Gwynne was what might be politely termed *a character*. He burned through an inheritance in no time whatsoever, getting caught up in all sorts of scandalous goings on. Not only did he strongly support the succession of Sophia and her descendants, but he had left England under something of a cloud when his financial dealings were called into question. Eventually Gwynne washed up in Hanover where he found an unlikely friend in George Augustus. Gwynne readily allowed Leibniz to use his name on the pamphlet, seeing it as the perfect way to curry favour with the heirs to the throne. In fact, his gamble proved to be badly mistaken. When Leibniz's open letter - signed by Gwynne - was translated and published, it was widely interpreted as an attempt to antagonise Queen Anne with the full support of Sophia.

The open letter purportedly from Gwynne was addressed to the Earl of Stamford and outright accused him of attributing Sophia's willingness to visit England to 'the Artifices of the Jacobites', with every intention of establishing a court in direct opposition to that of the queen. Besides, Leibniz noted with ill-disguised mischief, 'all the World knows, that the Electoress may come over whenever she pleases, without being invited.'

Queen Anne knew that all too well.

Gwynne, however, had badly misjudged the mood and in the Houses of Parliament, both Tories and Whigs alike denounced the letter as 'a scandalous, false and malicious Libel, tending to create a Misunderstanding between her Majesty and the Princess Sophia.'[33] In her official reply, Queen Anne graciously thanked Parliament and assured the members that 'nothing can be more acceptable to me, than so seasonable an Instance of your Concern to preserve a good Understanding between me and the Princess Sophia, and of your Care to defeat the Artifices of designing and malicious Men.'[34] In reality, despite her gracious words, she was livid. Sophia, waiting in Hanover in vain for her invitation to England, was no happier.

In fact, Sophia was perfectly happy for her letter to the archbishop to be published because she *did* believe that the Whigs had destroyed her chance of being invited to England. She also suspected that Queen Anne wouldn't be in the least bit disappointed about that, sure that the sovereign wanted to keep her successor as far away as possible for as long as possible. In Hanover, with his mother unrepentant, George Louis wisely entered damage limitation mode. He was all too aware that representatives of Queen Anne would soon be arriving in Hanover to confer the title of Duke of Cambridge upon his son and the last thing he wanted was for them to arrive whilst all of this trouble was rumbling on.

Though he was outside of the reach of his own nation, Gwynne wasn't immune from punishment for his part in the pamphlet's publication. George Louis dismissed him from the court and he wandered miserably into Hamburg. Here he remained, firing occasional salvos in the direction of Queen Anne or Sophia in search of money and favours, none of which were forthcoming. Eventually George Louis did take the wheedling Gwynne back into his favour and the wily Whig was at the new king's side when he set foot in his new realms, but he had *plenty* of time to kill before that far off day[35]!

By the time those envoys arrived in Hanover all was well. Marlborough wrote that, 'I had a very long conversation with this elector, who did not want many arguments to convince him that his and the queen's interest were the same. He has commanded me to assure her majesty that he will never have any thoughts but what may be agreeable to her's.'[36]

In order to paper over whatever cracks *might* have remained, the snappily-titled, *An Act for the Naturalization of the Most Excellent Princess Sophia, Electress and Dutchess Dowager of Hanover, and the Issue of her Body*, was passed by Parliament. As Sophia was not an Englishwoman by birth, this act naturalised her and her issue, to ensure no problems might arise when the moment of succession came. It was a clear sign of the restored accord between the two courts and the press was happy to report that all was once again up to speed.

'Yesterday Her Majesty came to the House of Peers with the usual Solemnities, and gave the Royal Assent to an Act for Naturalizing Her Royal Highness the Princess Sophia of Hanover and Her Issue.'[37]

The Retiring Life

With no chance now remaining that she might be called to England to experience life in the land of her mother before duty summoned her there, Sophia relaxed once more into her retirement. All intrigue was ended, Leibniz's knuckles were gently rapped by George Louis and the dowager electress found that her son's hands on the reins of succession were tighter than ever.

She contented herself with family, welcoming the news that her first great-grandchild was due in 1707, courtesy of George Augustus and Caroline of Ansbach. At the first reports of her pregnancy the court had held its breath not out of expectation, but out of anxiety. The previous year Caroline had similarly believed that she was pregnant, but had in fact been suffering from dropsy. This time there was to be no disappointment and in a bitter winter, she gave birth to a baby boy. This was Frederick[38], son of George Augustus and Caroline of Ansbach, and fourth in line to the throne of Great Britain.

At first Sophia was furious that Caroline had elected to give birth in private and had not even allowed her grandmother-in-law access to the room. When she saw Frederick at his christening, however, that displeasure melted away into affection. She simply couldn't be angry at Caroline for long and faced with this healthy little boy, she was happy once more[39]. Sophia's second great-grandchild, born to Sophia Dorothea and Frederick William, fared less well. Also named Frederick, he was born in November 1707 but lived just six months before his death.

Sophia could comfort herself with Caroline though, for she adored her. Just as she had taken Liselotte under her wing decades earlier she now treated Caroline to the same care and when the young electoral princess fell victim to smallpox, the dowager electress was terrified that she might be lost. Even worse, George Augustus refused to leave Caroline's side and he too came down with what could be a deadly infection. Happily the couple survived and would go on to rule Great Britain as a formidable king and queen.

In 1708, Prince of George of Denmark, the husband of Queen Anne, died. The childless queen declared that she had no intention of remarrying and this meant only one thing: the succession of the heirs from Hanover was now guaranteed. Sophia wasn't ignorant of the gossips who claimed that Anne would actually have preferred it if the Pretender would agree to convert, thus wiping out the hopes of the family on the continent. But this was a faint hope and everyone knew it.

The future was Hanoverian.

The following year Sophia's only surviving sibling, Louise Hollandine, took her last breath. She had continued to paint and regularly received visits from Liselotte, who had watched sadly as the old abbess declined into frailty. Fifty years after she took holy orders, the talented artist died. She had been suffering with ill health for many years and Liselotte wrote that she, 'had reached an age beyond which it is difficult to go much further, because she was eighty-six years and nine months old. Nevertheless, her death has stricken me to the heart. […] I also fear that her death will upset our dear aunt, the Electress, very much, and that her health may suffer.'[40]

Liselotte underestimated Sophia, who had been through enough grief in her time to weather this latest storm. Besides, Queen Anne might be *younger* but she was far from healthy and somewhere in her heart, the dowager electress still held onto the unvoiced hope that she might, by sheer determination, live to call herself the Queen of Great Britain. Perhaps this was one of the things that was keeping a spring in her step.

As the years passed, Sophia seemed to be as robust as she ever had been. Yet she continued to dream of that faraway land to which she had never been invited and to her delight, she found a partner in ambition in Caroline of Ansbach. Caroline was inordinately proud that her husband had been awarded not only the Order of the Garter but also the title of Duke of Cambridge, and she believed that these should only be the precursor to even better honours.

Though Queen Anne had feared that George Augustus might use the title to lobby for a seat in the House of Lords it was actually his wife who made the overture. Caroline asked George Louis if he might be willing to send his son to England so that he could sit in the Upper House, but the elector refused in no uncertain terms. He had already fended off his mother's efforts, after all, so he wasn't about to cave into the wishes of his daughter-in-law. Besides, Queen Anne's health was in terminal decline and Hanover was filling up with English courtiers who were looking to establish themselves as favourites *before* the queen died, so perhaps George Louis thought his mother and daughter-in-law could indulge themselves without moving from home at all.

The dowager electress, however, was not getting any younger.

In 1713 Sophia fell terribly ill. The court and a disinterested George Louis waited for the inevitable as their 83-year-old year matriarch appeared to teeter on the brink of death, growing weaker with each passing dawn. Sophia had never been a fan of doing what people expected of her and this was no exception. She was still too doughty for the Grim Reaper to pluck her from her bed and to the surprise of everyone in Hanover, she rallied once more. As Sophia's strength returned so too did her resolve and she and Leibniz began to discuss their pet topic of uniting the churches of England and Rome, but all of this talk was soon transformed once again in a desire to go to her mother's homeland.

With the encouragement of Caroline of Ansbach, Sophia urged Georg Wilhelm Helwig Sinold von Schütz, the Hanoverian minister in London, to officially request permission for her grandson to take his seat in the House of Lords. She was still clinging to that dream when a letter from Queen Anne arrived that poured a bucket of ice cold water over her long held desire to see England.

'As the rumour increases, that my cousin, the electoral prince, has resolved to come over to settle, in my lifetime, in my dominions, I do not choose to delay a moment to write to you about this, and to communicate to you my sentiments upon a subject of this importance. I then freely own to you that I cannot imagine that a prince who possesses the knowledge and penetration of your electoral highness can ever contribute to such an attempt; and that I believe you are too just to allow that any infringement shall be made on my sovereignty which you would not choose should be made on your own. I am firmly persuaded that you would not suffer the smallest diminution of your authority; I am no less delicate in that respect; and I am determined to oppose a project so contrary to my royal authority, however fatal the consequences may be. Your electoral highness is too just to refuse to bear me witness, that I give, on all occasions, proofs of my desire that your family should succeed to my crowns; which I always recommend to my people, as the most solid support of religion and their laws. I employ all my attention, that nothing should efface those impressions from the hearts of my subjects; but it is not possible to derogate from the dignity and prerogatives of the prince who wears the crown, without making a dangerous breach on the rights of the successors; therefore, I doubt not but, with your usual wisdom, you will prevent the taking such a step; and that you will give me an opportunity of renewing to you assurances of the most sincere friendship, with which I am, &c.'[41]

The letter arrived on 6 June 1714 and in the years that followed, many questioned whether it might have played a part in the sad events that occurred later that week. Sophia was badly stung by the queen's communication and seemed out of sorts from the moment she read it, which is hardly surprising. Though polite the content was plain: *nobody* from the House of Hanover was going to set foot in England so long as Queen Anne still drew breath. In the scant days that remained to her Sophia sent the letter on to Marlborough, intending to have it published. That day never came.

On 8 June 1714, Sophia sallied forth at Herrenhausen to take her evening stroll through the gardens in the company of her ladies. Though a storm threatened to break later that night, the evening was warm and together the women ambled through the blossoms, discussing the English question. As a gentle shower began to fall the dowager electress hitched up her skirts and ran for cover just as she had dashed from Lord Halifax and the unflinching gaze of the portrait of the Pretender. After a few steps Sophia faltered and seemed to lose her footing. Then she stumbled and sank down onto the rain-washed grass, clutching at her stomach as her devoted granddaughter-in-law hurried to her aid.

As the storm broke overhead, Sophia drew her last mortal breath. The dowager electress died there in the garden that she loved just before 6.00 pm, with her beloved Caroline of Ansbach at her side.

The era of Sophia, Dowager Electress, was over.

Just two months later, Queen Anne died at the age of 49 and King George I succeeded to the throne of Great Britain.

Let's leave the last word to Liselotte, the little girl who loved to jump and more than that, loved the aunt who had raised her.

'The longer I live the more reason I have to regret my aunt, the Electress, and to respect her memory. You are very right in saying that in many centuries we shall not see her like again.'[42]

Appendix A

Dramatis Personae

The Winter King and Queen

Frederick V, Elector Palatine (1596-1632)
Elizabeth Stuart, Electress Palatine (1596-1662)

Their Children
Henry Frederick, Hereditary Prince of the Palatinate (1614-1629)
Charles I Louis, Elector Palatine (1617-1680)
Elisabeth of the Palatinate (1618-1680)
Rupert of the Rhine (1619-1682)
Maurice of the Palatinate (1620-1652)
Louise Hollandine of the Palatinate (1622-1709)
Edward, Count Palatine of Simmern (1625-1663)
Henriette Marie of the Palatinate (1626-1651)
Frederick of the Palatinate (1627-1650)
Charlotte of the Palatinate (1628-1631)
Sophia, Electress of Hanover (1630-1714) - See below for Sophia's own
    illustrious heritage!
Gustavus Adolphus of the Palatinate (1632-1641)

The Dukes of Brunswick-Lüneberg

George, Duke of Brunswick-Lüneberg (1582-1641)
Anne Eleonore of Hesse-Darmstadt (1601-1659)

Their Children
Magdalene of Brunswick-Lüneburg (1620-1620)
Christian Louis, Duke of Brunswick-Lüneburg (1622-1665)

George William, Duke of Brunswick-Lüneburg (1624-1705)
John Frederick, Duke of Brunswick-Lüneburg (1625-1679)
Sophie Amalie, Queen of Denmark (1628-1685)
Dorothea Magdalene of Brunswick-Lüneburg (1629-1660)
Ernest Augustus, Elector of Hanover (1629-1698) – See below for the
    royal dynasty he and Sophia began!
Anna Marie of Brunswick-Lüneburg (1630-1660)

The Elector and Electress

Sophia, Electress of Hanover (1630-1714)
Ernest Augustus, Elector of Hanover (1629-1698)

Their Children
George I, King of Great Britain (1660-1727)
Frederick Augustus of Brunswick-Lüneburg (1661–90)
Maximilian William of Brunswick-Lüneburg (1666–1726)
Sophia Charlotte (1668–1705)
Charles Philip of Brunswick-Lüneburg (1669–90)
Christian Henry of Brunswick-Lüneburg (1671–1703)
Ernest Augustus, Bishop of Osnabrück (1674-1728)

Appendix B

An Epithalamion, or Marriage Song, on the Lady Elizabeth and Count Palatine Being Married on St Valentine's Day, by John Donne

I

HAIL Bishop Valentine, whose day this is;
    All the air is thy diocese,
    And all the chirping choristers
And other birds are thy parishioners;
    Thou marriest every year
The lyric lark, and the grave whispering dove,
The sparrow that neglects his life for love,
The household bird with the red stomacher;
    Thou makest the blackbird speed as soon,
As doth the goldfinch, or the halcyon;
The husband cock looks out, and straight is sped,
And meets his wife, which brings her feather-bed.
This day more cheerfully than ever shine;
This day, which might enflame thyself, old Valentine.

II.

Till now, thou warmd'st with multiplying loves
    Two larks, two sparrows, or two doves;
    All that is nothing unto this;
For thou this day couplest two phoenixes;
    Thou makst a taper see
What the sun never saw, and what the ark
—Which was of fouls and beasts the cage and park—

Did not contain, one bed contains, through thee;
    Two phoenixes, whose joined breasts
Are unto one another mutual nests,
Where motion kindles such fires as shall give
Young phoenixes, and yet the old shall live;
Whose love and courage never shall decline,
But make the whole year through, thy day, O Valentine.

III.
Up then, fair phoenix bride, frustrate the sun;
    Thyself from thine affection
    Takest warmth enough, and from thine eye
All lesser birds will take their jollity.
    Up, up, fair bride, and call
Thy stars from out their several boxes, take
Thy rubies, pearls, and diamonds forth, and make
Thyself a constellation of them all;
    And by their blazing signify
That a great princess falls, but doth not die.
Be thou a new star, that to us portends
Ends of much wonder; and be thou those ends.
Since thou dost this day in new glory shine,
May all men date records from this day, Valentine.

IV.
Come forth, come forth, and as one glorious flame
    Meeting another grows the same,
    So meet thy Frederick, and so
To an inseparable union go,
    Since separation
Falls not on such things as are infinite,
Nor things, which are but one, can disunite.
You're twice inseparable, great, and one;
    Go then to where the bishop stays,
To make you one, his way, which divers ways
Must be effected; and when all is past,
And that you're one, by hearts and hands made fast,
You two have one way left, yourselves to entwine,
Besides this bishop's knot, of Bishop Valentine.

V.

But O, what ails the sun, that here he stays,
   Longer to-day than other days?
   Stays he new light from these to get?
And finding here such stars, is loth to set?
   And why do you two walk,
So slowly paced in this procession?
Is all your care but to be look'd upon,
And be to others spectacle, and talk?
   The feast with gluttonous delays
Is eaten, and too long their meat they praise;
The masquers come late, and I think, will stay,
Like fairies, till the cock crow them away.
Alas ! did not antiquity assign
A night as well as day, to thee, old Valentine?

VI.

They did, and night is come; and yet we see
   Formalities retarding thee.
   What mean these ladies, which—as though
They were to take a clock in pieces—go
   So nicely about the bride?
A bride, before a "Good-night" could be said,
Should vanish from her clothes into her bed,
As souls from bodies steal, and are not spied.
   But now she's laid; what though she be?
Yet there are more delays, for where is he?
He comes and passeth through sphere after sphere;
First her sheets, then her arms, then anywhere.
Let not this day, then, but this night be thine;
Thy day was but the eve to this, O Valentine.

VII.

Here lies a she sun, and a he moon there;
   She gives the best light to his sphere;
   Or each is both, and all, and so
They unto one another nothing owe;
   And yet they do, but are
So just and rich in that coin which they pay,

That neither would, nor needs forbear, nor stay;
Neither desires to be spared nor to spare.
    They quickly pay their debt, and then
Take no acquittances, but pay again;
They pay, they give, they lend, and so let fall
No such occasion to be liberal.
More truth, more courage in these two do shine,
Than all thy turtles have and sparrows, Valentine.

VIII.
And by this act these two phoenixes
    Nature again restorèd is;
    For since these two are two no more,
There's but one phoenix still, as was before.
    Rest now at last, and we—
As satyrs watch the sun's uprise—will stay
Waiting when your eyes opened let out day,
Only desired because your face we see.
    Others near you shall whispering speak,
And wagers lay, at which side day will break,
And win by observing, then, whose hand it is
That opens first a curtain, hers or his:
This will be tried to-morrow after nine,
Till which hour, we thy day enlarge, O Valentine.

Bibliography

Anonymous. *The Georgian Era, Vol I.* London: Vizetelly, Branston and Co, 1832.

Anonymous. *Memorials Of Affairs of State In The Reigns of Q. Elizabeth and K. James I, Vol III.* London: T Ward, 1725.

Anonymous (ed.). *University Library of Autobiography: Vol V.* New York, F Tyler Daniels, 1918.

Arkell, Ruby Lillian. *Caroline of Ansbach: George the Second's Queen.* Oxford: Oxford University Press, 1939.

Baxter, Stephen B. *England's Rise to Greatness.* Los Angeles: University of California Press, 1983.

Beacock Fryer, Mary, Bousfield, Arthur and Toffoli, Garry. *Lives of the Princesses of Wales.* Toronto: Dundurn Press, 1983.

Beatty, Michael A. *The English Royal Family of America, from Jamestown to the American Revolution.* Jefferson: McFarland & Co, 2003.

Beauclaire, Horric de. *A Mésalliance in the house of Brunswick.* London: Remington & Co, 1886.

Belsham, William. *History of Great Britain from the Revolution to the Accession of the House of Hanover, Vol II.* London: GG & J Robinson, 1793.

Belsham, William. *Memoirs of the Kings of Great Britain of the House of Brunswic-Luneburg, Vol I.* London: C Dilly, 1798.

Belsham, William. *Memoirs of the Reign of King William III and Queen Anne, Vol I.* London: GG & J Robinson, 1803.

Benger, Elizabeth Ogilvy. *Memoirs of Elizabeth Stuart, Queen of Bohemia, Daughter of King James the First, Vol I.* London: Longman, Hurst, Rees, Orme, Brown, and Green, 1825.

Benger, Elizabeth Ogilvy. *Memoirs of Elizabeth Stuart, Queen of Bohemia, Daughter of King James the First, Vol II.* London: Longman, Hurst, Rees, Orme, Brown, and Green, 1825.

Benjamin, Lewis Saul. *The First George in Hanover and England, Volume I.* London: Charles Scribner's Sons, 1909.

169

Black, Jeremy. *The Hanoverians: The History of a Dynasty*. London: Hambledon and London, 2007.

Borman, Tracy. *King's Mistress, Queen's Servant: The Life and Times of Henrietta Howard*. London: Random House, 2010.

Bradlaugh, Charles. *Free Thought*. London, Free Thought Publishing Company, 1713.

Bromley, George (ed.). *A Collection of Original Royal Letters, Written by King Charles I and II, King James II and the King and Queen of Bohemia*. London: John Stockdale, 1787.

Burnet, Gilbert and Burnet, Thomas. *Bishop Burnet's History of His Own Time, Vol IV*. Oxford: The Clarendon Press, 1823.

Burnet, Gilbert and Burnet, Thomas. *Bishop Burnet's History of His Own Time, Vol V*. Oxford: Oxford University Press, 1833.

Calabi, Donatella and Christensen, Stephen Turk (eds.). *Cities and Cultural exchange in Early Modern Europe, Volume 2: 1400-1700*. Cambridge: Cambridge University Press, 2006.

Campbell, Thomas. *Frederick the Great, His Court and Times. Vol II*. London: Colburn, 1844.

Campbell Orr, Clarissa. *Queenship in Europe 1660–1815: The Role of the Consort*. Cambridge: Cambridge University Press, 2004.

Chapman, Hester W. *Privileged Persons*. London: Reynal & Hitchcock, 1966.

Churchill, Sarah, Duchess of Marlborough. *Some Years of the Life of the Duke and Duchess of Marlborough*. London: J Davis, 1817.

Clarke. *The Georgian Era: Volume I*. London, Vizetelly, Branston and Co., 1832.

Clarke, John, Godwin Ridley, Jasper and Fraser, Antonia. *The Houses of Hanover & Saxe-Coburg-Gotha*. Berkeley: University of California Press, 2000.

Cowper, CS (ed.). *Diary of Mary, Countess Cowper, Lady of the Bedchamber to the Princess of Wales, 1714-1720*. London: J Murray, 1865.

Coxe, William. *Memoirs of John, Duke of Marlborough, Vol I*. London: Longman, Hurst, Reese, Orme and Brown, 1818.

Craik, George L. *The Pictorial History of England: Being a History of the People as Well as a Kingdom, Vol IX*. London: Charles Knight & Co, 1900.

Crompton, Louis. *Homosexuality and Civilization*. Cambridge: Harvard University Press, 2003.

Dalrymple, John. *Memoirs of Great Britain and Ireland, Vol II*. London: W Strachan and T Caddell, 1773.

Daybell, James and Norrhem, Svante. *Gender and Political Culture in Early Modern Europe, 1400–1800*. London: Routledge, 2016.

Doran, John. *Lives of the Queens of England of the House of Hanover, Volume I*. New York: Redfield, 1855.

Dryden, John. *The Works of John Dryden, Vol VIII*. London: William Miller, 1808.

Duggan, JN. Sophia of Hanover: *From Winter Princess to Heiress of Great Britain, 1630–1714*. London: Peter Owen, 2013.

Edwards, Averyl. *Frederick Louis, Prince of Wales, 1701–1751*. London: Staples Press, 1947.

Evelyn, John. *Memoirs of John Evelyn, Esq, Vol V.* London, Henry Colburn, 1827.

Field, Ophelia. *The Kit-Cat Club: Friends Who Imagined a Nation*. London: Harper Press, 2008.

Forester, H (trans.). *Memoirs of Sophia, Electress of Hanover, 1630–1680*. London: T Bentley & Son, 1888.

Goldsmith, Oliver. *The Miscellaneous Works of Oliver Goldsmith, Vol II*. London: Allan Bell & Co, 1834.

Granger, J. *A Biographical History of England from Egbert the Great to the Revolution, Vol I*. London: T Davies, 1769.

Green, Mary Anne Everett. *Elizabeth, Electress Palatine and Queen of Bohemia*. London: Methuen & Co, 1909.

Green, Mary Anne Everett. *Lives of the Princesses of England, From the Norman Conquest: Vol V*. London: Henry Colburn, 1854.

Gregg, Edward. *Queen Anne*. New York: Yale University Press, 2014.

Gregg, Pauline. *King Charles I*. Los Angeles: University of California Press, 1984.

Griffiths, Ralph & Griffiths, GE. *The Monthly Review, Or, Literary Journal*. London" R Griffiths, 1798.

Gwynne, Rowland. *A Letter from Her Royal Highness, the Princess Sophia, Electress of Brunswick and Luneburg, to His Grace the Archbishop of Canterbury. With Another from Hannover written by Sir Rowland Gwynne to the Right Honourable The Earl of Stamford*. London: B Bragge, 1706.

Halliday, Andrew. *A General History of the House of Guelph*. London: Thomas and George Underwood, 1821.

Hanmer, Thomas. *The Correspondence of Sir Thomas Hanmer, Bart.* London: Edward Moxon, 1838.

Hatton, Ragnhild. *George I.* London: Thames and Hudson. 1978.

Hunt, Margaret. *Women in Eighteenth-Century Europe.* New York: Routledge, 2010.

Impelluso, Lucia. *Gardens in Art.* Los Angeles: The J P Getty Museum, 2005.

Inglis, Lucy. *Georgian London: Into the Streets.* London: Viking, 2013.

Jesse, John Heneage. *Memoirs of the Court of England: Vol II.* London: Richard Bentley, 1843.

Jordan, Ruth. *Sophia Dorothea.* New York: George Braziller, 1972.

Kiste, John van der. *The Georgian Princesses.* Stroud: The History Press, 2013.

Kiste, John van der. *King George II and Queen Caroline.* Stroud: The History Press, 2013.

Kroll, Maria (ed.). *Letters from Liselotte.* London: Allison & Busby, 1998.

Kroll, Maria. *Sophie, Electress of Hanover.* London: Victor Gollancz, 1973.

Leibniz, Gottfried Wilhelm Freiherr von, Clarke, Samuel and Alexander, Henry Gavin. *The Leibniz-Clarke Correspondence.* Manchester: Manchester University Press, 1956.

Lewalski, Barbara Kiefer. *Writing Women in Jacobean England.* Cambridge: Harvard University Press, 1993.

Morand, Paul. *The Captive Princess: Sophia Dorothea of Celle.* Florida: American Heritage Press, 1972.

Nichols, John. *The Progresses, Processions, and Magnificent Festivities, of King James the First, Vol II.* London: JB Nichols, 1828.

Oman, Carola. *Elizabeth of Bohemia.* London: Hodder and Stoughton Ltd, 1938.

Orléans, Charlotte-Elisabeth, duchesse d'. *The Letters of Madame, Vol II.* London: JW Arrowsmith Ltd, 1925.

Orléans, Charlotte-Elisabeth, duchesse d'. *Life and Letters of Charlotte Elizabeth, Princess Palatine and Mother of Philippe d'Orléans, Regent of France, 1652–1722.* London: Chapman and Hall Ltd, 1889.

Parker, Geoffrey. *The Thirty Years' War.* London: Routledge, 2006.

Redworth, Glyn. *The Prince and the Infanta.* New Haven: Yale University Press, 2003.

Shawe-Taylor, Desmond and Burchard, Wolf. *The First Georgians: Art and Monarchy 1714–1760.* London: Royal Collection Trust, 2014.

Bibliography

Sinclair-Stevenson, Christopher. *Blood Royal: The Illustrious House of Hanover*. London: Faber & Faber, 2012.

Smucker, Samuel M. *A History of the Four Georges, Kings of England*. New York: D Appleton and Company, 1860.

Strickland, Agnes and Strickland, Elizabeth. *Lives of the Queens of Scotland and English Princesses, Vol VIII*. London: William Blackwood and Sons, 1859.

Thackeray, William Makepeace. *The Four Georges*. London: Smith, Elder, & Co, 1862.

Thurloe, John. *A Collection of the State Papers of John Thurloe, Vol II*. London: The Executor of the late Mr Fletcher Gyles, 1741.

Toland, John. *An Account of the Courts of Prussia and Hanover; Sent to a Minister of State in Holland*. London: John Darby, 1705.

Walpole, Horace. *The Letters of Horace Walpole, Earl of Orford: Vol I*. London: Lea and Blanchard, 1842.

Ward, Adolphus William. *The Electress Sophia and the Hanoverian Succession*. London: Longmans. Green and Co, 1909.

Ward, Sean (trans.). *Memoirs (1630–1680)*. Toronto: Centre for Reformation and Renaissance Studies and ITER, 2014.

Wendland, Anna (ed.). *Briefe der Elizabeth Stuart*. Bohemia: Litterarischer Verein in Stuttgart, 1902.

Wilkins, William Henry. *Caroline, the Illustrious Queen-Consort of George II and Sometime Queen-Regent: A Study of Her Life and Time, Volume I*. London: J Murray, 1901.

Wilkins, William Henry. *The Love of an Uncrowned Queen*. London: Hutchinson & Co, 1900.

Williams, Robert Folkestone. *Maids of Honour*. London: Henry Colburn, 1845.

Williams, Robert Folkestone. *Memoirs of Sophia Dorothea, Consort of George I, Vol I*. London: Henry Colburn, 1845.

Williams, Robert Folkestone. *Memoirs of Sophia Dorothea, Consort of George I, Vol II*. London: Henry Colburn, 1845.

Wormeley, Katharine Prescott (ed. and trans.). *The Correspondence of Madame, Princess Palatine, Mother of the Regent; of Marie-Adélaide de Savoie, duchesse de Bourgogne; and of Madame de Maintenon, in Relation to Saint-Cyr*. Boston: Hardy, Pratt & Company, 1899.

Worsley, Lucy. *Courtiers: The Secret History of the Georgian Court*. London: Faber and Faber, 2011.

Newspapers

All newspaper clippings are reproduced © The British Library Board; in addition to those cited, innumerable newspapers were consulted.

Collection for Improvement of Husbandry and Trade (London, England), Friday, 15 March 1695; Issue 137.

Flying Post or The Post Master (London, England), 2 May 1702 – 5 May 1702; Issue 1091.

Flying Post or the Post Master (London, England), 1 December, 1705 –4 December 1705; Issue 1652.

London Gazette (London, England), 5 February,1685 – 9 February 1685; Issue 2006.

London Gazette (London, England), 22 July 1689 – 25 July 1689; Issue 2473.

London Gazette (London, England), 5 March 1702 – 9 March 1702; Issue 3790.

Mercurius Publicus Comprising the Sum of Foreign Intelligence (London, England), 31 May 1660 – 7 June 1660; Issue 23.

Post Boy (London, England), 30 July 1700 – 1 August 1700, Issue 829.

Post Boy (1695) (London, England), 23 January 1701 – 25 January 1701; Issue 905.

Publick Intelligencer (1655) (London, England), 17 December 1655 – 24 December 1655; Issue 12.

Websites Consulted

British History Online (http://www.british-history.ac.uk)

British Newspapers 1600–1950 (http://gdc.gale.com/products/19th-centurybritish-library-newspapers-part-i-and-part-ii/)

Hansard (http://hansard.millbanksystems.com/index.html)

Historical Texts (http://historicaltexts.jisc.ac.uk)

House of Commons Parliamentary Papers (http://parlipapers.chadwyck.co.uk/marketing/index.jsp)

JSTOR (www.jstor.org)

The National Archives (http://www.nationalarchives.gov.uk)

Oxford Dictionary of National Biography (http://www.oxforddnb.com)

State Papers Online (http://go.galegroup.com/mss/start.do?prodId=SPOL&authCount=1)

The Times Digital Archive (http://gale.cengage.co.uk/times-digital-archive/times-digital-archive-17852006.aspx)

Endnotes

Introduction

1. Granger, J (1769). *A Biographical History of England from Egbert the Great to the Revolution, Vol I*. London: T Davies, p.346.

Princess

1. In very simple terms, a cadet branch is a noble house that has descended from another via a younger son.
2. The Golden Bull of 1356 laid out the constitution of the Holy Roman Empire and all electorates were expected to abide by its terms. It took its name from its opulent golden seal.
3. Frederick IV was at the head of the Protestant Union. Established in 1608, this unified the Protestant states in Germany in one coalition.
4. Two of Frederick's sisters had married powerful Protestant princes. Luise Juliane became the bride of Frederick's guardian, John II, Count Palatine of Zweibrücken, whilst Elizabeth Charlotte wed George William, Elector of Brandenburg.
5. Anonymous (1725). *Memorials Of Affairs of State In The Reigns of Q. Elizabeth and K. James I*. London: T Ward, p.421.
6. Drury was a politician. He died in 1615.
7. Ibid., p.406.
8. Besides Henry, James and Anne had also lost Margaret in 1600 and Robert in 1602, followed by Mary and Sophia, who both died in 1607.
9. See Appendix C.
10. Frederick and Elizabeth had thirteen children. Nine lived to adulthood.
11. The garden became known as the *Eighth Wonder of the World*. It was still unfinished when Frederick and Elizabeth went into exile and was left to fall into ruins.
12. In 1609 the Holy Roman Emperor, Rudolf II, signed a document known as the *Letter of Majesty*, which guaranteed religious freedom to the people of Bohemia, regardless of whether they were Protestant or Catholic.

13. Green, Mary Anne Everett (1854). *Lives of the Princesses of England, From the Norman Conquest: Vol V*. London: Henry Colburn, pp.483–484.

14. The Sophias in question were Sophia, Countess of Hohenlohe, and Sophia Hedwig, Countess of Nassau-Dietz.

15. Gustavus Adolphus' widow, Maria Eleonora of Brandenburg, suffered a breakdown as a result of her husband's death. She kept his embalmed body in the castle of Nyköping for more than twelve months and had his heart removed and placed in a golden casket. Her bedroom was transformed into a chamber of mourning, draped in black, the windows shuttered and candles the only source of light. Over the bed hung the casket containing the heart of Gustavus Adolphus. Sophia made her 7-year-old daughter, Christina, sleep with her in that bed every night and every day was spent in loud displays of hysterical grief, which nobody could calm. Eventually a magnificent funeral was held for Gustavus Adolphus. He and his heart now rest in Stockholm's Riddarholm Church.

16. Frederick was buried at Frankenthal and remained there until 1635, when Spanish soldiers marched into Germany. Ludwig Philipp of Pfalz-Simmern-Kaiserslautern had the body disinterred and fled Frankenthal for Kaiserslautern with the remains of Frederick in his custody. What became of the late king of Bohemia's earthly remains after this is unconfirmed and his last resting place remains a mystery.

17. There are various translations of Sophia's memoirs. For the purposes of this volume, I have used two translations. The first is the original English translation by H Forester. Additional insight has been provided by Sean Ward's marvellous modern translation, in which he reimagines Sophia's writings for a twenty-first century audience. He also restores the missing portions of the text that Forester cut, fearful that it might offend the sensibilities of respectable readers.

18. She married Christian Friedrich von Harling, a member of Hanover's Privy Council, in 1662.

19. Lady Goring was the daughter of Richard Boyle, 1st Earl of Cork, and wife of the notorious Royalist, George Goring.

20. In fact, they were far from too old to start again, as we shall discover later!

21. One of Sophia's favourite anecdotes involving Elisabeth and her infamous nose occurred during this period. Elisabeth preferred not to appear in public during the periods in which her nose was red but on one occasion her sister, Princess Louise, invited her to visit their mother. 'Would you have me go with this nose?', asked Elisabeth. Her sister, much to Sophia's delight, replied, 'Will you wait until you get another?'

22. Later to rule as Stadtholder of the United Provinces of the Netherlands.

23. Anne was one of the daughters of Sir Robert Carey. Carey was guardian of Queen Elizabeth's brother, the future Charles I, and her sister, Mary, was great

friends with Elizabeth. She and the future queen of Bohemia were educated together and Mary later became Elizabeth's maid of honour.

24. Craven gave his name to Craven County, in North Carolina.

25. She ultimately married Frederick William, Elector of Brandenburg, and became a noted politician, with great influence over her husband.

26. Charles Louis had not endeared himself to his uncle, Charles I. During a prolonged visit to England during the early days of the English Civil War, Charles Louis came to the conclusion that a victory for the Parliamentarians might prove rather more palatable for the beleaguered Palatinate. After Charles I refused to lend his military might to Charles Louis' efforts to regain control of his ancestral homeland, the elector became convinced that Parliament was far more sympathetic to his cause than the king. Charles Louis returned to England again in 1644 and took the Solemn League and Covenant, much to the horror of his brothers, Maurice and Rupert, who had fought for the English king. Convinced that his Palatinate nephew was hoping to be placed on the English throne by Parliament, Charles I refused to have any further contact with Charles Louis. The two men did not reconcile before Charles I was executed. In fact, the doomed king refused to see his nephew and went to his death believing that Charles Louis was a traitor.

27. Of course, the fate of the embattled English king is infamous today. Following his return to England he was put on trial and ultimately executed.

28. Charles became King Charles II of England, Scotland and Ireland after the restoration in 1660. Two years later, he married Catherine of Braganza.

29. Known as Mistress Barlow, Lucy Walter was the mother of James, Duke of Monmouth, with her royal lover.

30. Green, Mary Anne Everett (1909). *Elizabeth, Electress Palatine and Queen of Bohemia*. London: Methuen & Co, p.382.

31. Wendland, Anna (ed.) (1902). *Briefe der Elizabeth Stuart*. Bohemia: Litterarischer Verein in Stuttgart, p.9.

32. Elisabeth became princess-abbess of Herford Abbey, a protestant convent. Louise Hollandine was considerably more controversial and converted to Catholicism to join the order of Maubisson.

33. The Fronde was a series of civil wars that occurred between 1648 and 1653. It began as a backlash against the policies of Cardinal Richelieu and Louis XIII, who attempted to curtail the powers of the nobility and hand more influence to the king's government. With the death of Louis XIII, the Parlement of Paris proposed a limit on royal power and requested that control of taxation be returned to the upper classes. The ensuing stalemate led to war.

34. Despite her brother's annoyance, Henriette Marie was very happy in her marriage. Tragically, she died of tuberculosis less than three months after the wedding took place. Within six months of his new wife's death, her husband also passed away.

35. Strickland, Agnes and Strickland, Elizabeth (1859). *Lives of the Queens of Scotland and English Princesses, Vol VIII*. London: William Blackwood and Sons, p.308.

36. Wendland, Anna (ed.) (1902). *Briefe der Elizabeth Stuart*. Bohemia: Litterarischer Verein in Stuttgart, p.38.

37. His brother became King Charles X Gustav of Sweden when Queen Christina abdicated in 1654.

38. Elizabeth Beatrice Brahe's death came after four years of marriage. The couple's son predeceased her and died in 1652.

39. Adolph John did rather better when he married a second wife, Elsa Elizabeth Brahe, in 1661. The couple had nine children and four of these, including two sons, survived to adulthood though in 1688, accusations of child abuse resulted in the couple having their children taken from their custody. Despite his ambitions of greatness, neither Adolph John nor any of his children ruled Sweden. Charles X Gustav eventually fathered a son, also named Charles, in 1655 and when he appointed a regency to govern his kingdom in the event that he might die before his son came of age, Adolph John's name was not among those he chose. It proved to be a germane decision because Charles X Gustav died in 1660, when little Charles was 4-years-old.

40. John Thurloe was secretary to the Protectorate's council of state and in his later role of Paymaster General and spymaster to Cromwell, prevented the planned assassination of the Lord Protector.

41. The cause of Charles II.

42. 'State Papers, 1654: October (1 of 5)', in *A Collection of the State Papers of John Thurloe, Volume 2, 1654*, ed. Thomas Birch (London, 1742), pp. 642–655. *British History Online* http://www.british-history.ac.uk/thurloe-papers/vol2/pp642-655 [accessed 1 February 2018].

43. Wendland, Anna (ed.) (1902). *Briefe der Elizabeth Stuart*. Bohemia: Litterarischer Verein in Stuttgart, p.48.

44. Strickland, Agnes and Strickland, Elizabeth (1859). *Lives of the Queens of Scotland and English Princesses, Vol VIII*. London: William Blackwood and Sons, p.296.

45. 'State Papers, 1654: October (1 of 5)', in *A Collection of the State Papers of John Thurloe, Volume 2, 1654*, ed. Thomas Birch (London, 1742), pp. 642–655. *British History Online* http://www.british-history.ac.uk/thurloe-papers/vol2/pp642-655 [accessed 1 February 2018].

46. The chosen representative was George Christopher von Hammerstein, a trusted associate of the brothers. His daughter was later a favoured courtier of George I.

47. 'State Papers, 1655: November (3 of 8)', in *A Collection of the State Papers of John Thurloe, Volume 4, Sept 1655 – May 1656*, ed. Thomas Birch (London,

1742), pp. 172–186. *British History Online* http://www.british-history.ac.uk/thurloe-papers/vol4/pp172-186 [accessed 31 January 2018].

48. *Publick Intelligencer (1655)* (London, England), 17 December 1655 – 24 December 1655; Issue 12.

49. Ranuccio was the grandson of the famed Cosimo II de' Medici, Grand Duke of Tuscany. Although his pursuit of Sophia failed, he eventually married three times.

50. In fact, he was far from impotent and fathered four daughters.

51. Signed on 24 October 1648, the Treaty of Westphalia ended the Thirty Years' War. It was the culmination of a peace conference that had opened four years earlier and included representatives from nearly two hundred states. The conference was a comedy of errors in which months were lost as the delegates argued who should enter the room first and once they were all there, who would sit where. Despite a mountain of bureaucracy eventually an accord was reached. The conference effectively ended hopes for a Roman Catholic domination of Europe.

52. The engagement to George William.

53. Wendland, Anna (ed.) (1902). *Briefe der Elizabeth Stuart*. Bohemia: Litterarischer Verein in Stuttgart, pp.94–95.

54. Bromley, George (ed.) (1787). *A Collection of Original Royal Letters, Written by King Charles I and II, King James II and the King and Queen of Bohemia.* London: John Stockdale, pp.299–300.

55. Charlotte continued to regard the divorce as illegal until her death in 1686. Over the years, her temper did not improve. Charles Louis and Luise remained married until her death in 1677 and together had thirteen children, of which nine lived to adulthood. Two years after Luise's death Charles Louis married Elisabeth Hollander von Bernau, who was more than four decades his junior. Although the couple had a son, Charles Louis died in 1680, before his last child was born.

Duchess

1. Liselotte needs no introduction to aficionados of French history. As the wife of Philippe I, Duke of Orléans, she was mother to Philippe II, Regent of France.

2. She eventually died in 1702, at the age of 78.

3. Orléans, Charlotte-Elisabeth, duchesse d' (1889). *Life and Letters of Charlotte Elizabeth, Princess Palatine and Mother of Philippe d'Orléans, Regent of France, 1652–1722.* London: Chapman and Hall Ltd, p.5.

4. She was also, eventually, the grandmother of Marie-Antoinette.

5. Wendland, Anna (ed.) (1902). *Briefe der Elizabeth Stuart*. Bohemia: Litterarischer Verein in Stuttgart, p.126.

6. Ibid., p.123.

7. Orléans, Charlotte-Elisabeth, duchesse d' (1925). *The Letters of Madame, Vol II*. London: JW Arrowsmith Ltd, pp.256–257.

8. Wendland, Anna (ed.) (1902). *Briefe der Elizabeth Stuart*. Bohemia: Litterarischer Verein in Stuttgart, p.122.

9. Ibid., p.125.

10. *Mercurius Publicus Comprising the Sum of Foreign Intelligence* (London, England), 31 May 1660 – 7 June 1660; Issue 23.

11. Orléans, Charlotte-Elisabeth, duchesse d' (1925). *The Letters of Madame, Vol II*. London: JW Arrowsmith Ltd, p.239.

12. Strickland, Agnes and Strickland, Elizabeth (1859). *Lives of the Queens of Scotland and English Princesses, Vol VIII*. London: William Blackwood and Sons, p.308.

13. Count Franz Wilhelm von Wartenberg died on 1 December. The Treaty of Westphalia ruled that the office would alternate between Catholic and Protestant holders. Since von Wartenberg was Catholic, the next holder must be Protestant and that Protestant was Ernest Augustus.

14. The bride was a Miss von Landas, her groom one of Ernest Augustus' former equerries named *von Lenthe*. In his insightful translation of Sophia's memoirs, Sean Ward speculates that this was most likely Kurt Wilhelm von Lenthe, the latest member of his family to serve as an equerry to the dukes of Brunswick-Lüneburg.

15. He was 37-years-old.

16. The long-time, ceaselessly loyal retainer died in 1702. As a mark of esteem for their service, she and her husband were laid to rest at the Neustädter Hof-und Stadtkirche St. Johannis zu Hannover, alongside other senior, esteemed courtiers.

17. Wilkins, WH (1900). *The Love of an Uncrowned Queen*. London: Hutchinson & Co, p.8.

18. "It's the French fashion."

19. Her sister, Hortense, was famously the mistress of King Charles II.

20. The other was the Principality of Calenberg.

21. Frederick III of Denmark was married to Sophie Amalie, the sister of Ernest Augustus and his brothers.

22. Sophia records that Susanne later died after purchasing medicine from an untrustworthy vendor. Unfortunately, what she believed to be harmless proved to be poison.

23. In a tragic twist of fate the couple's daughter, Marie Louise of Orléans, also died at the age of 26. Just like her mother, she too complained of a sharp abdominal pain before death and it's thought that she was suffering from appendicitis.

24. Liselotte died in 1722, having survived her husband by twenty-one years.

25. This was another term for a morganatic marriage.

Endnotes

26. Éléonore fell pregnant three more times but each pregnancy ended in miscarriage.

27. Wilkins, WH (1900). *The Love of an Uncrowned Queen*. London: Hutchinson & Co, p.31.

28. Éléonore had been among Tarente's attendants.

29. Wilkins, WH (1900). *The Love of an Uncrowned Queen*. London: Hutchinson & Co, p.25.

30. He eventually married Queen Anne of Great Britain.

31. Orléans, Charlotte-Elisabeth, duchesse d' (1925). *The Letters of Madame, Vol II*. London: JW Arrowsmith Ltd, p.234.

32. Later Prime Minister of Hanover.

33. She would briefly become a mistress of George Louis too.

34. In the event, one of these daughters did indeed marry her cousin, with Christine Sophia and Duke Augustus William of Brunswick-Lüneburg marrying in 1681.

35. Williams, Robert Folkestone (1845). *Memoirs of Sophia Dorothea, Consort of George I, Vol I*. London: Henry Colburn, pp.36–40.

36. She did manage to secure the title of princess for Sophia Dorothea though.

37. Years earlier Louise Hollandine had hoped to be married to James Graham, Marquis of Montrose. Tragically, the Royalist Montrose was captured by the Scottish in 1650 and sentenced to death. He was hanged, drawn and quartered that spring. Montrose's remains were on public display for over a decade before they were eventually buried at the church of St Giles eleven years later.

38. Marie Louise sank into deep depression in Spain and died just ten years later. Her husband lived until 1700, outliving two wives despite extensive health problems as a result of inbreeding. He had little power and the Spanish court descended into infighting, ruled by regents and favourites. When he died, his autopsy notes read, '[His corpse]... did not contain a single drop of blood; his heart was the size of a peppercorn; his lungs corroded; his intestines rotten and gangrenous; he had a single testicle, black as coal, and his head was full of water.' Quite a catch!

39. Louis, Grand Dauphin, married Duchess Maria Anna of Bavaria in 1680. Figuelotte married Frederick I of Prussia in 1684.

40. The world of European royal protocol was a dizzying one. Who should sit on an armchair, a high-backed seat, a stool; who might stand; who should go through a door first or walk ahead in the garden were all matters of vital diplomatic importance. A mistake could have serious consequences!

41. An ongoing complaint Sophia suffered from.

42. She based the memoirs on her letters to Charles Louis, though she burned his according to his wishes. Sadly, Sophia's letters to Liselotte and those she wrote to Figuelotte are also lost.

43. Burnet, Gilbert and Burnet, Thomas (1823). *Bishop Burnet's History of His Own Time, Vol IV*. Oxford: The Clarendon Press, p.198.

44. Wilkins, WH (1900). *The Love of an Uncrowned Queen*. London: Hutchinson & Co, p.81.

45. Louis XIV married Madame Maintenon within months of becoming a widower.

46. Wilkins, WH (1900). *The Love of an Uncrowned Queen*. London: Hutchinson & Co, p.102.

47. *London Gazette* (London, England), 5 February,1685 – 9 February, 1685; Issue 2006.

48. Sophia Dorothea, the daughter of George Louis and Sophia Dorothea of Celle, married her cousin, Frederick William I of Prussia, Figuelotte's son, who ate that worrisome shoe buckle. The couple eventually numbered among their children Frederick the Great.

49. Of Figuelotte's children, only Frederick William survived.

Electress

1. Wilkins, WH (1900). *The Love of an Uncrowned Queen*. London: Hutchinson & Co, p.420.

2. The seven were Charles Talbot, 1st Duke of Shrewsbury, William Cavendish, 1st Duke of Devonshire, Thomas Osborne, 1st Duke of Leeds (all were then mere earls), Richard Lumley, 1st Earl of Scarborough (at the time a viscount), Henry Compton, who was Bishop of London, Edward Russell, later 1st Earl of Orford, and Henry Sydney, the author of the letter and later 1st Earl of Romney.

3. Dalrymple, John (1773). *Memoirs of Great Britain and Ireland, Vol II*. London: W Strachan and T Caddell, p.22.

4. *London Gazette* (London, England), July 22, 1689 – July 25, 1689; Issue 2473.

5. Strickland, Agnes and Strickland, Elizabeth (1859). *Lives of the Queens of Scotland and English Princesses, Vol VIII*. London: William Blackwood and Sons, p.352.

6. Maximilian William eventually settled in Austria, where he died in 1726.

7. 'William and Mary: February 1691', in *Calendar of State Papers Domestic: William and Mary, 1690–1*, ed. William John Hardy (London, 1898), pp. 241–286. *British History Online* http://www.british-history.ac.uk/cal-state-papers/domestic/will-mary/1690-1/pp241-286 [accessed 22 February 2018].

8. Hanover didn't formally complete its formal conversion into an electorate until 1708, but it was recognised as such long before that.

9. George Louis barely escaped with his life from an engagement at the Battle of Neerwinden too.

Endnotes

10. *Collection for Improvement of Husbandry and Trade* (London, England), Friday, 15 March, 1695; Issue 137.

11. *Post Boy (1695)* (London, England), 23 January 1701 – 25 January 1701; Issue 905.

12. Thackeray, William Makepeace (1862). *The Four Georges*. London: Smith, Elder, & Co, pp.24–26.

13. Ibid., p.37.

14. *Post Boy* (London, England), 30 July 1700 – 1 August 1700, Issue 829.

15. Strickland, Agnes and Strickland, Elizabeth (1859). *Lives of the Queens of Scotland and English Princesses, Vol VIII*. London: William Blackwood and Sons, p.345.

16. Known to history as *the Old Pretender*.

17. Wilkins, WH (1900). *The Love of an Uncrowned Queen*. London: Hutchinson & Co, p.409.

18. Craik, George L (1900). *The Pictorial History of England: Being a History of the People as Well as a Kingdom, Vol IX*. London: Charles Knight & Co, pp.112–113.

19. Orléans, Charlotte-Elisabeth, duchesse d' (1889). *Life and Letters of Charlotte Elizabeth, Princess Palatine and Mother of Philippe d'Orléans, Regent of France, 1652–1722*. London: Chapman and Hall Ltd, p.151.

20. A wine from the Rhine, as a poet might say.

21. Toland, John (1705). *An Account of the Courts of Prussia and Hanover; Sent to a Minister of State in Holland*. London: John Darby, pp.59–61.

22. Ibid., pp.62–63.

23. Ibid., pp.65–68.

24. Ibid., pp.69–71.

25. *London Gazette* (London, England), 5 March 1702 – 9 March 1702; Issue 3790.

26. *Flying Post or The Post Master* (London, England), 2 May 1702 – 5 May 1702; Issue 1091.

27. Arkell, Ruby Lillian (1939). *Caroline of Ansbach: George the Second's Queen*. Oxford: Oxford University Press, p.7.

28. Wilkins, William Henry (1901). *Caroline, the Illustrious Queen-Consort of George II and Sometime Queen-Regent: A Study of Her Life and Time, Volume I*. London: J Murray, pp.29–30.

29. Kiste, John van der (2013). *King George II and Queen Caroline*. Stroud: The History Press, p.12.

30. Cowper, CS (ed.) (1865). *Diary of Mary, Countess Cowper, Lady of the Bedchamber to the Princess of Wales, 1714–1720*. London: John Murray, pp.149–150.

31. Sophia named the Archbishop of York, the Dukes of Somerset, Ormonde, Bolton, Marlborough, and Montagu, and the Earls of Bridgewater, Manchester, Peterborough, Rivers, Stamford, Sunderland, Radnor, and Oxford. Last but not

least were the Barons Wharton, Mohun, Raby, Lexington, and Somers. She crossed out the name of Lord Halifax, the man who delivered the document to Hanover!

32. Gwynne, Rowland (1706). *A Letter from Her Royal Highness, the Princess Sophia, Electress of Brunswick and Luneburg, to His Grace the Archbishop of Canterbury. With Another from Hannover written by Sir Rowland Gwynne to the Right Honourable The Earl of Stamford*. London: B Bragge, p.1.

33. 'The second parliament of Queen Anne: First session - begins 25/10/1705', in *The History and Proceedings of the House of Commons: Volume 3, 1695–1706* (London, 1742), pp. 442–473. *British History Online* http://www.british-history. ac.uk/commons-hist-proceedings/vol3/pp442-473 [accessed 22 February 2018].

34. Ibid.

35. Gwynne died in 1726.

36. Coxe, William (1818). *Memoirs of John, Duke of Marlborough, Vol I*. London: Longman, Hurst, Reese, Orme and Brown, p.362.

37. *Flying Post or the Post Master* (London, England), 1 December, 1705 – 4 December 1705; Issue 1652.

38. He was born on 1 February 1707.

39. Caroline would fall pregnant nine further times. One of these pregnancies ended in miscarriage and of the surviving children, seven (including Frederick) lived to adulthood. Sophia Dorothea, meanwhile, fared considerably better. Of fourteen pregnancies, ten children survived to adulthood.

40. Orléans, Charlotte-Elisabeth, duchesse d' (1925). *The Letters of Madame, Vol II*. London: JW Arrowsmith Ltd, p.23.

41. Craik, George L (1900). *The Pictorial History of England: Being a History of the People as Well as a Kingdom, Vol IX*. London: Charles Knight & Co, p.292.

42. Wormeley, Katharine Prescott (ed. and trans.) (1899). *The Correspondence of Madame, Princess Palatine, Mother of the Regent; of Marie-Adélaide de Savoie, duchesse de Bourgogne; and of Madame de Maintenon, in Relation to Saint-Cyr*. Boston: Hardy, Pratt & Company, p.168.

Index